How We Think They Think

University of **Chester**

CHESTER CAMPUS
LIBRARY
01244 392738

How We Think They Think

Anthropological Approaches to Cognition, Memory, and Literacy

Maurice E. F. Bloch

Westview Press
A Member of Perseus Books Group

The chapters in this book orginally appeared in slightly different versions in the following locations:

"Language, Anthropology and Cognitive Science," Man (n.s.), 1991, Vol. 26, No. 2, pp. 183–198. "What Goes Without Saying: The Conceptualization of Zafimaniry Society," in *Conceptualizing Society*, A. Kuper (ed.). 1992. London: Routledge. "Le Cognitif et L'ethnographique," *Grahdiva*, 1995, No. 17. "Domain Specificity, Living Kinds and Symbolism," in *Cognitive Aspects of Religious Symbolism*, P. Boyer (ed.). 1993. Cambridge: Cambridge University Press. Reprinted with the permission of Cambridge University Press. "Internal and External Memory: Different Ways of Being in History," *Suomen Antropologi*, 1992, Vol. 17, No. 1. "The Resurrection of the House Amongst the Zafimaniry of Madagascar," in *About the House: Levi Strauss and Beyond*, J. Carsten and S. Hugh-Jones (eds.). 1995. Cambridge: Cambridge University Press. Reprinted by permission of Cambridge University Press. "Time, Narratives and the Multiplicity of Representations of the Past," *Bulletin of the Institute of Ethnology*, Academica Sinica, 1993, No. 75 (Spring), pp. 29–45. "Autobiographical Memory and the Historical Memory of the More Distant Past," *Enquete*, 1996, No. 2, pp. 59–78. (Translation of the article "Mémoire autobiographique et mémoire historique. . . .") "Astrology and Writing in Madagascar," in *Literacy in Traditional Societies*, J. Goody (ed.). 1968. Cambridge: Cambridge University Press. Reprinted with the permission of Cambridge University Press. "Literacy and Enlightenment," in *Literacy and Society*, M Trolle-Larsen and K Sousboe (eds.). 1989. Publications of the Centre for Research in the Humanities. Copenhagen: Akademisk Forlag. "The Uses of Schooling and Literacy in a Zafimaniry Village," in *Cross Cultural Approaches to Literacy*, B. Street (ed.). 1994. Cambridge: Cambridge University Press. Reprinted with the permission of Cambridge University Press. "Why Do Malagasy Cows Speak French?" in *Kung!, the magazine of the LSE Anthropological Society*. 1971.

Copyright © 1998 by Westview Press, A Member of Perseus Books Group

Published in 1998 in the United States of America by Westview Press, 5500 Central Avenue, Boulder, Colorado 80301-2877, and in the United Kingdom by Westview Press, 12 Hid's Copse Road, Cumnor Hill, Oxford OX2 9JJ

A CIP catalog record for this book is available from the Library of Congress.
ISBN 0-8133-3373-3 (hc). — ISBN 0-8133-3374-1 (pb)

The paper used in this publication meets the requirements of the American National Standard for Permanence of Paper for Printed Library Materials Z39.48-1984.

PERSEUS
POD
ON DEMAND   10   9   8   7   6   5   4   3

Contents

Introduction   vii

PART 1
COGNITION

1 Language, Anthropology and Cognitive Science   3

2 What Goes Without Saying:
   The Conceptualization of Zafimaniry Society   22

3 Cognition and Ethnography   39

4 Domain-Specificity, Living Kinds and Symbolism   54

PART 2
MEMORY

5 Internal and External Memory:
   Different Ways of Being in History   67

6 The Resurrection of the House Amongst the
   Zafimaniry of Madagascar   85

7 Time, Narratives and the Multiplicity of
   Representations of the Past   100

8 Autobiographical Memory and the Historical Memory
   of the More Distant Past   114

PART 3
LITERACY

9 Astrology and Writing in Madagascar   131

10 Literacy and Enlightenment   152

11   The Uses of Schooling and Literacy in a
     Zafimaniry Village   171

12   Why do Malagasy Cows Speak French?   193

Index   197

Introduction

As the title of this book suggests, the essays gathered here concern issues of cognition, memory, and literacy as they relate to anthropology. However, because similar general theoretical questions are addressed throughout, the division under three headings hides a more fundamental unity. Every chapter deals in different ways with what is a central concern: the relation between what is, on the one hand, explicit and conscious—that is to say, the type of informants' knowledge that anthropologists can hope to access easily—and, on the other hand, what is inexplicit or unconscious, but perhaps more fundamental.

The chapters grouped in the "Cognition" section continue an argument that was begun in two earlier articles (Bloch 1977, 1986). These articles were concerned with the elaboration of a criticism of the proposition that culture and cognition could be equated—something that I argued was implicitly claimed in much anthropology. Rather, I maintained that what anthropologists were talking about when they claimed to represent a particular culture was usually based only on what was explicit, either because this was stated by informants or because it could be deduced from what was acted out in ritual. Such material was insufficient to tell us about the understanding of the world of the people concerned. Not to differentiate culture and cognition was misleading, since it presented what were a particular type of representations as though they were the collective representations about which Durkheim had been talking—that is the very foundation of all knowledge, the categories of understanding that had for centuries been the concern of philosophers.

This error was harmful in another way also, because the image of culture so produced grossly exaggerated the impression of cultural variability, not to say relativism, that existed in different human populations. This false image was consequent on the fact that the building materials used to create constructions that were claimed to be "culture" were (1) only those statements by informants that seemed odd and therefore interesting to anthropologists and their readers, while, at the same time, other, more familiar images were ignored as unworthy of interest; and (2) representations drawn from ritual contexts that are, as is argued in Chapter 4, by their nature counterintuitive negations of understandings of what the world is believed to be normally like (Boyer 1994). Such selectivity of raw material for creating accounts of the cultures of different groups of people around the globe could not avoid, because it concentrated on the odd, to exaggerate misleadingly the exotic and diverse character of human knowledge.

A justified criticism of the two earlier articles mentioned above, made by several authors and subsequently echoed by myself (Bloch 1989), was that, although they pointed out the mistake of seeing certain exceptional and strange cultural manifestations as constitutive of the foundations of all knowledge, and that, to a certain extent, they also accounted for the atypical nature and presence of those manifestations, my early studies nonetheless left untheorised what such exceptional ideological representations were contrasted with: that is, everyday knowledge. This seemed almost taken for granted as obvious, which it certainly is not. The purpose of the cognition chapters of this book is precisely to remedy this omission, or error, by attempting to discuss why everyday knowledge is, and must be, inexplicit, how it is enmeshed in action, and how work by cognitive scientists, especially cognitive psychologists, can help anthropologists understand the nature of everyday knowledge and therefore how we can represent it. This is the aim of Chapter 1. The chapters entitled "What Goes Without Saying" (Chapter 2) and "Cognition and Ethnography" (Chapter 3) are attempts to apply the more general and theoretical ideas of the first chapter to a particular ethnographic context, that of the Zafimaniry of Madagascar, whom I have been studying for more than 20 years.

Chapter 5, which opens the section "Memory," is different from most of the others in this book in that instead of arguing for the need for anthropologists to pay attention to cognitive studies, it calls instead for the reverse, a recognition of the value of anthropological studies concerned with notions of the person, in general, and of kinship, in particular, for psychological work. In the end, however, the general message is the same: Social sciences and psychological sciences cannot, and should not, forget what the others have learnt.

The remaining three chapters in the section on memory are particularly closely linked because they rely extensively on ethnographic data from the Zafimaniry study and because they deal with the way the awful events of 1947 are remembered in a small forest village, when, during a terrible but little-known colonial war, more than 100,000 people were killed in Madagascar. The village was burnt down during that war. Some of its inhabitants died, and the rest were forced to hide in the forest for almost two years, during which time they endured great hardships. Only recently have the villagers been willing to talk about these events amongst themselves and with me. The first chapter concerned with the memory of this period, Chapter 6, focuses on an account of this time and of the villagers' return to their village, as well as on the return of hope and social reproduction. The account is told in a well-rehearsed narrative, recounted on important occasions by the elders of the village. Chapter 7 also deals with narrative accounts of the war, but it is also, in many ways, a theoretical criticism of the earlier essay from the perspective developed in the cognition chapters in this volume. It argues that memory of what then happened cannot be equated with any particular narrative account. The line taken is similar to the much more general point that culture in general, and historical knowledge in particular, is a very different phenomenon than that which can be explained in words and cannot, therefore, be equated with what is explicit. Chapter 8 continues the same argument as Chapter 7 but goes on to discuss how it is possible for the memory of historical events to be transmitted between generations even without the medium of narratives.

The "Literacy" section opens with Chapter 9. This is a much older essay than the other papers in this book, but it nonetheless makes a related point, again with the help of ethnography from Madagascar. In this chapter I argue that many of the more elaborate cultural schemes—such as written astrological texts, which have been seen by certain anthropologists as frameworks of Malagasy culture—are actually hardly known by ordinary people. In fact, such schemes, if they are generally known at all, are understood merely as exotica and have power simply because of this fact and not because they are a fundamental framework for thought. In other words, I argue that in this case, the effect of literacy has not been to revolutionise the nature of cognition, as has been argued by some (Goody 1977), but rather to parenthesise certain forms of knowledge that, therefore, have only peripheral effects on the understanding of the world in general. This theme is taken up again in Chapters 10 and 11. In Chapter 10, I contend that the relationship of writing to language, and then to thought, is different in different contexts and also varies according to the technical character of the writing itself—for example, whether it is phonetic or ideographic. There can thus not be any general arguments about the effects of the introduction or presence of "writing" that can apply equally to the type of literacy found in, say, Japan and Europe. Chapter 11 considers the significance, and the insignificance, of the uses of literacy for present-day Zafimaniry, only some of whom can read and write, and those only since the 1940s. It goes on to show the significance of these arguments for the social character of schooling in this type of setting. The book closes with Chapter 12, a short piece about the uses of French by Malagasy peasants, who deny any knowledge of that language but who nonetheless use it to address their animals.

References

Bloch, M. 1977. The past and the present in the present. *Man* n. s. 13: 21–33.
_____. 1986. From cognition to ideology. In *Knowledge and power: anthropological and sociological approaches* (ed.) R. Fardon. Edinburgh: Scottish University Press.

_____. 1989. Foreword. *Ritual, history and power: selected papers in anthropol-
ogy,* LSE Monographs in Social Anthropology, No. 58. London: Athlone Press.
Boyer, P. 1994. *The naturalness of religious ideas.* Berkeley: University of California
Press.
Goody, J. 1977. *The domestication of the savage mind.* Cambridge: Cambridge
University Press.

Part One

Cognition

Chapter One

Language, Anthropology and Cognitive Science

The text of this chapter was originally given as a lecture in memory of the British anthropologist Sir James Frazer. The arguments it advances are the most general in the book and form the basis for the subsequent chapters. The chapter makes a number of fundamental points. First, it argues for the importance of cognitive science for anthropologists. Second, it argues that what people say is a poor guide to what they know and think. Third, it argues that the knowledge used in practice must be organised in such a way that it can be accessed at amazing speed and cannot therefore be lineal in nature. Fourth, it looks at the significance for anthropology of the process of becoming an expert in certain practices. Fifth, it argues theoretically for the importance of participant observation. The chapter turns to connectionist theory to make several of its points, but this does not indicate so much a commitment to any particular form of this theory as an emphasis on the need for this kind of theory.

*   *   *

I

Cognitive science is usually described as the attempt to bring cognitive psychology, philosophy, neurophysiology, artificial intelligence, linguistics and anthropology together in order to understand cognition. In this alliance anthropology is, in fact, a rather shadowy partner. Only cognitive anthropology is usually taken into account by cognitive scientists and, even then, only the further reaches of cognitive anthropology which many anthropologists, especially European anthropologists, would fail to recognise as their business at all. This state of affairs is unfortunate, because some of the theories emerging in cognitive science are *central* to the concerns of anthropology, whether social or cultural, and should lead anthropologists to re-examine many of the premises of their work. Other cognitive scientists, however, have much to learn from the central concerns of anthropology and particularly, if rather unexpectedly, from the traditional method of social anthropology: participant observation.

Cultural anthropologists study culture. This can be defined as that which needs to be known in order to operate reasonably effectively in a specific human environment.[1] Social anthropologists traditionally study social organisation and the behaviour by means of which people relate to each other. Both cultural and social anthropologists, however, are well aware that the distinction between the two branches of the discipline is not absolute. Cultural anthropologists know that they cannot get at culture directly, but only through the observation of communicative activity, verbal or otherwise, natural or artificially simulated. Social anthropologists are aware that they cannot understand action, verbal or otherwise, if they do not construct, probably in imagination, a representation of the culture of the people they study, since this is the only way to make sense of their activities (Winch 1958).

Some concept of culture is therefore essential to all social and cultural anthropologists. However, a further assumption of anthropology, sometimes stated and sometimes unstated, is that this culture is inseparably linked to language, on the grounds either that culture is thought and transmitted as a text through language, or that culture is ultimately 'language like', consisting of linked linear propositions. It is these two assumptions about culture that I want to challenge here.

If culture is the whole or a part of what people must know in a particular social environment in order to operate efficiently, it follows first, that people must have acquired this knowledge, either through the development of innate potentials, or from external sources, or from a combination of both, and secondly that this acquired knowledge is being continually stored in a manner that makes it relatively easily accessible when necessary.[2] These obvious inferences have in turn a further implication which is that anthropologists' concerns place them right in the middle of the cognitive sciences, whether they like it or not, since it is cognitive scientists who have something to say about learning, memory and retrieval. Anthropologists cannot, therefore, avoid the attempt to make their theories about social life *compatible* with what other cognitive scientists have to say about the processes of learning and storage.

Perhaps all this may seem commonplace but it is striking how often anthropologists' theories of learning, memory and retrieval have *not* been compatible with those of other cognitive scientists. The exception is the small group of cognitive anthropologists, largely confined to the United States,[3] who have paid serious attention to recent developments in cognitive science. Things are nevertheless beginning to change, and I hope that in this article I am swimming with the tide, but a tide which has only just

started to flow and which has not reached, especially in Europe, the heart-
land of anthropological theory where it is perhaps most needed.[4]

Of course I do not claim that other cognitive scientists have figured out
how the mind works, and that anthropologists have only to slot culture
into this well-advanced model. Cognitive scientists' understanding of the
mind-brain is dramatically incomplete and tentative. Nonetheless, some
findings are fairly clear and we should take these into account. Moreover,
the hypotheses of cognitive scientists, however speculative, fundamentally
challenge many unexamined anthropological assumptions in a way that
should not be ignored.

II

As noted above, my main concern is with only one aspect of the broad
topic of the relation between cognitive science and anthropology, namely
the importance or otherwise of language, or language-like phenomena, for
cultural knowledge. A good place to start is with a consideration of concept
formation, particularly classificatory concept formation, a topic about
which much has been written, and which is often recognised as of relevance
to anthropology.

In discussing this topic I am not concerned with the traditional anthropological issue, recently reviewed by Atran, of the extent to which classificatory concepts have an innate basis (Atran 1990), though it is quite clear
that in the past, anthropologists have grossly exaggerated cultural variation, and that the traditional questions of cultural anthropologists concerning very broad areas of knowledge should be rephrased from 'How are
these things learned?' to 'How is culturally specific knowledge produced
out of universal predispositions?'. Such rephrasing is too easily obscured in
anthropological references to 'cultural models' (Holland & Quinn 1987).

Leaving this fundamental question aside, it is nonetheless clear that all
classificatory concepts are at least partially learned, and recent work in this
area has brought about certain fundamental changes in the way we envisage the process. The old idea that the child learns classificatory concepts as
minimal and necessary definitions, an idea taken for granted in most of anthropology and which was more particularly implied in structuralism and
ethnoscience, was shown to be untenable some time ago (Fillmore 1975;
Rosch 1977; 1978; Smith 1988). The more generally accepted position now
is that such concepts are formed through reference back to rather vague
and provisional 'prototypes' which anchor loosely-formed 'families' of specific instances. For example, the concept of a house is not a list of essential
features (roof, door, walls, and so on) which have to be checked off before
deciding whether or not the thing is a house. If that were so we would have
no idea that a house which has lost its roof is still a house. It is rather that

we consider something as 'a house' by comparing it to a loosely associated group of 'houselike' features, no one of which is essential, but which are linked by a general idea of what a typical house is.

Thus, as suggested by Markham and Seibert (1976), classificatory concepts are in fact based on an appraisal of their referents in the world, on how we think of the construction and make-up of these referents, or on our understanding of the way they are constituted. It therefore seems that the mental form of classificatory concepts, essential building blocks of culture, involves loose and implicit practical-cum-theoretical pattern networks of knowledge, based on the experience of physical instances sometimes called 'best exemplars' (Smith *et al.* 1988: 372). A significant aspect of looking at classificatory concepts in this way is that it makes them isomorphic with what are known as 'scripts' and 'schemata', although these latter may be on a much larger and more elaborate scale. These 'scripts' and 'schemata' are, in effect, chunked networks of loose procedures and understandings which enable us to deal with standard and recurring situations, for example 'getting the breakfast ready', that are clearly culturally created (Abelson 1981; Holland & Quinn 1987; D'Andrade 1990).[5]

If classificatory concepts such as 'scripts' and 'schemata' are not like dictionary entries, but are instead small networks of typical understandings and practices concerning the world, then the question of their relation to words becomes more problematic than it was with the old 'checklist of necessary and sufficient conditions' view. That there is no inevitable connexion between concepts and words is shown by the now well-established fact that concepts can and do exist independently of language. This is made clear in the many examples of conceptual thinking in pre-linguistic children, first presented by Brown (1973). Children have the concept 'house' before they can say the word. We also have studies which show that the acquisition of lexical semantics by children is very largely a matter of trying to match words to already formed concepts. This is the so called 'concept first' theory.

Contrary to earlier views in cognitive anthropology (Tyler 1969), therefore, language is not essential for conceptual thought.[6] It is possible to go beyond this initial distancing between the lexicon and mental concepts, however, thanks to work on semantic acquisition by Bowerman (1977). This demonstrates a continual back and forth movement between aspects of classification which are introduced through language and mental concepts, as the child learns to express these concepts through words. This dialectical movement is not only interesting in itself but also suggests a much more general process, to which I shall return, by which originally non-linguistic knowledge is partly transformed as it becomes linguistic, thereby taking on a form which much more closely resembles what structuralists, among other anthropologists, had assumed to characterise the organisation of all human knowledge (Keil & Batterman 1984).

This brief review of concept formation enables us to reach the following provisional conclusions: (1) that much of knowledge is fundamentally non-linguistic; (2) that concepts involve implicit networks of meanings which are formed through the experience of, and practice in, the external world; and (3) that, under certain circumstances, this non-linguistic knowledge can be rendered into language and thus take the form of explicit discourse, but changing its character in the process.

III

Another area of joint concern to anthropology and cognitive psychology also reveals the importance of non-linguistic knowledge. This is the study of the way we learn practical, everyday tasks. It is clear that we do not usually go through a point-by-point explanation of the process when we teach our children how to negotiate their way around the house or to close doors. Much culturally transmitted knowledge seems to be passed on in ways unknown to us. Perhaps in highly schooled societies this fact is misleadingly obscured by the prominence of explicit instruction, but in non-industrialised societies most of what takes people's time and energy—including such practices as how to wash both the body and clothes, how to cook, how to cultivate, etc.—are learned very gradually through imitation and tentative participation.

The cultural specificity, complexity and embeddedness of such tasks, and their character as not linguistically explicit, have often been commented upon by anthropologists, for example by Mauss (1936), Leroi-Gourhan (1943) and Haudricourt (1968), but have rarely been studied satisfactorily. The few studies we do have tend to deal with unusual tasks necessary for specialised crafts which require formal apprenticeships. In these cases, also, anthropologists have noted that language seems to play a surprisingly small role in the transmission of knowledge. For example, in her study of weavers in Ghana, Goody (1978) was amazed at the small part played by questioning and speaking in teaching apprentices. Similarly, Lave, in her study of Liberian tailors, notes that what she calls 'apprenticeship learning', which relies on the 'assumptions that knowing, thinking, and understanding are generated in practice' (Lave 1988; 1990:310), is more effective than formal teaching based on linguistic, socratic forms. If this is so for these relatively specialised tasks there is no doubt that the same conclusions would be reached even more emphatically in studies of learning more common, though not necessarily less skilled, everyday tasks.

The significance of such findings is much more important than we might at first suppose. This is because the fact that the transmission of knowledge in West African weaving or tailoring is largely non-linguistic may have less to do with the culture of education in these places than with a general feature of the kind of knowledge that underlies the performance of complex practical tasks, which *requires* that it be non-linguistic.

That this is so is suggested by various studies of learning in which, by contrast to the examples just mentioned, the original teaching is received through language, or at least in propositional form, but in which the process of becoming an expert seems to involve the transformation of the propositions of the teacher into fundamentally non-linguistic knowledge (Dreyfus & Dreyfus 1986: ch. 1).[7] Thus Anderson (1983) points out how people who are taught driving through a series of propositions have to transform this knowledge into non-linguistic, integrated procedures before the task can be effected rapidly, efficiently and automatically—one might say properly. Only when they do not think about what they are doing in words are drivers truly experts.[8] Probably some teaching needs to be done verbally, but there are also advantages in the non-linguistic transmission of practical skills typical of non-industrial societies since such transmission by-passes the double transformation from implicit to linguistically explicit knowledge made by the teacher and from linguistically explicit to implicit knowledge made by the learner.

It could be objected that my stress on the non-linguistic side of practical activities is somewhat exaggerated. After all, language also plays a role in the performance of many familiar practical actions, though not necessarily driving. Even this fact, however, may bear less on the extent to which knowledge is linguistic than might appear at first sight.

Let me take an example which is in part derived from the semantic work of Johnson-Laird (1988: ch. 18; see also Johnson-Laird 1983: 396–447), modified by Sperber and Wilson's (1986) theory of relevance and which is also indirectly inspired by Malinowski's (1935) study of the role of language in Trobriand agriculture. Imagine a Malagasy shifting cultivator with a fairly clear, yet supple mental model, perhaps we could say a script, stored in long-term memory, of what a 'good swidden' is like; and that this model, like that of a roundabout in the mind of the expert driver, is partly visual, partly analytical (though not necessarily in a sentential logical way), partly welded to a series of procedures about what you should do to make and maintain a swidden. This Malagasy is going through the forest with a friend who says to him 'Look over there at that bit of forest, that would make a good swidden'. What happens then is that, after a rapid conceptual-isation of the bit of forest, the model of 'the good swidden' is mentally matched with the conceptualised area of forest, and then a new but related model, 'this particular place as a potential swidden' is established and stored in long-term memory. This stored mental model, however, although partly created by the linguistic event and understood in terms of the rele-vance of the statement to both the mental model of the 'good swidden' and to that of the area of forest, is not likely to include the linguistic statement tagged onto it. The intrusion of language has therefore not made the mental model any more linguistic.

To return to the example of car driving: we have seen that driving expertly seems to require that the information be stored non-linguistically if it is to be accessible in an efficient way. Why should this be so?

In order to begin to answer this question we need to turn again to the process involved in becoming an expert. It is not surprising that practice in performing a complex task makes the practitioner more efficient, but studies of expertise show that the increase in efficiency is more puzzling than might at first appear. For example, when people are repeatedly asked to read a page of text upside down they gradually do this faster and faster, but the increase in speed is not continuous, nor does it go on for ever. At first there is a rapid increase in efficiency which continues for a while, then it begins to slow down, until eventually there is no further increase. The shape of the curve of increased efficiency suggests (Johnson-Laird 1988: 170, citing Newell & Rosenbloom 1981) that the process of learning involves the construction of a cognitive apparatus dedicated to cope with this sort of task. The establishment of that apparatus is slow, and while it is in construction there is significant improvement; however once it has been set up no further improvement becomes possible. A chunk or apparatus concerned with a familiar activity has thus come into existence in the brain as a result of repeated practice (Simon 1979: 386 sqq.).

A more complex and much discussed example of what happens when someone becomes an expert comes from studies of master chess players. It has been convincingly argued that expert chess players do not differ from novices (who are not complete beginners) in knowing the rules of chess or in performing such motor tasks as moving one piece without knocking the others down. What seems to distinguish the expert from the novice is not so much an ability to handle complex strategic logico-mathematical rules, but rather the possession, in memory, of an amazingly comprehensive and organised store of total or partial chessboard configurations, which allows the expert to recognise the situation *in an instant* so as to know what should be done next (Dreyfus & Dreyfus 1986: 32–5). However, bearing in mind the example of driving, what is surely happening is that the expert is not just remembering many games but that she has developed through long practice a specific apparatus which *enables her to remember* many games and configurations much more easily and quickly than the non-expert. She has learned how to learn this kind of information. This would explain how the expert can cope, not only with situations which she recognises, but also with situations which are new, so long as they fall within the domain which she has learned to cope with efficiently.

Learning to become an expert would therefore be a matter not simply of remembering many instances, but of constructing a dedicated cognitive mechanism for dealing with instances of a particular kind. Such a mechanism, because it is concerned only with a specific domain of activity, can cope with information relating to that domain of activity remarkably quickly and efficiently, whether this be information about chess-piece configurations, motorway scenarios, or potentially useful areas of forest, and even though the specific cases of chess, motorway or forest have not been previously encountered in exactly that way (Dreyfus & Dreyfus 1986: ch. 1).

If becoming an expert does involve the creation of apparatuses dedicated to handle families of related tasks, then this is surely something which an anthropologist must bear in mind. For what she studies is precisely people coping with familiar yet ever novel situations (Hutchins 1980). It seems reasonable to assume that the construction of dedicated apparatuses for dealing expertly with certain areas of activity is going on in the process of cultural learning of all common practical tasks. Indeed some recent work suggests that learning to become an expert in familiar areas is a necessary preliminary to other types of learning and to being able to cope with the less familiar and less predictable. The reason seems to be partly neurological.

In the case of car driving, it seems that as a person becomes an expert, not only does she drive better, not only does she transform what was once linguistic propositional information into something else, she also seems to employ much less neurological potential in doing the necessary tasks (Schneider & Shiffrin 1977), thereby freeing her for other mental tasks, such as talking on a car phone. Similarly, the extraordinary feats of memory of the chess master seem to be made possible by the efficient packing of information through the use of the expert apparatus for coping with novel situations of play.

Such observations suggest the general conclusion that the ability to learn more is largely a matter of organising what one has already learned in packed chunks so that one has room for the new. Some cognitive scientists have therefore argued that the problems young children have in doing the tasks which, as Piaget showed, only adults can do, stem not from the immaturity of the children's brains, but from the fact that this 'packing' has not yet taken place. Once the essential preliminary procedures have been sufficiently organised, their implementation will only require limited neurological capacity, leaving enough 'room' for the child to perform further supplementary tasks. These are the tasks which the child had earlier seemed unable to perform; but really the problem was that they could not normally be performed simultaneously with their necessary preliminaries (Smith *et al.* 1988).

There is therefore considerable evidence that learning is not just a matter of storing received knowledge, as most anthropologists implicitly assume when they equate cultural and individual representations, but that it is a matter of constructing apparatuses for the efficient handling and packing of specific domains of knowledge and practice. Furthermore, as suggested by the case of learning to drive, evidence shows that once these apparatuses are constructed, the operations connected with these specific domains not only *are* non-linguistic but also *must* be non-linguistic if they are to be efficient.[9] It follows that much of the knowledge which anthropologists study necessarily exists in people's heads in a non-linguistic form.

Before proceeding further, an ambiguity in what has been argued so far must be removed. To say that knowledge concerned with the familiar must be non-linguistic could mean one of two things. It could mean simply that this knowledge is not formulated in natural language. On the other hand it could mean something much stronger. It could mean that this knowledge is in no way 'language like', that it is not governed by the characteristic sentential logic of natural and computer languages.[10] Here I adopt the stronger of the two alternatives because I believe that the studies on expertise discussed above suggest that the knowledge organised for efficiency in day-to-day practice is not only non-linguistic, but also not language-like in that it does not take a sentential logical form. To argue this and to make my argument less negative I now turn to the admittedly controversial assumptions of what has been called 'connectionism'.

IV

What is particularly interesting for anthropology in connectionism is not so much connectionism itself, but the reasons why a theory like it is necessary. Simply put, a theory such as connectionism is necessary because a sentential linear model of the mind-brain, sometimes called the sentence-logic model (Churchland & Sejnowski 1989), which is broadly similar in form to the semantics of natural language, cannot account for the speed and efficiency with which we perform daily tasks and cope with familiar situations.

The sentence-logic or sentential linear model is intuitively attractive for a number of reasons, and these explain why it is implicit in anthropological theory and was accepted unchallenged for a long time in cognitive psychology. First of all, and probably most significantly, it is *the* model of folk psychology, as anthropologists have nicely demonstrated (D'Andrade 1987). Sentential logical forms are how we think we think. Secondly, sentential logical models work well for the semantics of natural language; and thirdly, they worked well for those metaphors for the mind—the von Neumann or digital computers.

However, these three arguments in favour of the sentence-logic model are very weak. First, folk psychology, whatever the majority of anthropologists may say, need not, as Churchland and Churchland (1983) point out, be any more valid than folk physics as a basis for scientific accounts. Secondly, what applies to language need not apply to other forms of mental activity.

Thirdly, digital computers come nowhere near to doing the jobs we humans can do, and so they must be, in some way, inappropriate as metaphors for the mind-brain.

The case for connectionism is best made by considering an example, and by using this type of example we can see the relevance of the theory for anthropology. Remember the Malagasy peasant. When the man said to his friend, 'look over there . . . that piece of forest would make a good swidden', an unbelievable mental feat seems to have then been achieved by the man addressed. He recalled from long-term memory the complex yet highly flexible mental model or schema 'the good swidden', then he conceptualised the piece of forest indicated, taking in information about the vegetation, the slope, the surrounding countryside, the hydrology, the soil, etc., then he matched the two intricate conceptualisations in what could not be just a simple comparison but a highly complex set of transformations. When put in this way, the total task seems Herculean, but in reality even the moderately talented Malagasy farmer would come to some assessment in just a few seconds. Furthermore, this computational feat is no more difficult than many other similar tasks which human beings perform all the time. Why then does such a task appear so impossibly complicated when we think about what it entails? The reason is that we are explaining the behaviour of the Malagasy farmer in terms of our own folk psychology, including a model of language-like semantics. This makes an easy task, which we know the farmer can perform in an instant or two, seem absolutely awesome. There must, indeed, be something wrong about how we think we think.

Connectionism is an alternative theory of thought which makes such commonplace feats as that of our Malagasy farmer possible to envisage. It suggests that we go about the whole process of thought in a quite different way from what we had previously and loosely assumed. The problem with the folk way of describing thought procedures, for example of how a decision is reached, is that we tend to see the activity as a serial process of analysis carried on along a single line by a single processor. For complex yet familiar tasks such processing would be impossibly clumsy and lengthy. Instead, connectionism suggests that we access knowledge, either from memory or as it is conceptualised from perception of the external world, through a number of processing units which work in parallel and feed in information simultaneously. It suggests, too, that the information received from these multiple parallel processors is analysed simultaneously through already existing networks connecting the processors. Only with this multiple parallel processing could complex understandings and operations, like those about the swidden, be achieved as fast as they are. Otherwise, given the conduction velocities and synaptic delays in neurons, it is a physical-cum-biological impossibility for the number of steps required by a logical-sentential model of the mind-brain to be carried out in the time within which even the simplest mental tasks are ordinarily performed. A connectionist brain, on the other hand, could (at least hypothetically) work sufficiently fast (Feldman & Ballard 1982).

It is much too early to say whether connectionism will prove to be an accurate analysis of the working of the brain, and, in any case, I am not in a position to be able to evaluate its neurological validity. What matters here, above all, is that the theory offers the kind of challenge to sentential logical models which anthropology requires, and it offers the kind of answers which would cope with the situations we seek to understand.

Support for connectionism does not, however, all come from first principles. Some psychological experimental work seems to confirm the theory (Rumelhart *et al.* 1986). The fact that computer programs which enable digital computers to work on something like parallel processing seem to be able to get them to do tasks which ordinary digital computers working with classical programs are unable to do, such as reading and reproducing in three dimensions grey shaded images, is also encouraging. There are, however, two other aspects of the theory which make it particularly attractive to the anthropologist.

The first is that connectionism can cope well with what Johnson-Laird (1983: 438–47) called the 'provisional' character of mental models, while sentential logical models imply a much greater rigidity which is quite unlike what we find in natural situations. The mental model of 'the good swidden' cannot be a checklist of characteristics to be found in a particular configuration or even an example of the kind of 'fuzzy' digital models recently proposed. With such fundamentally fixed models the Malagasy farmer would never find the right plot. The model cannot require absolutely any particular characteristic or configuration; just a general flexible theoretical-practical hypothesis. Connectionism can handle this type of 'fairly loose' practical-theoretical thinking, which as we saw is also implied in prototype theory, while other theories cannot.

Secondly, a connectionist model can account for the length of the process of becoming an expert at a particular task, a fact which itself is quite a puzzle. With such a model we can understand what would be happening when a person is learning to handle a family of related tasks, such as learning how to learn chess configurations. The person would be creating connected networks dedicated to specific domains of cognition, and procedures which, once set up, could be accessed quickly and efficiently by multiple parallel processing. Such a process for complex tasks, such as becoming a car driver or a chess expert, would require a good deal of packing and quite a bit of connecting, but once the job was done it would be highly efficient.

Since much of culture consists of the performance of these familiar procedures and understandings, connectionism may explain what a great deal of culture in the mind-brain is like. It also explains why this type of culture cannot be either linguistic or 'language like'. Making the culture efficient requires the construction of connected domain-relevant networks, which by their very nature cannot be stored or accessed through sentential logical forms such as govern natural language. Furthermore, as the discussion of apprenticeship learning shows, it is not even necessary for this type of knowledge ever to be put into words for it to be transmitted from one member of the community to another. The highly efficient non-linear packing in purpose-dedicated domains, formed through the practice of closely related activities, also explains why the transfer of one type of knowledge from one specific domain to another is so difficult. Lave's (1988) observation that there is no carry-over between school maths and coping with mathematical problems in a supermarket may well be due to the fact that the latter are dealt with in such a well chunked and connected domain that it cannot easily admit knowledge of such a different kind as sentential-logically organised school maths.[11]

V

To claim that much of culture is neither linguistic nor 'language like' does not imply that language is unimportant. Nevertheless, contrary to what anthropologists tend to assume, we should see linguistic phenomena as a *part* of culture, most of which is non-linguistic. Instead of taking language for granted, we should see its presence as requiring explanation. I cannot, in the space of this article, review all the circumstances and reasons for the occurrence of language in cultural life. Nonetheless, even here, cognitive science can offer provocative suggestions.

As we have seen, everyday practical actions and knowledge are probably packaged fairly hermetically into networks that take the form presumed by connectionist models. This packaging works very well for quick and efficient operations in familiar domains, but occasionally these networks can also be unpacked into linear sentential sequences which can then be put into words. If such transformations are commonplace, as I believe they are, we should then see culture as partly organised by connectionist networks and partly consisting of information organised by sentential logic, with a fluid transformative boundary between the two.[12]

The process of putting knowledge into words must require such a transformation in the nature of knowledge that the words will then have only a distant relationship to the knowledge referred to. But the process may also involve gains in different areas, as suggested by work, cited earlier in this article, on the transformation of prototype concepts into classical concepts (concepts which can be defined by a checklist of necessary and sufficient features).

For example, the extension of aspects of knowledge, normally chunked in a particular domain, into another domain may be one of the processes that require verbalisation, and such extension may well be linked with the process of innovation, as some of the work on the significance of analogical thinking for creativity suggests (Sternberg 1985). Indeed, we should perhaps see culture as always balanced between the need for chunking for efficiency, on the one hand, and, on the other, linguistic explicitness which allows, *inter alia*, for innovation and for ideology. With such a perspective we might be able to envisage a kind of general 'economy' of knowledge, which social anthropologists could then place in specific social and historical situations.

VI

In mentioning one of the possible reasons for explicitness I am suggesting a direction which would take me far from the limited concerns of this article. But even without going into these issues our discussion of the ways in which knowledge is organized has fundamental implications for anthropology. The first point is that culture is probably a different kind of phenomenon from what it has previously been thought to be, with the result that our understanding of culture has remained partial and superficial. Up to now, anthropology has tried to analyse culture through folk models of thought applicable only to sentential logical knowledge which, as noted, is but a small part of all knowledge. Dreyfus and Dreyfus (1986: 28) point out how social scientists use a 'Hamlet model' of decision making where the actor is assumed to weigh up and analyse alternatives in a self-conscious, logical fashion. In this respect it is interesting to note that unlike most of our informants doing familiar tasks, when Hamlet was trying to decide what to do next he was putting his thoughts into words. It is striking how many of the theories which have been popular in anthropology, such as transactionalist theories and other forms of methodological individualism, fall foul of Dreyfus and Dreyfus's strictures.

Then there are methodological implications. If the anthropologist is often attempting to give an account of chunked and non-sentential knowledge in a linguistic medium (writing), and she has no alternative, she must be aware that in so doing she is not reproducing the organisation of the knowledge of the people she studies but is transmuting it into an entirely different logical form. To effect such a transmutation is not impossible—after all we can describe things which are not linguistic. But in the attempt to evoke such knowledge we should avoid stylistic devices which turn attempts at description into quasi-theory, as was the case with structuralism and transactionalism. Perhaps we should make much more use of description of the way things look, sound, feel, smell, taste and so on—drawing on the realm of bodily experience—simply for heuristic purposes, to remind readers that most of our material is taken from the world of non-explicit expert practice and does not only come from linear, linguistic thought.

Above all we should beware the temptations of folk psychology. Folk psychology is indeed a form of competence employed in certain limited circumstances by the people we study, and it is therefore an object of research for anthropologists, but it is not something we want, or need, to carry over into anthropological explanation.

Thus, when our informants honestly say 'this is why we do such things', or 'this is what this means', or 'this is how we do such things', instead of being pleased we should be suspicious and ask what kind of *peculiar* knowledge is this which can take such an explicit, linguistic form?[13] Indeed, we should treat all explicit knowledge as problematic, as a type of knowledge probably remote from that employed in practical activities under normal circumstances.

Of course such conclusions raise the question of how we are ever going to get at this connected, chunked knowledge. But here I believe anthropologists have an advantage over other cognitive scientists in that they already do have a technique advocated by Malinowski but perhaps never followed by him: participant observation.

Because of its long-term character, involving continuous and intimate contact with those whom we study, participant observation makes us learn the procedures which these people have themselves learned and enables us to check up on whether we are learning properly by observing our improving ability to cope in the field with daily tasks, including social tasks, as fast as our informants. For example, as a result of fieldwork I too can judge quickly whether a bit of forest in Madagascar would make a good swidden. Indeed, I find that as I walk through the forest I am continually and involuntarily carrying out this sort of evaluation. Once this level of participation has been reached we can attempt to understand chunked knowledge through introspection.

Introspection is, of course, a notoriously dangerous procedure, and fear of introspection is what led anthropologists, especially cognitive anthropologists, to adopt research procedures which imitate the laboratory studies of others in order to 'harden' their findings. To me this approach seems misguided for two reasons. First, even in psychology, now that it has emerged from its behaviourist phase, the value of 'ecologically' based studies (Neisser 1975) and the merit of introspection as a theoretical starting point are once again becoming recognised. Secondly, much 'hard' evidence has proved on critical examination to be much 'softer' than the information obtained through participant observation. For example, one lesson which seems to follow from my argument is that ethnography backed up by our informants' 'actual words' may often be quite misleading.

In any case, I believe that anthropologists who have done prolonged fieldwork have always obtained the basis of their knowledge about the people they study from informal and implicit co-operation with them, whatever they might have pretended. I am fairly sure that the way I proceed in giving an account of the Malagasy cultures I study is by looking for facts, and especially for statements, that *confirm* what I already know to be right because I know how to live efficiently with these people, or, if you will, because I have established in my brain non-linguistic chunked mental models which enable me to cope with most things in daily life at great speed. Like other anthropologists, I then pretend that the linguistic confirmations of these understandings, which I subsequently obtain from what my informants say, are the *basis* of what I understand, but this is not really so. My knowledge was established prior to these linguistic confirmations.[14]

To recognise this is not shameful and should help us to avoid what is our greatest betrayal as anthropologists. One fact we always and rightly stress when explaining how our way of going about things contrasts with that of other social or cognitive scientists is the importance we attach to the everyday and how we believe that the most important aspects of culture are embedded in the basic mental premises of action. Anthropologists are particularly aware of this because many work in foreign cultures and so the exotic-in-the-everyday cannot but be prominent. We are also reminded of the importance of everyday practical culture because we do long-term fieldwork and participate for very long periods indeed. This learning about the practical is the best thing about anthropology, yet it often hardly features in our ethnographies; rather we rush to studies of rituals which could have been done in a week, or to analyses of economic organisation which could be done better by geographers and for which participant observation is, in any case, unsuitable.

Anthropologists worried about the difficulty of applying the kind of rigorous confirmation procedures of other disciplines should not worry too much. They certainly should not give up altogether and pretend, as has recently been fashionable, that they are merely involved in some literary exercise. They should learn to respect their own work rather more, and in cognitive matters they should remember that the basis of cognitive science is a *combination* of different disciplines, each with a contribution to make, but with a single aim.

The greatest contribution of anthropology to this totality can perhaps be to specify how cognition is employed in a natural environment, and in this way to help to decide what kinds of hypotheses and findings are required from those other cognitive sciences which work in more controlled conditions. It is because I am familiar with daily life in a Malagasy village, and also because I look for general explanations of what is going on, that I see the central problems to be solved as those of accounting for such intellectual feats as that of the peasant looking at the forest in search of a swidden site. Dreyfus and Dreyfus are quite right to point out that, by failing to pay attention to the way real human experts operate, cognitive scientists have attempted to create artificial intelligences along lines that ignore the very characteristics of human practice, but this is not a reason for arguing, as they do, for giving up the attempt altogether. It is a reason why, in the same way as anthropologists need other cognitive scientists, these other cognitive scientists would also benefit from co-operation with anthropologists having experience of participant observation.

Notes

The research on which this article was based was financed by The Spencer Foundation. I also benefited greatly from the hospitality of the anthropology department of Bergen University where I was able to develop some of the ideas presented here. I would also like to thank F. Cannell, C. Fuller, D. Holland, N. Quinn and G. Strauss for helpful comments on an earlier draft. Above all I would like to thank D. Sperber for introducing me to the subject and making many useful suggestions for the improvement on the text of the lecture as it was originally delivered.

1. I do not want to imply that all members of a community need possess all cultural knowledge. Discussions of 'distributed cognition' by Cicourel and others suggest that this may not be so.

2. See Sperber (1985) to find this point fully argued.

3. Among American anthropologists who have discussed connectionism are Quinn and Strauss (1989), Hutchins (1988) and D'Andrade (1990).

4. It is true that structuralism, at least in its Lévi-Straussian form, paid attention to memory in that it assumed that the source of structuration was the need to encode information so that it could be kept and retrieved. In retrospect, however, as was shown by Sperber, the structuralist's view of memory was much too simple. In particular it assumed, with other types of cognitive anthropology, that what an individual received from others was stored in the same form as it had been communicated and that all information was equally memorable (Sperber 1985).

The theories of learning implicit in structuralism are even more problematic since they cannot account for the inevitably gradual construction of structured knowledge, a criticism which has been made in a variety of ways by Piaget (1968), Turner (1973), Sperber (1985) and myself (1985). Admittedly, such writers as Bourdieu (1972) have tried to remedy this situation, but in his case with a theory of learning *habitus* which is psychologically vague and which, because of its reintroduction of the notion of individual 'rational' choice, runs into some of the difficulties which I go on to discuss.

5. Holland and Quinn (1987: 19) draw attention to the significance of these for our understanding of culture.

6. Work on deaf and dumb children also seems to show that advanced conceptual thought does not require language (Petitto 1987; 1988). I am grateful to L. Hirschfeld for pointing out the significance of this work for my argument.

7. Although I am relying extensively on Dreyfus and Dreyfus's characterisation of expertise (1986), I do this to reach quite different conclusions.

8. I am told that in Norway, although the normal driving test involves both a practical section and a question and answer section, some people seem totally unable to do the language part of the test, and so a more difficult practical test has been devised for them which eliminates the need to do the language part. There is apparently no evidence that people who have obtained their test in this way are worse drivers than the others.

9. The point has already been made by Schank and Abelson (1977).

10. After all, it is possible to argue, as Fodor does, that although thought is not a matter of speaking to oneself silently, it still is ultimately 'language like' and involves series of 'grammatically' (though not the grammar of the surface structure of natural languages) linked representations and propositions. This suggestion enables Fodor to talk of a 'language of thought', though it might be better to say a 'quasi-language of thought' (Fodor 1987).

11. The fact that people who are unable to perform Wason's task (a logical test performed under laboratory conditions with two-sided cards) when faced by his cards can do it when it is reproduced in a context familiar to them points to similar conclusions (Johnson-Laird & Wason 1977). See the discussion of this point in Dreyfus and Dreyfus (1986: 19).

12. Such a reconciliation of rule and representation models with connectionist ones has been proposed by Bechtel (1990).

13. These explicitly linguistic forms may have different relations to knowledge (see Barth 1990).

14. An attempt to write an ethnography along these lines is to be found in Bloch (1992).

References

Abelson, R. 1981. Psychological status of the script concept. *Am. Psychol.* **36**, 715–29.

Anderson, J.R. 1976. *The architecture of memory.* Cambridge, MA: Harvard Univ. Press.

Atran, S. 1990. *Cognitive foundations of natural history.* Cambridge: Univ. Press.

Barth, F. 1990. The guru and the conjurer: transactions in knowledge and the shaping of culture in southeast Asia and Melanesia. *Man* (N.S.) **25**, 640–53.

Bechtel, W. 1990. Connectionism and the philosophy of mind: an overview. In *Mind and Cognition* (ed.) W. Lycan. Oxford: Blackwell.

Bloch, M. 1985. From cognition to ideology. In *Power and knowledge: anthropological and sociological approaches* (ed.) R. Fardon. Edinburgh: Scottish Univ. Press.

——. 1992. What goes without saying: the conceptualisation of Zafimaniry society. In *Conceptualising society* (ed.) A. Kuper. London: Routledge.

Bourdieu, P. 1972. *Esquisse d'une theorie de la pratique.* Paris: Droz.

Bowerman, M. 1977. The acquisition of word meaning: an investigation in some current concepts. In *Thinking: readings in cognitive science* (eds) P. Johnson-Laird & P. Wason. Cambridge: Univ. Press.

Brown, R. 1973. *A first language: the early stages.* Harmondsworth: Penguin.

Churchland, P.M. & P.S. Churchland 1983. Stalking the wild episteme. *Nous* **17**, 5–18 (reprinted in *Mind and cognition* (ed.) W.L. Lycan. Oxford: Blackwell, 1990).

Churchland, P.S. & T. Sejnowski 1989. Neural representation and neural computation. In *Neural connections, mental computations* (eds) L. Nadel *et al.* Cambridge, Mass.: M.I.T. Press.

D'Andrade, R. 1987. A folk model of the mind. In *Cultural models in language and thought* (eds) D. Holland & N. Quinn. Cambridge: Univ. Press.

_____. 1990. Some propositions about the relations between culture and cognition. In *Cultural psychology* (eds) J. Stigler *et al.* Cambridge: Univ. Press.

Dreyfus, H. & S. Dreyfus 1986. *Mind over machine: the power of intuition and expertise in the era of the computer.* Oxford: Blackwell.

Feldman, J. & D. Ballard 1982. Connectionist models and their properties. *Cogn. Sci.* **6**, 205–54.

Fillmore, C. 1975. An alternative to checklist theories of meaning. In *Proceedings of the first Annual Meeting of the Berkeley Linguistic Society,* 123–31.

Fodor, J.A. 1987. *Psychosemantics.* Cambridge, MA: M.I.T Press.

_____. 1983. *Modularity of mind: an essay on faculty psychology.* Cambridge, MA.: M.I.T. Press.

Goody, E. 1978. Towards a theory of questions. In *Questions and politeness: strategies in social interaction* (ed.) E. Goody. Cambridge: Univ. Press.

Haudricourt, A.-G. 1968. La technologie culturelle: essai de méthodologie. In *Ethnologie générale* (ed.) J. Poirier. Paris: Pléiade.

Holland, D. & N. Quinn (eds) 1987. *Cultural models in language and thought.* Cambridge: Univ. Press.

Hutchins, E. 1980. *Culture and inference: a Trobriand case study.* Cambridge, MA.: Harvard Univ. Press.

_____. 1988. Where's the expertise in expert navigation? Paper delivered at the annual meeting of the American Anthropological Association at Phoenix, Arizona.

Johnson-Laird, P. 1983. *Mental models: towards a cognitive science of language, inference and consciousness.* Cambridge: Univ. Press.

_____. 1988. *The computer and the mind: an introduction to cognitive science.* London: Fontana.

_____. & P. Wason 1977. A theoretical analysis of insight into a reasoning task. In *Thinking: readings in cognitive science* (eds) P. Johnson-Laird & P. Wason. Cambridge: Univ. Press.

Keil F.C. & N. Batterman 1984. A characteristic-to-defining shift in the development of word meaning. *Verb. Learning and verbal Behav.* **23**, 221–36.

Lave, J. 1988. *Cognition in practice.* Cambridge: Univ. Press.

_____. 1990. The culture of acquisition and the practice of understanding. In *Cultural psychology* (eds) J. Stigler *et al.* Cambridge: Univ. Press.

Leroi-Gourhan, A. 1943. *Evolution et techniques.* Paris: P.U.F.

Malinowski, B. 1935. *The language of magic and gardening (Coral Gardens and their Magic* Vol. 2). London: Allen & Unwin.

Markham, E.M. & J. Seibert 1976. Classes and collections: internal organisation and resulting holistic properties. *Cognit. Psychol.* **8**, 561–77.

Mauss, M. 1936. Les techniques du corps. *J. Psychol.* **32**, n. 3–4.

Neisser, U. 1975. *Cognition and reality: principles and implications of cognitive psychology.* San Francisco: Freeman.

Newell, A. & P.S. Rosenbloom 1981. Mechanisms of skill acquisition and the law of practice. In *Cognitive skills and their acquisition* (ed.) J.R. Anderson. Hillsdale, NJ: Erlbaum.

Petitto, L.A. 1987. On the autonomy of language and gesture: evidence from the acquisition of personal pronouns in American sign language. *Cognition* 27, 1–52.

_____. 1988. Language and the prelinguistic child. In *The development of language and language researchers: essays in honor of Roger Brown* (ed.) F.S. Kessel. Hillsdale, NJ: Erlbaum.

Piaget, J. 1968. *Le structuralisme*. Paris: P.U.F.

Quinn, N. & C. Strauss 1989. A cognitive cultural anthropology. Paper prepared for the session on "Assessing Developments in Anthropology" of the American Anthropological Association Annual Meetings, 1989.

Rosch, E. 1977. Classification of real world objects: origins and representations in cognition. In *Thinking: readings in cognitive science* (eds) P. Johnson-Laird & P. Wason. Cambridge: Univ. Press.

_____. 1978. Cognitive representations of semantic categories. *J. exp. Psychol.* **104**, 192–223.

Rumelhart, D., G. Hinton & J. McClelland 1986. A general framework for parallel distributed processing. In *Explorations in the microstructure of cognition,* vol. **1.** (eds) D. Rumelhart & J. McClelland. Cambridge, MA.: M.I.T. Press.

Schank, R. & R. Abelson 1977. *Scripts, plans, goals and understanding.* Hillsdale, NJ: Erlbaum.

Schneider, W. & R. Shiffrin 1977. Controlled and automatic human information processing, 1: detection, search and attention. *Psychol. Rev.* 84, 1–66.

Simon, H. 1979. *Models of thought.* New Haven: Yale Univ. Press.

Smith, E.E. 1988. Concepts and thought. In *The psychology of human thought* (eds) R.J. Sternberg & E.E. Smith. Cambridge: Univ. Press.

Smith, L., M. Sera & B. Gattuso 1988. The development of thinking. In *The psychology of human thought* (eds) R.J. Sternberg & E.E. Smith. Cambridge: Univ. Press.

Sperber, D. 1985. Anthropology and psychology: towards an epidemiology of representations. *Man* (N.S.) **20**, 73–89.

_____. & W. Wilson 1986. *Relevance: communication and cognition.* Oxford: Blackwell.

Sternberg, R.J. 1985. *Beyond I.Q.: a triadic theory of human intelligence.* Cambridge: Univ. Press.

Turner, T. 1973. Piaget's structuralism. *Am. Anthrop.* 75, 351–73.

Tyler, S. (ed.) 1969. *Cognitive anthropology.* New York: Holt, Rinehart & Winston.

Winch, P. 1958. *The idea of a social science.* London: Routledge & Kegan Paul.

Chapter Two

What Goes Without Saying: The Conceptualization of Zafimaniry Society

This chapter is an attempt to put into practice some of the ideas concerning ethnography and cognition outlined in Chapter 1 and to apply them to the ethnography of the Zafimaniry, a small group of forest dwellers whom I have been studying for more than 20 years. The basic concept used here is that of the mental model, *which is close to the notion of* schema *discussed in Chapter 3.*

*   *   *

A problem which lurks uneasily in the prefaces of most anthropological monographs and worries, or should worry, all fieldworking anthropologists is that the way anthropologists conceptualize the societies they have studied in their ethnographic accounts almost always seems alien, bizarre, or impossibly complicated to the people of those societies. Perhaps this would not matter if ethnographies claimed only to be description from the outside; however, most accounts attempt, at least in part, to represent a society and ways of thinking about it from the insiders' point of view. Perhaps, then, we could get rid of the difficulty by saying that this disturbing lack of recognition was just a problem of vocabulary; after all, most people in most parts of the world are unacquainted with the technical terms and literary conventions of academic anthropology. But one has to face the fact that, if this were all there was to it, anyone who was reasonably good at paraphrase would surely be able to cross the communication gap and produce a non-technically worded ethnography with which informants would largely agree. Clearly, this is not often the case. The problem of lack of validation by the people with whom anthropologists work begins, then, to look like a very serious one.

In fact, the basis of the problem lies in something much more damaging than is normally recognized. Anthropological accounts, I believe, work from a false theory of cognition. As a result, when they attempt to represent the way the people studied conceptualize their society, they do so in terms which do not match the way *any* human beings conceptualize *anything* fundamental and familiar in *any* society or culture. In imagining how the people they study conceptualize society anthropologists use the common folk view of thought current in both Western and many other societies. But there is considerable evidence that this folk theory is as wrong about psychological processes as the folk theory of physics is wrong about the nature of energy (see Bechtel 1990; Churchland and Sejnowski 1989).

The folk model, which is also widely assumed in Western philosophy, is that thought is logic-sentential and language-like. We tend to imagine thinking as a kind of silent soliloquizing wherein the building blocks are words with their definitions and the process itself involves linking propositions by logical inferences in a single lineal sequence. By contrast, much recent work in cognitive science strongly suggests that everyday thought is not 'language-like', that it does not involve linking propositions in a single sequence in the way language represents reasoning. Rather, it relies on clumped networks of signification which *require* that they be organized in ways which are not lineal but multi-stranded if they are to be used at the amazing speed necessary to draw on complex stored information in everyday activity. If that is so, anthropologists are presented with two problems.

The first is that the people we study are unlikely to be able easily to describe their thought processes for anthropologists through what they say, since language is an inappropriate medium for evoking the non-lineal organization of everyday cognition. (This, like several other points I make in this chapter, was pointed out in a different way by Bourdieu in 1972.) Furthermore, since having to explain to others what one thinks through an inappropriate medium, viz., language, is a familiar problem in all cultures, informants asked to give retrospective accounts of their thought processes—a common enough occurrence in normal life—are able to fall back on the conventions by which the problem is normally avoided. These conventions of everyday discourse usually involve reinventing a hypothetical quasi-linguistic lineal, rational thought process which appears to lead satisfactorily to the conclusions reached. But it does so deceptively in terms of the way we, and they, think we think because it follows the folk theory of thought shared by the anthropologist and the informant. In other words, the problem of explaining to others how we reach a decision is solved by what we would normally call *post hoc* rationalizations, and these are what anthropologists are given when they too ask for retrospective explanations of actions.

The second problem which arises from the impossibility of matching the organization of everyday thought to the semantics of natural language relates to the anthropologists' own accounts of their informants' thought processes. Anthropologists write books, in which information is inevitably presented by means of language, and so their medium makes them slip far too easily into representing the hypothesized thought processes of those they study as though these also inevitably assumed the organizational logic of the semantics of language. Furthermore, the problem is not just one of medium; anthropologists naturally attempt to produce accounts of intellectual processes which will prove persuasive to their readers, and readers, along with the anthropologists' informants, expect accounts of the thought of the people studied to match the folk theory of thought. As a result, a kind of double complicity is all too easily established between anthropologists and their readers and between anthropologists and their informants—a double complicity which leads to representations of thought in logic-sentential terms.

But in fact, although a plausible account is thereby produced, it leaves all the main participants uncomfortable. Informants feel that anthropologists' accounts are not right. Readers are also suspicious of accounts of the culture of others which, although plausible, are quite unlike the way they experience their own culture. Anthropologists themselves are worried by the fact that the acceptable ethnographies they produce with such effort have somehow lost 'what it was really like'. This is something which they sometimes wrongly attribute to the difficulty of rendering one text into another, while what they should be thinking about is the problem of rendering into a text something which is not a text.

Fortunately, as suggested above, recent work in cognitive science helps us resist the insidious influence of the folk theory of thought by suggesting an alternative to it. This work, although still tentative, provides scientific ammunition against the logic-sentential folk model of thought implied by language and suggests another way in which thought is organized which, furthermore, is intuitively attractive to a field-working anthropologist. This is so because, while the *post hoc* overlinguistic rationalizations of most ethnography seem distant from what one feels is going on in real situations in the field, the newer theory of thought intuitively seems to correspond to the way informants actually operate in everyday situations.

It is impossible to discuss fully here the theoretical basis of this alternative view of cognition (but see Churchland and Sejnowski 1989; Bloch 1991). The core of the approach, usually known as connectionism, is the idea that most knowledge, especially the knowledge involved in everyday practice, does not take a linear, logic-sentential form but rather is organized into highly complex and integrated networks or mental models most elements of which are connected to each other in a great variety of ways. The models form conceptual clumps which are not language-like precisely because of the simultaneous multiplicity of ways in which information is integrated in them. These mental models are, what is more, only partly linguistic; they also integrate visual imagery, other sensory cognition, the cognitive aspects of learned practices, evaluations, memories of sensations, and memories of typical examples. Not only are these mental models not lineal in their internal organization but information from them can be accessed simultaneously from many different parts of the model through 'multiple parallel processing'. This is what enables people to cope with information as rapidly as they, and probably other animals, do in normal, everyday situations.

There is, of course, no question of anthropologists' studying these mental models directly in any detail. However, the awareness that cultural knowledge is likely to be organized in this way should modify the way in which we represent actors' ways of thinking in general and their conceptualizations of society in particular. It should make anthropologists suspicious of overlinguistic, over-logic-sentential conceptualizations and prompt them to search for alternatives which could correspond to the clumped models just discussed. Furthermore, in going in this direction I believe we will find that much of the often-expressed discomfort with ethnography may disappear and that the problem that the people we study cannot relate to our accounts of them may be diminished.

This paper is an attempt to go some way towards writing ethnography in such a way that actors' concepts of society are represented not as strings of terms and propositions but as governed by lived-in models, that is, models based as much in experience, practice, sight, and sensation as in language. In trying to do this there can be no avoiding the problem that inevitably this information is presented in a medium, language, whose semantic organization leads back to the kind of presentation from which I am trying to escape, but it is also true that language can be used, if not without difficulty, to talk about processes and patterns which are not in any way language-like. We should not mistake our account for what it refers to.

There is also another difficulty. Normally anthropologists who are trying to persuade their audience that what they are saying is a fair account of the concepts of the people they study tend to fall back on quoting their informants. This apparently innocent procedure is, however, for the reasons just discussed, potentially misleading, since people's explanations probably involve *post hoc* rationalizations of either a conventional or an innovative character. So, although I do use what people say in attempting to convey these mental models, these statements are merely purpose-specific periphery to the foundations of conceptualization. But then where do my data come from, and how can I persuade my readers of their relevance? Here I propose an awkward solution.

Through intimate participant observation over long periods of time, anthropologists learn how to live in a relatively coordinated way with their informants. In order to do this they must learn and internalize a great deal of the knowledge that the people they study must themselves have learnt and internalized. Now, if indeed anthropologists have learnt these clumped non-logic-sentential mental models which organize the cultures they study, they should be able to make at least plausible assertions of how their informants conceptualize the world as a result of their own introspection. I believe that readers who are convinced that anthropologists have carried out the kind of fieldwork necessary for this kind of understanding should be willing to give them the benefit of the doubt. This may seem to be asking a lot; in fact it does not call for more intellectual generosity than is normally required from the readers of academic texts, and sometimes perhaps not for such good reasons. Anthropologists' accounts of the thought processes of their informants accompanied by many verbatim statements, which therefore superficially appear based on irrefutable evidence, will on examination turn out to require almost as much trust from the reader because of the arbitrary way in which these statements must be selected. Furthermore, such language-based accounts are likely to be misleading because the style of presentation will inevitably suggest that the core of the actors' conceptualizations is these few selected verbal statements.

In this paper I shall therefore try to give, for the sake of demonstration, an ethnographic account of the conceptualization of society by a small group of people I studied in Madagascar called the Zafimaniry.[1] My description relies on the evocation of a few linked central mental models[2] which I believe are, when put together, sufficient to organize their conceptualization and practice of society. These models, as connectionist theories would lead us to expect, are not principally propositional in the traditional sense of the term, though they can be accessed in part through language, but partly visual, partly sensual, partly linked to performance. They are all anchored in practice and material experience, and this is what makes them 'obvious' to anybody, anthropologist or informant, who participates in Zafimaniry life. For this reason, my account would not, I am sure, appear in any way strange to my informants. Indeed, their reaction is that since what I am talking about is merely about what things 'are like'—people, trees, sex, gender, houses, and so on—it is a waste of time to talk much about them.[3]

In doing this I am implicitly criticizing some aspects of my earlier attempt at giving an account of their society (Bloch 1975). This article dealt with many other topics than the Zafimaniry's conceptualization of their society, and by these I stand. I tried to give an account of their social organization, especially their kinship organization, largely in terms of a fairly hazy moiety organization, complex marriage and filiation rules, and kinship terminology. After subsequent fieldwork I now find this attempt, although on the whole acceptable in terms of the facts it presented, to suffer precisely from giving the impression that the Zafimaniry's conceptualization of society could be given in the logic-sentential form criticized above, though this is precisely how social anthropologists traditionally proceed.[4]

The Zafimaniry are a group of shifting cultivators numbering about 20,000 who live in the eastern forest of Madagascar. Although they have in the past been incorporated into various states and kingdoms, they have, by and large, maintained a remarkable degree of autonomy up to the present day, and in most matters their villages, varying in size between 300 and 3,000 inhabitants, are practically self-governing. Here I attempt to give an account of how they conceptualize their society in terms of five linked mental models from which all the main principles of their social organization seem to flow: (1) the mental model of what people are like and how they mature, (2) the mental model of the differences and similarities between women and men, (3) the mental model of what a good marriage is like, (4) the mental model of what trees and wood are like, and (5) the mental model of what houses are like. These are all very simple models which misleadingly appear to the participants as merely emanations of the empirical, but when they are put together they produce the highly specific conceptualization of society which characterizes the Zafimaniry's view.

What People Are Like and How They Mature

The Zafimaniry conceptualization of the maturation of the body focuses not so much on growth as on hardening and straightening. Thus Zafimaniry often play with the soft bodies of their babies and laugh over their bendability, calling the children, in an amused fashion, by the common Malagasy term for babies, which literally means 'water children'. In a similar mood they show each other the baby's fontanelle and the watery substance it covers. The change from bendable wetness to straight hardness is rarely commented upon in discourse, but its importance can be guessed at from continual allusions to the straight leg and arm bones of elders and ancestors and from the fact that people talk of the elders' 'straightening' the young as they show them the proper ways of behaving according to ancestral rules. Less direct is the way people expect to break their leg and arm bones more and more easily as they get old because, they sometimes say, the bones are 'harder'. Equally suggestive is the way people note and sometimes comment on the drying out of the skin of the old in relation to that of the young. All these cognitions, practices, and chance or more formal remarks indicate a general understanding of the maturing body which is unproblematically communicated without the anthropologist's necessarily being aware of the exact manner of this transmission.

This physical change in the body accompanies psychological development. Babies cannot talk and cannot be expected to do much for themselves. They do not exercise any moral judgement. This amoral unpredictability continues through youth and in some ways increases as the children get bigger and cause more chaos. Their behaviour soon becomes tinged with boisterous and unstable sexuality, and the boys tend to become aggressive. But a change occurs for both boys and girls at marriage. Marriage calms people down; their minds turn to practical matters to do with making their marriage successful, in particular rearing and being able to support children who themselves produce children, and so on. Later the psychological state typical of the married person is, and should be, gradually replaced by the *gravitas* of elders. Elders are calm, very stable people whose psychological disposition is the exact opposite of the playful quarrelsomeness of the young in that they are peacemakers who value unity and morality above all things.

This general process of psychological development is often commented upon and even explained by the Zafimaniry, but it is not the basis of the model any more than statements are the basis of the cognition of bodily development. The basis is the demonstrated and observed behaviour of people of different ages, together with the disapproval or surprise expressed when people display psychological behaviour inappropriate for their ages.

The model of maturation also has an aspect which concerns occupation. When the young are old enough to get about, they soon become little foragers. At first this happens in the village, and then, little by little, their activities take place ever farther away, sometimes deep in the forest, involving ever bigger finds and game. The children start with berries and insects, then move on to small fish and crustacea and then to birds and larger mammals. This period of foraging ends with marriage, but because boys marry later than girls (since girls mature earlier) the foraging stage continues longer and develops towards an extreme for young men when their hunting becomes associated with larger animals such as wild boar. This last stage of the foraging period also involves wage labouring; this consists exclusively of forestry work, which is easily assimilated to hunting and foraging both because it takes place deep in the forest and because the young male workers behave as if they were on a hunting trip, with boisterous mock aggression and the singing of hunting songs.

The foraging of the young is for the Zafimaniry an adventurous but not a serious form of activity; they say and demonstrate by their actions that it is a form of play. Consequently the product of such activity, although it is very important nutritionally and economically, is not, nor in their evaluation should it be, taken seriously. For example, when little girls sold some delicious forest fruit at a market for quite a lot of money, everybody commented that this was ridiculous. With marriage, the foraging of the young gives way to agriculture, which is and is recognized to be the typical activity of the married middle-aged. Unlike foraging, this is a serious business, and it is closely associated with the need to support children and grandchildren. Finally, middle age, dominated by agriculture and marriage, is gradually replaced by elderhood. In elderhood other types of activities dominate. At first carpentry and the carving of the wood which will strengthen and beautify the house become central activities for the relatively young male elder. Then, for both genders, various forms of highly valued oral activities come to the fore. These include making formal speeches, amongst them requests or thanks to the ancestors, speeches involved with formal visiting, church addresses, and above all the oratory of dispute settlement.

Maturation is therefore not just a matter of physical and psychological development but also a matter of changing occupation. This totality can be more completely grasped by briefly looking at two further facets of the model: language and locality.

The language of the young is and is often noted to be a tumble of rushed, often unfinished sentences. Their conversational style is marked by continual interruptions and what Karl Reisman called 'contrapuntal conversation' (Reisman 1974). In many ways it too is an aspect of play. The language of the middle-aged also relates to the character of the activities which dominate their lives. It is typically earnest conversation in which the different speakers do not interrupt each other and in which the intention of conveying information and of negotiation seems to govern the style of intercourse. Finally, the speech typical of elders is highly formalized, highly decorated, and largely formulaic in that it follows predictable models for thanks, greetings, prayers, etc. The manner of speaking is quiet and as if not addressed to anybody; it seems beyond dialogue. However, in contrast with the styles of conversation typical of the young and the middle-aged, the style of elders is employed only when they are *being* elders; the rest of the time they speak like middle-aged people.

Finally, there is a spatial aspect to all this. The young are always running about, as soon as they can they go off in search of forest products and adventure. The middle-aged also move about a lot, but they are ever more anchored to the house of their marriage. This stabilization and localization increase still further with the elders, who, as we shall see, gradually merge with the house itself.

The Differences and Similarities Between Women and Men

Gender is not for the Zafimaniry the prime identity that it may be in some cultures. First one is a child, an adult, an elder, a parent, etc., and *then* one is a special kind of child, a special kind of parent, etc., that is female or male. Furthermore, the relative prominence of gender differentiation varies with age. Gender becomes more important at adolescence and then becomes gradually less so.

However, women and men have certain bodily characteristics which mean that they are different. These bodily differences concern the linked activities of sex and the production of children. Because sex and reproduction require both women and men, these differences are complementary and not a matter of more or less. At the same time, there is a hierarchical aspect to gender. Insofar as they are comparable, women are usually physically weaker and, in a way which appears to the Zafimaniry inevitably linked, probably also mentally inferior to men, although in certain circumstances (which although unusual are not rare) it is possible for women to be intellectually superior and stronger than men. This is so, for example, if a wife fulfils her duties while a husband does not or if the man is weakened by disease or other infirmity or simply if she is big and he is small.

What a Good Marriage Is Like

The model of the good marriage is as central to Zafimaniry conceptualization as that concerning the maturation of people. The core of the model is the image of a complementary, loving, fruitful union of two spouses engaged in joint domestic and agricultural tasks.[5]

Fruitfulness manifests itself first of all in the number of children produced and then in the number of children produced by these children, and so on. Again, it is manifested in the success, principally the agricultural success, of the parents in providing for these children, grandchildren, and so on, so that they thrive. A fruitful marriage is one in which the combination of the spouses leads to the growth of a unity which they have created. This means that the children of the marriage are the continuation of this unity, and therefore siblings are part of a single totality since they are the outgrowth of the original unity produced by loving complementarity.

The centrality and character of this image of loving complementarity can be conveyed by a few hints provided by Zafimaniry ethnography. One of these is that parents who arrange that their children should marry keep this a secret from them. It is felt that parents can only point their children in the right direction, and mutual compatibility can only be achieved if it is believed by the parties to be spontaneous. Another hint is the fact that Zafimaniry diviners, in contrast to those in other parts of Madagascar, normally find the cause of sterility to be not a problem the woman has but the lack of compatibility of the pair. Then there is the total absence of public quarreling between spouses in a society where nothing much can be kept private and the fact that people say that if such quarreling became public the marriage would immediately break up.

At the heart of the model is the image of the couple cooperating harmoniously in the performance of single domestic and agricultural activities through different but complementary tasks. Most agricultural tasks are indeed carried out by husband-and-wife pairs working together, and this is often commented upon favourably. People often pointed out to me the emblematic significance of the particularly heavy work involved in carrying crops from the field to the house; this is a task that spouses share, although their ways of carrying, one on the head the other on the shoulder, are different.

Marital harmony is the product of the psychological and physiological compatibility of the spouses, but for the Zafimaniry this requires that a *balance* be established between the two parties. If the family of either the groom or the bride is much weaker, there cannot be a proper marriage, because a proper marriage requires that equal respect be paid to the origin of both spouses. Sexual unions in which this is not the case often occur, but to the Zafimaniry they are not marriages because marriage is marked by mutuality and reciprocal exchange at all levels. Balance is always threatened by the difficult intrusion of an element of imbalance brought about by the superiority of the man over the woman. Much of the Zafimaniry conceptualization of society flows from the attempt to reintroduce in this situation the balance of the good marriage.

A Zafimaniry marriage is the result of the stabilization of what starts as a playful, fleeting relationship between two very young persons who are like that because of their state of maturation. As the children grow up and form couples who begin to have regular sexual relationships, this fact becomes noticed, and the young people are forced to appear before the girl's parents in a simple ritual which is called *tapa maso* (literally, 'the breaking of the eyes'). This refers to the fact that it is very wrong for people of different generations, especially if they are of different sexes, to have knowledge of each other's sexual activity. The appearance of the young couple together asking for the girl's father's blessing therefore breaks this avoidance—it 'breaks the father's eyes'.

After the *tapa maso* the couple will most probably stay with the girl's parents until the next ritual, which is called the *fanambarana* (literally, 'the making clear'). The essential element of this ritual is the groom's fetching of the bride and her trousseau of kitchen furniture to his family's locality. The reason it is the bride who follows the groom and not the other way round is that the man is stronger than the woman. This fact, however, contradicts the image of balance, and so various strategies are adopted to restore it.

First of all, attempts are made during the *fanambarana* to produce a downright denial that an imbalance exists. The marriage is said to be a swop; everybody repeats the well-worn phrase that the marriage is 'an exchange of a male child for a female child', implying that the parents of the boy gain a daughter and the parents of the girl gain a son—and, indeed, from then on the spouses address their parents-in-law with the same terms as they use for their own parents. Similarly, people say that a marriage is 'the exchange of male orange for a female orange'. This gnomic statement is then explained as meaning that it is an exchange of like for like, since no one can tell the difference between the two sorts of oranges.

Other ways of lessening imbalance concern specific practices. The spouses must spend much time with the girl's parents, and they will seek the blessings of both sides equally for any important task. Their children are considered to be equally the grandchildren of both sides. Imbalance is also temporarily corrected by the fact that the obligations of the couple to the girl's parents have priority over their obligations to the boy's parents because, as they say, 'they are less often with the former'. Most important, the imbalance caused by gender is corrected by the introduction of the concept of the unity of siblings. This comes into play in two ways.

Since siblings are part of a unity, marriage to a particular person implies, to an extent, marriage to his or her siblings, including those of the other gender. The siblings of ego's spouse are also ego's spouses. Thus Zafimaniry men refer to the brothers of their wives and the husbands of their sisters by a term (*vady lahy*) which literally means 'male spouse', and Zafimaniry women refer to the sisters of their husbands and the wives of their brothers by a term (*vady vavy*) which literally means 'female spouse'. By stressing these 'marriage' relationships and the reciprocal and equal cooperation which exists between 'female spouses' and especially between 'male spouses', the marriage relationship regains a gender-free balance which the difference between women and men threatens to disrupt.

The unity of siblings is also used to recover the balance essential for the good marriage in an even more radical way. This involves making a specific marriage part of a reciprocal exchange wherein pairs of cross-sex young people classed as siblings by the kinship terminology intermarry simultaneously. Zafimaniry have a strong preference for marriage of a brother and a sister to sister and brother. This creates a pattern very similar to that familiar to anthropologists as cross-cousin marriage, and it has similar sociological effects in that it leads to a loose moiety system, something I discussed in a previous publication on the Zafimaniry (Bloch 1975). That this is so should not, however, make us forget that this moiety system is conceptualized as the result of the need for balance in a good marriage, not in the traditional description by means of rules and terminology which characterized my earlier attempt.

What Trees and Wood Are Like

The importance of trees and wood, two words which are translated into Malagasy by the single word *hazo*, is central to the Zafimaniry. As shifting cultivators they depend on burning wood to make fields; because the climate is so cold and damp they must have wood fires continually burning in their houses. Besides this they used to, and to a certain extent still do, make their cloth from the bark of trees, and their houses and most of their utensils are made of wood. It is not surprising, therefore, that all Zafimaniry possess very extensive scientific knowledge about wood, about the many species of trees, about the many different qualities of the woods they yield, and about the way different woods must be treated to prepare them for the various uses to which they are put.

The most valued trees and also the rarer ones are those which produce the kind of wood used in house building, and these must contain what the Zafimaniry call *teza*. The *teza* of trees is a dark impacted core which is much harder than the outer part, called by a term which normally refers to white of egg. It is often compared to the bones of animals and humans, which can also be called by the same word. A central image of *teza* is that it is what remains after a swidden has been fired, since this hardened core does not normally burn. Indeed, the word *teza* is the root of the verb *mateza,* 'to last or to remain'.

The maturation of trees with *teza* is of the greatest significance to the Zafimaniry. Young trees have no *teza* at all; then, as the tree gets older, stronger, and less bendable, the *teza* starts to develop as a tiny core surrounded by a very extensive 'white of egg'. Gradually, over many years, this proportion will change, so that in very old, very tall trees the *teza* will occupy most of the trunk, leaving a small outer ring of 'white of egg'. Such trees are the greatest and the most useful of all trees, since their *teza* can be used for the building of long-lasting houses and other artefacts which partake of the lasting nature of *teza* because they are made of it.

The presence of *teza* is awe-inspiring; it is a thing worthy of respect. It is the product of a maturation similar to the maturation of human beings in that it implies a straightening and a hardening of an inner core, but the *teza* of trees goes farther in that process than human beings can. Humans soon reach their peak of straightness and hardness and then go into reverse in old age and death; trees with *teza,* in contrast, continue to harden and become more and more lasting. As hard, dried wood, they outlast transitory human beings.

It is this lasting apotheosis of the *teza* of the noblest wood that is celebrated in the Zafimaniry carvings which are famous throughout Madagascar. These are low-relief geometrical patterns which cover the wooden parts of houses. Many writers have attempted with little success to understand what these carvings represent. In fact they represent nothing; they are a celebration of the lasting qualities of the *teza* which they cover.

What Houses Are Like

As is the case for people, marriages, and trees, the best way of understanding the Zafimaniry mental model of the house is to see it as a process of maturation. Indeed, the model of the maturation of the house is intimately tied to the model of the maturation of a marriage.

The first sign of appearance of a Zafimaniry house is usually the beginning of a flimsy building to the south of a young man's parents' house. Since a son owes his parents respect, this position is chosen because the south is an inferior direction to the north. The building will be very flimsy; apart from the four corner posts, it will be made of flexible woven bamboo and mats. It will most probably not possess the two focal features of the Zafimaniry house—the central house post, made of the *teza* of the hardest wood known to the Zafimaniry, and the hearth. These two crucial features are added only when the young man feels that his marriage is sufficiently well advanced to move his wife and children into the house. Then, with the permission of his father, he will erect the central house post and build the hearth. These will become the twin foci of the house. The central house post will be associated with the man for the rest of his life, and his normal place will be leaning against it. The hearth is little more than three stones which support a cooking pot and under which a fire can be lit. However, it will be furnished with the pots and cooking utensils which the bride brings with her after the *fanambarana* ceremony, and after that it will become permanently associated with the woman of the marriage. Before the house can be fully lived in, that is, before eating, cooking, or having sexual intercourse in it is allowed, a ritual of inauguration will be held wherein the elders of the families of both spouses will bless the house, especially the hearth and the central house post.

This ceremonial opening is, however, only a stage in a very long process during which the house will become harder and more permanent. What this means is that the soft and perishable parts of the house will gradually be replaced by the massive *teza* of great trees shaped so as to slot into each other. These are called the 'bones of the house', and they make the house extraordinarily lasting. The process of strengthening and beautifying the house is very long drawn out. It takes a long time for the house to become completely wooden, and before this some wood may already have had to be replaced. As the house is becoming more wooden, the wood itself will be gradually carved to 'celebrate' (to give *vonahitra* to) the *teza* of the posts, of the planks, and of the whole house itself. This hardening and beautifying is carried out at first by the husband working in marital cooperation with his 'male spouses', especially his wife's brothers. Then, as the spouses grow older, the task will be taken over by sons and daughters' husbands, then by grandsons and granddaughters' husbands, and so on. Thus the house which began with the marriage of two people will grow and become beautiful together with the fruitful balanced compatibility which they achieve. If the marriage continues to be fruitful, that is, if further descendants are born to it, this process of house growth will continue long after their death.

This is possible partly because of the unity of the group descended from a marriage and partly because of a symbolic substitution made conceivable by the association of people and trees via the notion of *teza*.[6] After the death of the couple the man will come to be represented by the central house post and the woman by the hearth and especially the furniture for it which she brought at her marriage. These remaining (*mateza*) objects become relics representing the original couple, and they are addressed as such and offerings are made to them by the descendants, especially on the occasions when they gather in the house, by then referred to as *trano masina* ('holy house'). These meetings will principally be to make requests for blessings from the house/ancestors and to settle disputes among descendants. A successful marriage therefore becomes an ever harder and more beautiful house which never stops growing as descendants in both male and female lines continue to increase. For these people it remains their 'house', though what this means is that it is a place of cult for them.

There is, however, a further aspect to all this. The couple in the house will itself have been the balanced product of two different houses: that of the parents of the bride and that of the parents of the groom. This fact is well recognized by the Zafimaniry. Thus young spouses with children, normally living in a house which has only just begun to harden with bones, are also children of two other couples. In fact, both the woman and the man are children of two couples, because, as we have seen, the marriage has made them the children of each other's parents. This dual filiation is demonstrated by the fact that the young couple and their children spend much time in the houses of their two sets of parents and will go and seek blessings from both sets whenever an important decision has to be made. In fact, of course, they will in theory also do this in the four sets of grandparents' houses, and so on, except that for these more remote ascendants it will not be the actual couples who are visited and asked for blessings but the paired house posts and hearths of holy houses.

It might seem as if everybody would belong to a near-infinity of ascendant houses, but the reality is usually much simpler. The reason is that the strong preference for marriages which overcome the imbalance caused by differences in gender (such as marriages between two pairs of cross-sex siblings) means that most marriages tend to occur between pairs of localities or moieties originating from two holy houses. The repetition of marriages means that most couples need only be concerned with two holy houses in which their respective groups originated as well as the two houses where their parents live. Intermediary houses tend to be forgotten.

The Conceptualization of Society

We have looked at five mental models of the sort which, according to connectionist theory, we would expect to be at the basis of people's conceptualizations of society. From my experience of life with the Zafimaniry these seem to me the central notions which organize these matters for them. To the Zafimaniry, and perhaps to us, these seem very 'obvious', very 'well-founded' observations of how things are. Yet we have seen how, when they are put together, they produce a distinctive conceptualization of society. Had we not proceeded in the way we did here—starting from these apparently 'obvious' understandings of 'how things are'—we would have ended with a description of Zafimaniry society which would have fallen foul of all the problems of misrepresentation I described in the introduction to this paper. This description would probably have been very similar to the account I gave in my first article on the Zafimaniry (Bloch 1975), and the reader who is in any doubt about the difference in the way ethnography is handled here from classical models should refer to that earlier attempt. The structure of the argument would be very familiar, and therefore acceptable, to other anthropologists, but it would suffer from the same problems of representing Zafimaniry ideas of society as if they took a logic-sentential form which in fact they do not take. Most probably, such an account would be totally foreign to the Zafimaniry, whereas I am encouraged by the fact that they find the account presented here to be not 'alien' but so obvious that they think it pointless.

What, then, are the implications of going about things in this way? First, this account is much more likely to be compatible with theories which describe the mental/neural processes of storage and retrieval that people use in everyday life than would be the case for an account based on logic-sentential models. The Zafimaniry 'know' perfectly well that this is how people are and how they mature; they 'know' that trees grow like this and develop *teza;* it is 'obvious' that men and women are physiologically different, but it is equally 'obvious' that girls and boys are equally the children of their parents; 'clearly' a strong, hard, decorated house is the house of a couple whose children and other descendants are many and successful; it 'goes without saying' that a good marriage involves balance, cooperation, and mutuality. Of course, all this obviousness is ultimately misleading; anthropologists know, usually because they originate from another culture, what the informant does not know—that the 'obvious facts' are, partially at least, the product of specific and in the short term arbitrary historical processes. This, however, is not a reason for giving a false account of how people conceptualize their society.

In fact, there are other advantages in such an approach which can only be suggested here. The anchoring of conceptualization in the material—the body, houses, wood, styles of speaking—and in practices—cooking, cultivating, eating together—means that the cultural process cannot be separated from the wider processes of ecological, biological, and geographical transformation of which human society is a small part (a point made powerfully by Descola in this volume). Culture is not merely an interpretation superimposed on these material facts but integrated with them. When we are talking of mental processes, as we must when we are talking of conceptualization, we are talking of the interaction of one biological process with other biological and physical processes. Finally, seeing the conceptualization of society as flowing from mental models which are in great part conceptualizations of material things and practices suggests something about the way living in a society is learnt. It is not principally learnt by absorbing verbal rules and lexicographic definitions; rather it is learnt as one learns as a baby to negotiate the material aspect of one's house, as one follows other children in looking for berries in the forest, as one watches the stiff gait of one's grandfather, as one enjoys the pleasure of working harmoniously with a spouse, as one cooks with the implements of the hearth, as one sees one's grandfather lean against the central post, as one cuts through a massive tree trunk, and as one sees the beauty of the house of a fruitful marriage.[7]

Notes

1. I carried out two prolonged periods of fieldwork among the Zafimaniry, for six months in 1971 and then for another six months in 1988–9. I was familiar with their culture and language before I started, having previously carried out fieldwork for several years among the closely related Merina. Previous accounts of the Zafimaniry include Vérin (1964), Coulaud (1973), Bloch (1975), and Raminosoa (1971–2). The research on which this paper is based was funded by a generous grant from the Spencer Foundation of Chicago. I am grateful for comments on earlier seminar presentations from members of the anthropology departments of the University of Bergen and the London School of Economics. Above all I am grateful for suggestions and help in preparing the manuscript from Fenella Cannell and J. Parry.

2. The term 'mental model' is Johnson-Laird's (1983). What I am referring to is similar to the 'cultural model' used by some anthropologists, but this term usually implies a reliance on language which I am trying to avoid (Holland and Quinn 1987).

3. The fact that these models are anchored in practice and material experience means that even to a non-Zafimaniry they may appear 'obvious'. This is significant, since such an approach rules out many of the wider claims of certain forms of cultural relativism.

4. I am ignoring variation within Zafimaniry culture in this account because when dealing with the fundamental models with which I am concerned I do not believe that there is much variation. This occurs at more superficial levels.

5. It is very interesting to compare this with the account of American marriage given by Quinn (1987). In many ways Quinn is aiming for the same kind of data as I am, but in contrast she depends almost exclusively on linguistic information.

6. This jump from people to things involves cognitive processes very different to those which can be discussed here (see Bloch 1991).

7. The parallel with Bourdieu's (1973) discussion of the Berber house will be clear, but differences arise from a completely different view of the nature of mental processes; Bourdieu uses precisely the logic-sentential notion of thought which I am criticizing here.

References

Bechtel, W. (1990). 'Connectionism and the philosophy of mind: an over-view', in W. Lycan (ed.) *Mind and Cognition*, Oxford: Blackwell.

Bloch, M. (1975). 'Property and the end of affinity', in M. Bloch (ed.) *Marxist Analyses and Social Anthropology*, London: Malaby Press.

_____. (1991). 'Language, anthropology, and cognitive science', *Man* n.s. 26: 183–198.

Bourdieu, P. (1972). *Esquisse d'une théorie de la pratique précédé de trois études d'ethnologie Kabyle*, Paris: Droz.

_____. (1973). 'The Berber house', in M. Douglas (ed.) *Rules and Meanings*, Harmondsworth: Penguin.

Churchland, P.S. and Sejnowski, T. (1989). 'Neural representation and neural computation', in L. Nadel, P. Cooper, P. Culicover, and R. Harnish (eds) *Neural Connections, Mental Computations*, Cambridge, MA: M.I.T. Press.

Coulaud, D. (1973). *Les Zafimaniry: Un groupe ethnique de Madagascar à la poursuite de la fôret*. Antanarivo: F.B.M.

Holland, D. and Quinn, N. (1987). *Cultural Models in Language and Thought*, Cambridge: Cambridge University Press.

Johnson-Laird, P. (1983). *Mental Models: Towards a Cognitive Science of Language, Inference, and Consciousness*, Cambridge: Cambridge University Press.

Quinn, N. (1987). 'Convergent evidence for a cultural model of American marriage', in D. Holland and N. Quinn (eds) *Cultural Models in Language and Thought*, Cambridge: Cambridge University Press.

Raminosoa, N. (1971–2). 'Système éducatif de la femme et sa fonction dans la société Zafimaniry', *Bulletin de Madagascar* 307: 936–51; 308: 3–30; 309: 107–39; 310: 215–34.

Reisman, K. (1974). 'Contrapuntal conversations in an Antiguan village', in R. Bauman and J. Sherzer (eds) *Explorations in the Ethnography of Speaking*, Cambridge: Cambridge University Press.

Vérin, P. (1964). 'Les Zafimaniry et leur art: un groupe continuateur d'une tradition esthètique Malgache méconnue', *Revue de Madagascar* 27: 1–76.

Chapter Three

Cognition and Ethnography

The text of this chapter is a translation of a lecture given in French in memory of the French anthropologist Robert Hertz. It contains a defence of anthropology as necessarily involving both ethnographic interpretation and the attempt to generalise about human beings in general. As in Chapter 2, I argue here that the most important aspects of human knowledge must be implicit and I illustrate this by means of an example of the type of kinship that most concerned Lévi-Strauss.

*   *   *

The few texts which Robert Hertz[1] wrote in his short life have exerted an extraordinarily important influence on anthropology, especially British anthropology. His work reconciles the two characteristic constitutive elements of social anthropology: on the one hand, its scientific purpose in explaining the nature of human beings in society, and on the other, the interpretative work involved in ethnography. The scientific purpose no doubt came to him from Hertz's involvement in the Durkheimian school to which he belonged; his ethnographic skill is perhaps best seen in his study of the cult of Saint Besse, based, as it is, on the practice of ethnography dependent on intimate contact between researcher and the people studied. This uncomfortable combination of social anthropology, the desire to produce generalising work and the desire to understand "from the inside", poses many theoretical and philosophical problems, but nonetheless it is, I believe, what has been the key to its greatest successes. Malinowski provides a supreme example of this strange marriage in the way he combines the theoretical language of functionalism, derived from the natural sciences, with the evocation of the adventurous life of the Argonauts of the Pacific. Lévi-Strauss, too, at one moment seeks to penetrate the ambiguous statements of the magician about his craft, and at another advances theoretical propositions about the neurological organisation of knowledge.

Some anthropologists, however, would now maintain that this epistemological combination is inadmissible. Over the last few years, a spirit of what might be called fundamentalism has developed in the work of anthropologists who identify with only one side of this dual heritage and who consequently wish to "purify" anthropology of the other orientation. We are therefore faced with two movements which only have in common their rejection of the hybrid character of the discipline.

The Two Fundamentalisms

One type of fundamentalist insists on the hermeneutic and literary dimension of ethnography. Traditional ethnographic writing needs to be rethought because, in their view, its scientific claims are inappropriate and invalid. The other form of fundamentalism is aggressively naturalist and manifests itself in a number of ways. Here, I am concerned with only one of its forms in the work of those anthropologists who see in cognitive science, and cognitive psychology in particular, our only salvation. They believe that in order to progress theoretically, social anthropology needs to rethink itself so as to fit within the greater compass of these disciplines. Some even suggest that anthropology should become a kind of ancillary subject to a general science of cognition.

Although equally critical towards traditional anthropology, these two currents of thought rarely meet because their champions generally regard themselves as belonging to such totally antagonistic theoretical camps that they are unable to find any middle ground.

Those anthropologists who, following first Clifford Geertz and later James Clifford and George Marcus (1986) and Michael Taussig (1987), see anthropology as, above all, a literary enterprise, criticise the "objectivist" and scientific pretensions of the discipline. Their aversion to any link between anthropology and the hard sciences is probably due to the fact that they remember with legitimate distaste previous naively reductionist tendencies in anthropology such as cultural ecology or sociobiology; but they also share the general doubts about the independent nature of the scientific method which characterise our time.[2]

At the other extreme are the anthropologists interested in cognition, who are often impatient with the lack of scientific rigour in traditional ethnographic writing. They want ethnographers to supply more "serious" data, which could then be used with confidence in the attempt to build a genuine anthropology in the true meaning of the term. They almost seem to wish that ethnographers become cognitive psychologists working under quasi-laboratory conditions but in exotic settings.

However, such "experimental" field methods advocated by cognitive anthropologists can only be put into practice when they relate to extremely circumscribed areas of research: for example, the justly famous studies of plant classification of Brent Berlin, and others, which characteristically only look at the taxonomic status of living kinds (Berlin, Breedlove and Raven 1973). These methods yield data which is usually of marginal interest for answering the traditional questions at the heart of social anthropology. Furthermore, when these studies focus on more central problems, such as the study by D'Andrade of the meta-representations of "mind", it seems as if this kind of enquiry can only be attempted within the context of the researcher's own culture: when they and their subjects share the same background, which they can then take for granted (D'Andrade 1987).[3] This is because the very topic, mind in this case, only exists in terms of already culturally constructed concept, and the result of such enquiries cannot therefore supply the type of rigorous data for cross-cultural comparison which the method originally aspired to provide. Unlike categories within the hard sciences, concepts like mind are not fixed or defined by the world independently of cultural context; our objects of study, as soon as they are complex, cannot really be "known" without an in-depth familiarity with their culturally specific phenomenology. Consequently, we cannot make cross-cultural comparisons of the constituent elements as if they were, for example, metals. Such well-known difficulties, which are fundamental problems in the "idea of a social science" (Winch 1958), explain the poverty of many cognitive studies. These have lost the richness specific to more hermeneutic types of anthropology because the practitioners are not able to constantly redefine their analytical tools in the very process of research and analysis as does an anthropologist using participant observation who is continually reflecting on her relationship with the people studied. By abandoning this particular aspect of anthropological research, cognitive anthropologists—especially American ones—have in the end, through their concern to gain scientific credibility, thrown out the anthropological baby with the bath water.

Fundamentalism also makes its appearance in a very different form in the work of those interested in the interpretative aspect of anthropological writing. These, by contrast, stress the "internal" character of the object of the social sciences. The hermeneutic dimension of anthropological practice, upon which philosophers insist (Winch 1958), has long been recognised in anthropology, as the writings of Evans-Pritchard and Geertz clearly show. Such writers tend to also stress the false "objectivity" of ethnographic texts which claim to present facts "as they are". They rightly point to the large gap which exists between the lived experience of the ethnographer (attempts at participation, uncertain communications, the multiplicity of voices—none of which are explicit, the "imponderability of daily life", as Malinowski put it) and the nicely formulated representations that one finds in ethnographic monographs which give such satisfaction to the author and the reader. It is, therefore, a totally welcome development, though not exactly a new one, that such fundamental questioning of objectivism has penetrated the professional shell of our discipline. But we must also consider critically where the recognition of this problem has led us.

The first effect has been to a disenchantment with the informative capacity of ethnography. This has led to defeatism and, amongst some, a desire to abandon totally pretensions to objectivity and to view our writing as works of "fiction" (Tyler 1986). Secondly, it has sharpened our critical focus on the role of the ethnographic author, a critique which often brings with it a "liberal" or "post-liberal" bent to the denunciation of objectivism. For such authors ethnographic representation is neither different in nature nor better-founded than any other representation, and there is therefore no reason for anthropology to prefer pseudo-scientific language to that of informants. The ultimate conclusion of such an approach is that an honest ethnography should consist of, more or less, the verbatim recording of conversations which have taken place between the ethnographer and his informants. And because of the somewhat showy humility of the author in this type of work, the informant's words hold prime position. Since there is no reason to highlight the words of any particular individual, ethnographic texts ought to become merely an array of quotations. Quotations from women and men, old and young, important or not, all should be juxtaposed without order in a monograph without structure, since organising this text would result in the imposition of an author. By such means, anthropology would return to an "innocent and naive" state in which all scientific pretensions are abandoned (Dwyer 1982).

It is worth noting that this extreme post-modern approach is actually similar to a pre-Malinowskian conception which continues to inform certain contemporary ethnographies of a totally different character. These are ethnographies undertaken after short periods in the field involving no real participation, and which result in the direct publication of more or less structured interviews. Such ethnographies, both the old and the modern, again amount to no more than quotations of what certain informants, often described as experts, confided to a tape-recorder during officially organised visits.

The rationale behind all these ethnographic approaches is the same. It is based on what appears to these authors a self-evident question: Who could tell us better about a culture and a society than those who live within it? Thus the criticism of ethnography's scientific pretensions leads to simple acceptance of what our informants say. Their words supposedly offer direct access to their knowledge, culture, and society. In the end, therefore, this mock naive approach constitutes just as radical a theoretical fundamentalism as that of the cognitivists, though going in an opposite direction.

Cognition and Interpretation

These two tendencies both seem to offer good reasons for abandoning the hybrid character of social anthropology and to retain only one component. Is it possible, however, also to argue in favour of its continuation?

Dan Sperber, an advocate of the cognitive tendency, proposes one scenario for maintaining the link between the two apparently irreconcilable elements of the discipline. He posits the need for a preliminary divorce between ethnography, which must be interpretive, and anthropology, a generalising scientific subject, as an indispensable preliminary to their remarriage. This remarriage would be possible once a "descriptive commentary" is incorporated into ethnography, so that the relation of interpretation to the empirical basis experienced by the ethnographer might be critically evaluated. Ethnography would then provide usable raw material for a scientific anthropology (Sperber 1982). In this scenario, interpretive ethnography would only have an ancillary role.

For my part, I am less optimistic than Sperber about the value of his "descriptive commentary", and I doubt that ethnography, hermeneutic by definition, could ever straightforwardly provide anthropology with the type of data Sperber's anthropology would need. Furthermore, I am, in the first instance, an ethnographer, and I assign to ethnography a central position in anthropology, so I cannot accept the small role which Sperber gives it in his redefinition of the relations between ethnography and anthropology. Like him, however, I want to maintain the Hertzien double-sided character of social anthropology, albeit in a different way.

Sperber asks what it is that ethnography can bring to cognitive science. I prefer to ask here the opposite question: What is it that the various cognitive sciences can contribute to ethnographic practice? I, in fact, want to argue (1) that ethnographers cannot afford to ignore the findings of cognitive sciences if they want their work to lay some claim to objectivity, and (2) that they can do that without taking refuge in the study of phenomena marginal to most social anthropologists.

But why does the ethnographer need cognitive sciences? Simply because one of the essential aims of ethnography is to produce representations of the knowledge of the people we study, even if this knowledge can only be reached implicitly by observing practices and imagining their interpretations. If people's knowledge, in its broadest sense, is an essential object of what we study, it is necessary to reflect on its nature, its psychological organisation, and to be able to explain it in such a way that we can account for one of its most fundamental yet problematic features: the incredible speed and ease with which it can be used. I would argue that all ethnographers employ, whether they are aware of it or not, general psychological theories as soon as they try to make us understand how the people they study see the world and what motivates them in their actions. These theories cannot and, therefore, should not escape from critical examination, especially from disciplines specialising in the study of knowledge in use. In particular, these disciplines will teach us to be wary of the traps laid in our path by the received folk psychology of the ethnographer, which because of its misleadingly "obvious" character evades serious examination.

Lévi-Srauss was aware of this problem when, in the 1950s and 1960s, he used linguistics and cognitive psychology to create what he called structural anthropology. Such a step is still necessary today, but it must be repeated, in particular, since the cognitive psychology he then made use of has subsequently moved on significantly.

Speaking and Knowing

To understand the problems which stem from the use of folk psychology by ethnographers, it is useful, by way of example, to look at the relation of knowledge and language as it is implied to exist in the writings of a number of anthropologists.[4]

Most ethnographic monographs are based on the notion that the language of our informants provides direct access to their knowledge. This is a highly problematic proposition. I have already described the extreme position of those ethnographers who chose simply to record what their informants say and to leave it at that. But without going as far as that, many anthropologists confuse, for example, the rules that informants will occasionally spell out and effective control of social practices. They often tell us that certain words in the language of the people they study are "concepts", ignoring, or ignorant of, the extensive literature which shows how problematic such an equation is. Sometimes merely influenced by lexicographic features, they attribute a "cognitive" quality to relations of hierarchy or opposition which are then grandly qualified as structural. Such implicit but immense theoretical leaps beg many questions. To begin to suggest what these problems might be I turn to two examples, one drawn from a well-known experiment in cognitive psychology, and the other from my own fieldwork.

The experiment goes as follows. Subjects are briefly shown a picture of a totally ordinary office; secretaries are sitting on chairs in front of their work tables, upon which are placed folders, typewriters, computers, and so on, but on one of the typewriters there are two bananas. About half an hour later, the subjects are asked to draw up a list of all the objects in the picture. Nearly all of them, first of all, mention the bananas, and none of them ever forget to mention them somewhere in their list; by contrast, their memory of the other objects tends to be much more inexact (Friedman 1979). The results of this experiment are not surprising, but they illustrate nicely the kind of thing which cognitive psychology can teach the ethnographer.

We can easily explain the results of the experiment. The furnishing of the room is a familiar spectacle, and so attention is drawn towards the unusual, in this case, the bananas. This psychological capacity of paying attention to the uncommon is clearly useful: It allows us, in our daily life, to focus our interest immediately on what might require a less foreseeable and "automatic" response than an action motivated by objects whose presence is "taken for granted". But what is familiar to each and everyone in a particular historical context is precisely what anthropologists call culture.

To know a culture is therefore to have successfully stored in our memory knowledge of the type as what is a normal "office". This type of knowledge is often called a schemata in psychology (Schank and Abelson 1977).[5] Such a schemata permits us not only to recognise an office—the various elements which make up its furniture—but also to know how to react towards it in an appropriate manner. In fact, this type of schematic knowledge is a more complex phenomenon than it might first appear. It is clear that even in a relatively homogeneous culture, all actual examples of office furniture are different. Holding such a schemata enables the individual to recognise not just a particular office but all the occurrences of what could be an office and to act according to all the possible requirements of this category in a quasi-automatic fashion, without paying much conscious attention to the actions which an office is likely to entail for them. Paying attention, as here, also often implies speaking about it because, as we saw in the experiment, people speak about the unexpected and not about the familiar. The fact that the subjects of the test did not easily mention the usual furniture of an office, however, did not mean that the subjects of the test had completely forgotten the various elements which make up an office when they were asked what they had seen. In a sense, it could be said that they remembered these things too well but not in an explicit verbalised way. Thus even in such a straightforward case, as in this experiment, we see that "knowing" involves different types of activities. To know what offices are like within our own culture is to stock a whole series of implicit and closely interlinked theories. These theories enable us to recognise the occurrence of "offices" and to record rapidly a multitude of phenomena which are then "taken for granted", without normally having to consciously pay any great attention to them or speaking of them. Furthermore, these theories enable us to react extremely rapidly in terms of the schemata, "without thinking". On the other hand, knowing that there are bananas in this office is a different type of knowledge; it entails storing this information in one's memory in such a way as to be able to mobilise it consciously with ease, to speak of it, and to act consciously in response to it.

A great deal of work in cognitive science is relevant to this observation. For example, according to connexionist theories, the difference between these two sorts of knowledge takes on a very special significance. This theory, which admittedly does not enjoy universal acceptance, helps to formulate this type of problem better and to understand the reasons why it is so difficult to speak about familiar schema, or in other words, to provide an account of one's own culture. Knowledge of schemas, such as the office schema in our example, is probably organised in the brain in a radically different manner to the linear and sentential logic of language. In particular, such nonlinear organisation, in connectionist networks, would allow for the mobilisation of "fundamental" knowledge, at the very instant that we act in a familiar environment. Moreover, this process happens at sufficient speed for this knowledge not to occupy too much "space" in our brain and thus not to be easily put into words, and, by this means, leaves enough room for coping consciously, and therefore linguistically, with the unexpected.

The significance of this type of consideration for ethnographic practice is immense. The first lesson to be drawn is that one must not confuse what people say with what they know. Different types of knowledge are organised in different ways, each with its own specific relation to language and action. Normally, the most profound type of knowledge is not spoken of at all. Indeed, speaking of it transforms its nature, since it is because one is unable to speak of it that it can be used as such a basic guide, with such speed and suppleness. This type of knowledge must be implicit, which is a great nuisance for the ethnographer, since it is precisely knowledge of this sort that anthropological research claims as its subject matter.

Secondly, schema theory may help us understand better what it means when informants appear to hold different beliefs from one another. Without wishing to deny the existence of real differences, many of the differences that the ethnographer comes across might, in fact, hide more fundamental agreements, simply because informants do not speak about what is fundamental in their culture and which they therefore most likely share. What they will talk about might, on the contrary, simply be about what is most unexpected to them, which, by definition, is not shared.

Similarly, schema theory explains why it is that informants are generally incapable of explaining to us what they should do in rituals which the ethnographer cannot witness but that they can, nevertheless, perform with ease when the time comes. Such inexplicitness is partly due to the incongruity of the anthropologist's questions, but mainly because such knowledge is organised in such a way as to be simply accessible for practice, and thus speed, but not for verbal exposition. There is thus a contradiction between the ease with which we use knowledge and the extreme complexity involved in explaining linguistically the mechanism which enables us to do so.

Thirdly, what all this means is that the hermeneutic process which is most problematic because of the distance between knowledge and interpretation is not, as it is often assumed, that of ethnographic writing, but that which has to take place in the head of an informant when he or she is asked to explain a practice and its significance. If basic knowledge normally remains implicit and cannot be directly expressed in words because of its nonlinear organisation, then the informant who tries to answer us in language—which is necessarily linear—must proceed to a fundamental reinvention since no translation is possible. Anthropologists, such as Geertz, have correctly stressed the existence of two levels of interpretation in ethnography, but by refusing to take into account what cognitive psychology could teach us, they have lacked a framework with which to adequately deal with the problem which informants have to undertake when faced by an anthropologist. Similarly, anthropologists who simply reproduce informants' words are not getting any closer to their knowledge than those who apparently interpret most freely.

The foregoing remarks, although merely indicative, are intended to illustrate the relevance of cognitive psychology for ethnographic practice, even when ethnographers claim to be merely recording "naively" what others have said to them. We have to face the fact that we cannot speak about the knowledge of others, if we have not also seriously considered the nature of "knowledge". For such a task the implicit folk psychology of most anthropologists simply misleads.

A Malagasy Example

Some anthropologists might object here that the above discussion might well be true of the kind of phenomena dealt with in the office-and-banana experiment but that it has nothing to do with their usual concerns. To show that this is not so, I now turn to one of the most classical of anthropological subjects: the study of a kinship structure which Lévi-Strauss would characterise as an elementary structure with direct exchange, and which others would call Dravidian.

My example concerns the Zafimaniry of Madagascar, which I have been studying for over twenty years (Bloch 1992). In common with that of a number of South East Asian peoples, Malagasy society seems at first disconcerting in that it seems to lack clear organising social principles. As a result, a number of anthropologists have alleged that it is practically impossible to give satisfactory ethnographic accounts of such societies (Wilson 1977).

I could not help sharing these sentiments when I first arrived in Zafimaniry country. I was then interested in their marriage system, but it was impossible to obtain precise information on the subject from the Zafimaniry. Their explicit discourse was limited to a very few negative rules common to the whole island: The marriage of descendants of two sisters is forbidden (over a number of undefined generations), and one should not marry a classificatory mother or father—that is to say one should marry within one's own generation. The kinship terminology of reference is of the Hawaiian type; it operates with a minimum number of distinctions, and the terms which do exist to designate parents-in-law, sons-in-law, and daughters-in-law are rarely used. The terminology of address is simpler still: It does not even distinguish between parents and affines, and there is no term with which to refer to affines as a group. Other explicit principles are vague: It is good for a brother and a sister to marry a sister and a brother; couples should get on well together; partners should love each other, and so on. In other words, nothing explicit indicates the presence of an elementary structure.

It was therefore with much surprise that after tracing genealogies, I realised that the two parts of the village in which I worked, sometimes called "up" and "down" by the inhabitants, formed two quasi-exogamous moieties, which were exchanging spouses in a systematic and regular fashion. When I spoke to the Zafimaniry about this "discovery", they told me that they too had noticed this phenomenon and that they knew it existed in other villages in more or less the same way. My discovery did not interest them very much. I was not teaching them anything new; for them, it was totally natural to marry in this way, but they could not explain the pattern of alliances to me, just as they could not understand my interest in knowing about it.

After much uncertainty, I had to face a common ethnographic problem. Either I ignored the existence of a structure which was not spoken about and which the kinship vocabulary seemed to deny, and thereby implicitly attribute the marriage pattern to a statistical accident, or I had to try to somehow account for it. Choosing the latter option, I needed to explain how such a well-known pattern could occur without the presence of the rules and the vocabulary that we have all been taught necessarily accompanies such a structure.

Actually, the office-and-bananas experiment helps us in a preliminary way make sense of this type of situation, since it enables us not to be surprised by the lack of an explicatory discourse about a schemata, something which we now know are not normally verbalised.

But another aspect of the ethnographic enigma remains to be explained. Why does the kinship vocabulary not reflect, and why does it even, apparently, contradict a form of matrimonial alliance which has long existed among the Zafimaniry? According to kinship textbooks, kinship terminology and the alliance system should represent two sides of the same coin. But since nothing like this occurs among the Zafimaniry, we must ask how such a state of affairs could possibly be? However, this question originates in precisely one of those commonsense psychological theories which cognitive psychology warns us against. The notion that a given kinship terminology and an alliance system are closely related is based on a strong, but unproved, hypothesis that terms express clear and categorical concepts which, because of their classificatory nature, are logically interrelated and hence organise practices; in this case marriages. But cognitive psychologists' recent work on conceptualisation reaches two conclusions which cast fundamental doubt on such presuppositions.

First, anthropologists need to remember that concepts and words are not the same thing (Smith 1988).[6] This difference can be shown in different ways; the easiest is to note that some concepts are not verbalised. The Zafimanery can therefore easily possess and use the concept of "group of affines amongst whom we normally seek our spouses" without having a word to designate such a group; indeed, their very behaviour testifies to the existence of such an unnamed concept. For the same reason, the fact that they do not distinguish terminologically in address between father and father-in-law in no way excludes the possibility that the same word designates two very distinct concepts.

Furthermore, contrary to the assumptions implicit in structuralism and traditional ethnoscience, concepts are not defined by a list of abstract distinctive features (Smith 1988) which are locked into a closed system of contrasts and oppositions. Rather, we should understand concepts in terms of the analogy with a dazzling light, with an uncertain centre, which diffuses a multitude of aureoles and beams. Concepts are merely loosely bound mental associations and bits of knowledge according to which we can recognise certain phenomena as similar to each other and others as different. Above all, concepts allow us to organise actions which are well-adapted and foreseeable; they are not definitional tools. If concepts were organised according to the structuralist model and corresponded to words, they would indeed establish significant contrasts and definitions. Thus kinship terminology would allow one to know categorically whether an individual was conceptually a cross-cousin or not; it would be impossible that the same person could be considered both a cross-cousin and a parallel-cousin if the two terms existed. But if, as suggested above and as many psychologists now believe, concepts are vague in spite of significant cores—that is to say if they are organised around prototypes, i.e., ideal-typical occurrences to which empirical phenomena more or less correspond—it becomes possible for one individual to be conceived more or less as a cross-cousin and for another to be regarded as both cross-cousin and parallel-cousin. This is the case with the Zafimanery, who often treat the same individual differently—as kin or as a affine—depending on the context, and changing in this, from one moment to the next. The implacable and quasi-mathematical classificatory logic of classical kinship studies would make such examples highly problematic, but in fact there need be no problem if our understanding is informed by what cognitive psychology can tell us and not by the kind of folk psychology that is buried in anthropological theory.

Cognitive science can also, however, sometimes offer positive teachings to the ethnographer. For example, the above-mentioned theory of concepts and schemas also suggests a methodology for fieldwork that can make us observe and study with particular attention phenomena and practices of which we might otherwise not have taken much notice.

Let us return to the example of Zafimaniry marriage. Many cognitive psychologists believe that concepts and schemas are linked to prototype situations mostly defined in early childhood. If this is so, we need to study the process of socialisation to understand both the development of the conceptualisation of a kinship system and the formation and existence of nonverbal concepts. The study of the socialisation of children is not a new area of study in classical anthropology. But the latter, because of its lack of reference to cognitive psychology, has uncritically adopted the vague commonsense notions of behaviourism. In particular, the traditional ethnography of learning rarely addresses what is a central ethnographic problem; that is, the indirect relation between socialisation and the formation of concepts, verbal and nonverbal.[7]

Here I briefly indicate the type of phenomenon that would need to be studied in order to deal with such a question. Everything happens as if just after birth, a Zafimaniry child begins to acquire a notion of the kinship system in the form of prototypical concepts well before learning to speak. Such knowledge obviously owes nothing to language but seems to be derived from certain practices which create those concepts, which then implicitly come to organise the world of alliances.

Thus, young babies are often encouraged to breastfeed not only from their mother's breast but also from other women who nearly always belong to the same moiety as the mother. Similarly, small children are often systematically placed on the backs of older children, who also belong to their own side of the village. Such practices seem to contribute to the formation of a nonverbal conceptualisation of the contrast between the two moieties. One can even sometimes notice external manifestations of this psychological process. For example, even though most of the time, babies are passed from breast to breast, from hand to hand, and from back to back, within their own moiety, as soon as they are handed over to a person who is not familiar, which usually means from the other moiety, they immediately begin to struggle and cry and as this is expected of them this is encouraged through teasing. It is thus probable that babies begin to form one or more concepts or schema of their moiety, which incorporates a series of typical and expected behaviour from people belonging to their own moiety, and which they accept only from them.

Similarly, one can see in the child's behaviour the progressive development of a concept of the "other" moiety. This process is without doubt linked to the fact that adults from the child's moiety treat adults and children from the other moiety very differently. Indeed, many of them are treated as brothers-in-law and sisters-in-law, with whom a joking relationship, marked by a lack of respect, is maintained. Thus at a very young age, children adapt themselves to these differences in behaviour. These differences are often extremely subtle, but by providing an ever-present backdrop to village life, they are all the more powerful.

Children's progressive familiarisation with these subtle differences rapidly leads to behaviour which is more directly alliance-related. From early childhood, children play at "being married" and simulate sexual relations. These games are always organised in relation to the division of the village, and soon they become increasingly serious. In other words, childhood "alliances" are already governed by exchange between moieties. I have seen, for example, boys of about thirteen tease their playmate whose lover was a girl from his own moiety.

I do not mean to say by all this that Zafimaniry children reinvent the kinship system of their society by deducing the logic of practices they observe. Rather, they unconsciously take part in these practices, and in this way the system is incorporated and transmitted. The Kantian principle which postulates that categories are always prior to practices is thus reversed. In this respect, a practice so common that it can pass unnoticed by the observer proves illuminating. Young Zafimaniry children, up to the age of two or three, are nearly always carried in a piece of cloth which makes their whole body adhere to the backs of boys and girls, and men and women, who in their manner of speaking and of moving their bodies, produce and reproduce the implicit classification of kinship according to the conceptualisation which was transmitted to them. When a child is stuck to a back, his or her body is an integral part of another body, "connected" to another brain. It is thus through the activity of their own bodies that Zafimaniry children discover and integrate conceptualisations transmitted through culture. A child does not first learn the concepts which govern kinship and then put them into practice. On the contrary, by being part of another body, the child practices kinship even before knowing its principles.

There is therefore nothing mysterious about a kinship structure which operates without people knowing its rules or possessing a vocabulary to describe it. Such a kinship structure is thus the product of concepts and schema which are nonverbal and about which it is not necessary to speak. Unspoken, these concepts are nonetheless integrated into daily practice and organise knowledge and behaviour.

Conclusion

Was it necessary to have recourse to the cognitive science in general, and cognitive psychology in particular, to reach such conclusions? At least it seems that without such recourse our reasoning would have been quite different. My argument rests on the claim that observation must be guided by the dialectic between empiricism and theoretical hypotheses, in this case borrowed from the cognitive sciences. These hypotheses here concern the nature of schema and of concepts, and the relationships that exist between concepts and language, between concepts and practices, and between the learning of specific social practices. Such toing and froing between scientific theories and ethnography is precisely what the dual nature of anthropology has involved, and losing it would make us lose the possibility of this type of reasoning.

My fieldwork amongst the Zafimaniry followed the traditional approach inspired by Malinowski. This type of research is what cognitivists criticize because of its lack of precision and because of its anecdotal character. I did not ask myself a priori questions at the outset, which being defined outside of any ethnographic context could have provided a basis for cross-cultural comparison. On the contrary, like most other anthropologists, I let myself be guided to a great extent by the Zafimaniry themselves, towards what interested and mattered to them most. Thus, as my research and understanding progressed, I constantly redefined my questions. In this way, my informants participated in the definition of my objects of enquiry.

For me, as for Geertz, a hermeneutic process was essential and integral to ethnographic practice. But interpretation also has to be informed by a scientific tradition: It cannot simply be guided, as Geertz and even Weber have it, by vague intuitions of uncertain origin; hence the importance of cognitive sciences in the enterprise I seek to contribute to. By using cognitive science, we can analyse from an explicit and considered standpoint hypotheses we implicitly make about knowledge, about motivations for action, and about the actions of the people we study, to pay attention to phenomena in the field which we might otherwise have neglected or at least interpreted differently.

Notes

1. This text was given as the Robert Hertz Memorial lecture in Paris in 1993.

2. Marvin Harris's cultural ecology and sociobiology provide good examples of such theories.

3. I think we have to accept that we have failed to develop fieldwork research methods which succeed in combining the rigour of a psychology laboratory with the anthropological tradition of participant observation. Even if this were desirable, it would be too much to expect from just one person. A field worker studying the people with whom he lives cannot create events; he waits for them to happen. He holds conversations with others, but only when the right moment occurs. Should several ethnographers work together in the field? It would not be possible to divide the workload so that one person learns to know intimately the language and culture under study, while the other carries out psychological experiments. Both these researchers would need to undertake both aspects of the work, but then the advan-

tage of being two disappears. This idea is therefore not practicable. Only one researcher, Toren (1990), seems to have succeeded in undertaking, in an exotic setting, research informed by cognitive psychology but relevant to the central concerns in classical anthropology.

4. I am taking up a theme which I have argued elsewhere (Bloch 1991 and 1992).

5. Schank and Abelson (1977) use the term *script* for what I call here *schemata* (sing.) and *schema* (plur.).

6. Even if language necessarily uses words to express concepts.

7. For a counterexample, see Jean Lave 1988, *Cognition in Practice.*

References

Berlin, B., Breedlove, D. and P. Raven. "General principles of classification and nomenclature in folk biology". *American Anthropologist.* vol. 74. 1973: 214–242.

Bloch, M. "Language. Anthropology and Cognitive Science". *Man.* vol. 26. n 2. 1991: 183–198.

_____. "What goes without saying: the conceptualisation of Zafimaniry society", in A. Kuper (ed.). *Conceptualising Society,* London, Routledge. 1992.

Clifford, J. and G. Marcus (eds.). *Writing Culture.* Berkeley, University of California Press, 1986.

D'Andrade, R. "A Folk model of mind" in Holland, D. and Quinn, N., *Cultural Models in Language and Thought,* Cambridge, Cambridge University Press, 1987.

Dwyer, K. *Maroccan Dialogues: Anthropology in Question.* Baltimore, The John Hopkins University Press. 1982.

Friedman, A. "Framing Pictures: The role of knowledge in automatised encoding and memory for gist". *Journal of Experimental Psychology,* General 108, 1979: 316–355.

Hirschfeld, L. "Is the acquisition of social categories based on domain specificic competence or on knowledge transfer?", *in* L. Hirschfeld and S. Gelman (eds.), *Mapping the Mind,* Cambridge, Cambridge University Press, 1994.

Lave, J. *Cognition in Practice,* Cambridge, Cambridge University Press, 1988.

Schank, R. C. and R. P. Abelson. *Scripts. plans, goals and understanding.* Hillsdale, N. J., Lawrence Erlbaum Associates Inc., 1977.

Smith, E. "Concepts and thought", *in* R. J. Sternberg and E. E. Smith (eds.). *The Psychology of Human thought,* Cambridge, Cambridge University Press, 1988.

Sperber, D., *Le Savoir des anthropologues,* Paris, Hermann, 1982.

Taussig, M. *Shamanism, Colonialism, and the Wild Man,* Chicago, Chicago University Press, 1987.

Toren, C. *Making Sense of Hierarchy,* London, The Athlone Press, 1990.

Tyler, S. "Post-modern ethnography: From document of the occult to occult document", *in* J. Clifford and G. Marcus (eds.), *Writing Culture,* Berkeley, University of California Press, 1986.

Williams. P. *Nous, on n'en parle pas.* Paris, Éditions de la Maison des sciences de l'homme, 1993.

Wilson, P. "The problem with primitive folk", *Natural History* 81 (10). 1977: 26.

Winch, P. *The Idea of a Social Science,* London, Routledge and Kegan Paul, 1958.

Chapter Four

Domain-Specificity, Living Kinds and Symbolism

This chapter attempts to do what was called for in the previous chapter, that is, to move the study of cognition to the very heart of the traditional concerns of social anthropology—in this case, religious symbolism. Here I argue that in spite of the counterintuitive nature of many religious beliefs, it is still possible to see them as anchored in much less exotic forms of understanding, in this example the understanding of what living things are like, especially trees. The cognitive theories used here relate to the hypothesis of domain specificity, which has often been seen as incompatible with the connectionist theories used in Chapters 1 and 2. This incompatibility does not seem to me to be necessary, but, in any case, the point I am trying to make once again is the fruitful character of cognitive theory in general when applied to ethnography.

*   *   *

This chapter is highly speculative. It explores the possibility that some recent work in developmental cognitive psychology might help us to understand aspects of what has often been called ritual symbolism. In particular, it is concerned with the old question of the prominence in many religious practices of living kinds, both as objects and concepts.

In a number of recent articles S. Atran (1987) and D. Sperber (1985) have been making increasingly strong claims for the existence of a specific cognitive domain concerning 'living kinds'. In this they have been following recent suggestions made by Fodor (1983) which make the case for the existence of numerous such distinct cognitive domains. They have accompanied their claim for the existence of a specific cognitive domain for living kinds with suggestions concerning the significance the existence of such a domain might have for anthropology. For the purpose of this short chapter only, I shall assume that Atran and Sperber are right without further discussion, none the less, and in some ways, I shall want to go further than they do. I shall also be using their hypothesis to illuminate an area of concern which is not theirs.

Atran (1990, 1993) argues that in all cultures cognition about living kinds is governed by different rules than cognition about other kinds and that in all cultures the rules governing the cognition of living kinds are the same. Such an observation leads to the suggestion that there is an innate predisposition among all humans for constituting a 'living-kinds domain'. Such a predisposition to a particular form of cognitive development relevant to a limited area of human cognition would be similar to the much more certainly hypothesised innate predisposition for learning grammar or face recognition. According to Atran and Sperber, the child is pre-programmed, 'hard-wired' to use the common jargon, to learn particularly fast and in particular ways about living kinds and their implications. As a result, living kinds are not only learnt about in a different way, the very concepts of living kinds are different from, for example, categorical concepts of artefacts. For Atran the core of this difference lies in the fact that categorical concepts of living kinds presume an underlying nature while categorical concepts of artefacts are defined by functions.

Atran's evidence is circumstantial but suggestive. First of all, he turns to the extensive work done by such ethnoscientists as Berlin, Breedlove & Raven (1973) concerning the classification of plants and animals. This suggests striking regularities in the organisation of folk taxonomies of living kinds. In particular, these authors draw attention to what Berlin and his associates have called the generic level, a level which corresponds roughly to our 'species' level and which seems to be the basis of plant and animal classification in all cultures (but see Mandler & Bauer 1989). This basic character derives from the fact that other superordinate or subordinate levels are, according to these authors, always much less elaborated than the generic level and also always depend on it. For Berlin, Breedlove & Raven the generic level corresponds to what other cognitive psychologists have called the basic level.

The other type of evidence Atran turns to comes from the related work by psychologists such as Eleanor Rosch (1978) concerning prototypes and especially the work concerning bird classification, which in many ways established prototype theory. Atran seems to be arguing that prototypically organised concepts are characteristic of categorical concepts of living kinds but may not exist beyond this domain.

Finally, Sperber and Atran turn to independent evidence which seems to suggest that subjects, especially children, treat living kinds in a unique and distinctive way. Atran thus argues that once the child has understood that an animal, even an animal she has never seen such as a tiger, is indeed a representative of a living kind, she will make a number of very strong assumptions which she would not make for a representative of a non-living kind.

For example, the child will presume that even when the animal has lost all its empirical characteristics (stripes, legs, etc.) the thing will still remain for the child *essentially* a tiger.

Subsequent research by psychologists such as Mandler & Bauer (1989) and Carey (1978, cited in Smith, Sera & Gattuso 1988) seems to give some backing to Atran and Sperber's theories, since it shows that very young children seem to distinguish between animate and inanimate objects so early that it seems inconceivable that distinction could be learnt through interaction with the environment.[1] On the basis of this admittedly fragmentary evidence I feel justified to take, for purposes of presentation, Atran's and Sperber's highly tentative argument as though it were proved. None the less, even here, this argument sems to require serious qualifications.

Following Berlin, Breedlove & Raven, Atran argues that one of the distinguishing characteristics of cognition concerning living kinds, at least as far as 'the ordinary understanding of the everyday world' is concerned (Atran 1987: 28), is the certainty with which species are linked to superordinate and subordinate categories. This degree of certainty contrasts with the unsure and changing way concepts concerning artefacts are linked to other levels of classification.

In making this last point, Atran has to face some familiar objections. For example when discussing the categorical concept indicated by the word 'tomatoes', psychologists such as Rey (1983: 248) noted how tomatoes are ambiguously classed, sometimes as vegetables, sometimes as fruits. This, according to Atran, is irrelevant to theories concerning the cognition of natural kinds because such words as 'fruit' and 'vegetable' indicate concepts concerned with artefacts which are therefore *functionally* conceptualised in contrast to natural kinds.

The difficulty raised by a case such as 'tomatoes' may, however, be quite significant. Even though one may accept Atran's argument and one may have removed from one's mind any suspicion that we are simply dealing with a tautology, the apparent ambiguity of 'tomatoes' is much more suggestive to the anthropologist than might appear from Atran's dismissal. Atran says of such cases:

> In general, when living kinds enter the space of concern with human function and use, such as eating, gardening (weeds and flowers), farming (beasts of burden), entertainment (pets, circus and fair animals), they cease to be of taxonomic importance . . . For items that pertain to the conceptual space of human function and use, then, there may well be 'unclear cases' of category affiliation, but this has no relevance to folk biological classification. (1987: 43)

Such reasoning may be acceptable as a way of dealing with a specific theoretical difficulty, but it also highlights two quite different but related issues of fundamental importance.

First there is a practical side to this matter. One cannot but be struck by how important, literally vital, these 'awkward' conceptual bridges between living kinds and artefacts are for the survival of human beings, who, after all, rely on the transformation of living kinds into artefacts for their food and much more. It seems, therefore, unreasonable to make these 'passages' a minor issue of theory since they certainly cannot be a minor issue for people living in anything but the most artificial conditions.

Secondly, these cognitive 'bridges' between natural kinds and artefacts themselves reveal what must be a central cognitive process if we accept Atran's theory and the existence of specific cognitive domains. The fact that such things as tomatoes can be both living kinds and artefacts draws attention to an aspect of things which Atran seems to have forgotten. Atran's evidence for the differentiation of living kinds from other concepts comes presumably from adults or at the very least children who have learnt to speak. However, the manifestation of innate domain potentialities, leading to a specific cognitive mechanism for the formation of concepts of living kinds, seems to develop very early on. Subsequent to the formation of these very early concepts much development will follow. This subsequent development may mean that early concepts may be reformed to change character and perhaps to lose the prototype characteristics so typical of natural kinds concepts (Keil & Batterman 1984). Secondly, and probably closely related to the *characteristic-to-definition* shift, is the fact of greater systematic integration of knowledge which must occur during later stages of cognitive development (see Fentriss 1984). What this must surely mean is that although we may accept that there are specific distinct innate propensities for the cognition of different domains in the young child, a significant part of cognitive development must be the *linking* up of such domains, whether we believe that such linking up affects or does not affect the specificity of domains.

The linking up of domains seems to be a relatively unexplored area. However, it is fascinating that such a crucial coordination as that between the domain of artefacts and of living kinds, should imply both a reorganisation of general cognitive-patterns process and at the same time the cognition of an essential practical process. The possibility of such a correlation between cognition, cognitive development and the dialectics of life is thought-provoking enough for the anthropologist, but here I want to discuss yet a further related fact.

It would appear that much religious ritual symbolism is also concerned with these coordinations and passages between living kinds and artefacts, thereby somehow replicating what one may presume are fundamental sequences of cognitive development concerned with the essential processes of human life.

In recognising this parallel between symbolism, the fundamental processes of human interaction with the environment and the development of cognition it is not possible to posit a causal connection. However, in noting the cognitive trajectory of the symbolism and seeing what this trajectory might mean in terms of associations within domains and crossings over between domains, we might get a further insight into the mental processes operated by certain symbolic systems and even some intuition into the evocative power of this symbolism.

In this chapter I want to look briefly at an example of such a symbolic system which is central to the representations of a particular group of people. This will illustrate how symbolism so often seems to focus on the cognitive and practical significance of the transformation of living kinds into artefacts, the 'awkward' cases of Atran's theory.

The Zafimaniry

The Zafimaniry are a group of shifting cultivators living in Madagascar who rely mainly on maize, beans and taro.[2] They number approximately 20,000. They live in a narrow band of mountain forest at an altitude of approximately 1,400 metres. Like all Malagasy people, a central theme of their culture is a concern with the impermanence of living human beings. The most commonly quoted Zafimaniry proverb is: *ny tany tsy miova fa nyolombelona no moiva.*[3] This is best translated as 'While the land[4] does not change (or transform), the living people[5] change.' This proverb, and many others which are almost identical, reflect a constant awareness of the fragility and impermanence of human life in a world which is not concerned with their problems and which therefore affects them randomly; but such a saying also suggests a solution: the attaching of human beings to the permanent land by means of the mediation of permanent materials, in their case especially hard wood of which the houses should ideally be made.

The Zafimaniry conform surprisingly well to what Lévi-Strauss has called 'house-based societies' not only because certain houses are central religious focuses but also because the symbolism of houses is, as he predicted, closely linked with the supreme valuation of the unity of a married pair.

Zafimaniry sexual unions are extremely unstable but little by little some of these unions are proved to be successful by their fertility and they then become established. This long, uncertain and gradual process is marked by a complex series of rituals, among which the building and blessing of the house, the setting up of the central post and the hearth by the couple are particularly important. Like the marriage, the building of the house is a gradual process which is marked by the 'hardening' of the house. This occurs when flimsy impermanent materials, such as woven bamboos and mats are replaced by massive decorated wooden planks, which are called the 'bones' of the house. Again like the marriage, the growth and hardening of the house continues long after the death of the original couple as children, grandchildren, etc. continue to add to the structure and replace rotten wood. By then the house has become a 'holy house' (*trano masina*) which is a source of blessing for the descendants. What has happened is that the house has changed for the descendants from a structure sheltering the original couple to the original couple in a new, more mature form. The holy houses are, for the Zafimaniry, their ancestors made permanent. This is especially so for the central posts and hearth of the house. These are respectively the man and the woman of the original couple. When the descendants seek blessing from their ancestors they address the post and the hearth as though they were the ancestors of the group themselves. Again, when certain offerings to the ancestors are made these things receive the offerings by being given honey or rum and occasionally the blood of cattle.

What has therefore happened is that with the passage of time people become replaced by artefacts. It is the most impermanent aspect of people, their attraction to each other which becomes one of the most permanent Zafimaniry artefacts: the totally wooden house. In order fully to understand this transformation, however, it is important to turn not only to Zafimaniry ideas concerning houses, but also to their ideas concerning the wood and the trees of which the houses are made.

The Zafimaniry use the same word for both TREE and WOOD, *hazo*, thereby perpetrating the same 'muddle' which Atran noted for TOMATO, since in doing this they are merging a natural kind with an artefact. In one way this linguistic fact might be taken simply to indicate that the great divide stressed by Atran is ignored by Zafimaniry in their language and this might therefore throw doubt on the distinction between artefact and natural kind at least for adult Zafimaniry. However, this would be misleading, as the Zafimaniry are very aware of the distinction between natural kinds and artefacts and in this case the fact that a natural kind can become an artefact is continually discussed. Similarly, the ritual symbolism of the Zafimaniry also suggests an awareness of the paradox of living kinds becoming artefacts and, if anything, the symbolism emphasises the passage from one kind of thing to another. Zafimaniry never tire of pointing out that great trees start as soft pliable little plants 'like grass', but that these soft little plants end up as gigantic, hard, straight things which, in the form of wood, can last almost for ever.

The importance of trees for the Zafimaniry is very great. This is both because of the fact that they totally depend on wood and also because of the prominence of trees/wood as a topic of discourse. I have already noted how Zafimaniry houses are made of wood. Nearly all their implements also are made of wood. In the past, and to a certain extent still now, their clothes were made of wood because they were woven from bark fibre. Their medicines are exclusively powdered mixtures of different woods. Very importantly, it is wood and the burning of wood which makes the fields on which they grow their crops as a result of the clearing and fertilising of the land by fire. Finally, and probably most crucial of all, they warm themselves continually with woodfires. Without these continual fires life would be impossible in such a cold and wet country, and equally importantly it would be impossible to preserve crops. This is because in order to store maize, which is their main staple, they hang it from the rafters of the house so that the fire will dry it and cover it with a black shiny coating of soot which protects the cobs from being eaten by little weevils. The Zafimaniry are well aware of their symbiosis with wood and the forest to the extent that they say that people are not Zafimaniry, even though their ancestors were Zafimaniry, when they live in villages where, as a result of over-swiddening, the forest has disappeared.

The Zafimaniry call a set of very strong woods 'ancestor woods'. Then they distinguish amongst these by means of sibling terminology which marks differential seniority, so that the strongest wood of all, *nato* is the 'older sibling' of the second strongest, *amboneka*. Above all, what distinguishes ancestor woods is that they have something which is called *teza*. The importance of the concept of *teza* in Zafimaniry thought is central. One of the meanings of the word, which is Malagasy wide, is at the root of the verb which means 'to last a long time'. (Interestingly, but not surprisingly, Malagasy has several verbs which correspond to the English verb 'to last'.) The same word can also be used to mean human bones. In some contexts it can be used for ancestors. However, the typical meaning of the word, that is the one which Zafimaniry will give as a definition when asked about the word out of any particular context, refers to the core of ancestor trees (or wood).

These very hard woods develop, as they grow older, a clearly demarcated darker impacted core. This is called *teza*. This core is totally absent in young trees of these species but develops little by little so that in old trees it represents the majority of the tree. This is the hardest and most resistant part of the tree and the Zafimaniry will often point out with satisfaction that after the burning of a swidden the *teza* of those trees remains unburnt.

In Zafimaniry ideas about wood and about its straightness and *teza*, their central concepts about the body are involved, but they are displaced, so to speak, away from the human body to that of trees. One side of the association can be understood as a parallel. The growth of ancestor trees with *teza*, which can mean BONE and/or ANCESTOR, is like the growth of humans, starting soft, supple, wet and without hard straight bones; but with time the hard straight *teza* becomes defined and increases: ultimately, it will take over. This is like the hardening and straightening of bones which will ultimately mark elderhood and ancestorhood. However, trees achieve the process better than humans and are seen to do so. Unlike human bone, the bone of trees (*teza*) continues to grow, increase and harden progressively on a very long time scale, so that ultimately it practically takes over. Human *teza*, on the other hand, although it starts off all right, soon goes into reverse with old age and death, as human beings patently do. Trees can thus materially fulfil the ideal of what should happen to humans. They pass from fluid transformative things to things which are very hard, very permanent (very *teza*) and which can therefore form an almost permanent bond with the land and thereby share in its stasis, as the proverb quoted earlier in this chapter seems to demand.

Secondly, and probably because of the very fact that trees achieve materially the ideal of development which humans fail to achieve in their bodies, wood is made to gradually *replace* humans. This happens when the unstable marriage of young living people so hardens and stabilises that it becomes a hardening house, made of wood obtained from trees with *teza*, with its central post and hearth which are the source of blessing for descendants and which *are* the 'ancestors'.

Discussion

The brief outline of Zafimaniry symbolism given above none the less covers the most salient aspects of the system. The system is based on a set of transference from humans, to trees, to wood, to houses. The fragile relationship of two opposite-sex humans matures and hardens in a way that the Zafimaniry see as part and parcel of the maturing of the body of the pair. A process which is believed to involve both the proportional growth of bones as against flesh, as well as the hardening and straightening of these bones. This first transference which consists of passing from the stabilisation of the relation of the two partners to the maturing of their bodies is to the Zafimaniry fairly straightforward, since both processes are seen as merely two manifestations of the same general process of maturation which, for the Zafimaniry, links inseparably growth and reproduction.

The next passage, however, is more complex. The relationship of the body to trees can at first be seen as metaphorical. As the body grows, so do the trees; as the body becomes more rigid and straight, so do the trees; finally, as the bones in the body become defined and strong, so does the *teza* inside the trees. However, it is, I believe, quite wrong to see such a relationship simply as a kind of 'ritual metaphor' (Fernandez 1977). This is because all theories of metaphor imply a fixed relationship between vehicle and principal, while what is characteristic of symbolism, especially when it is linked to ritual, is that the relationship is a continually evolving one. What is characteristic of this case, and others like it, is that what starts out as a metaphorical parallel ends up as a substitution. The substitution occurs when the wood in the house comes to represent, or rather to *be* the original couple. This is a process which is only completed after the death of both members of the original couple, and when their house, 'hardened' through the contribution of planks and carvings from the descendants, becomes the couple and is addressed as such in, for example, ancestral evocations.

This passage from impermanent humans to permanent artefact, however, reveals on closer examination to be itself made up of several analytically distinguishable elements. First of all there is the jump from person to tree. One aspect of this jump seems to me to depend on the recognition of the fundamental unity of trees and humans deriving from the fact that both are living kinds. This underlying unity is seen above all in the common fact of growth and of maturation, which is one of the more salient characteristics of living kinds. Thus, the very general, and if we are to believe Atran and others, the very primitive concept of living kinds gives the basis for what still remains a fairly complicated and unexplored cognitive operation, involving the transformation of a metaphor into a substitution. This first element of the passage is, however, only a first stage in a further transformation where the living tree is transformed into an artefact: wood. This process is, as the Zafimaniry themselves continually stress, long drawn out. It involves the cutting of the tree, the drying and seasoning of the wood, the cutting of the trunk into manageable pieces, the making of planks which will become the 'bones' of the house, ultimately perhaps the decorating of these 'bones' with carvings.

Now this second process involves precisely what Atran had seen as the 'muddle' between a living kind: trees (in Zafimaniry *hazo*) and an artefact: wood (in Zafimaniry *hazo*). Alternatively, we could say it involves the crucial process of transformation between living kinds and artefacts on which life depends. I would suggest that there is a little truth in both formulations. What underlies the full process is the fact that the symbolic seems to play with the cognitive dissonance between living kinds and artefacts as well as the unity between humans and trees, on the one hand, and, on the other hand, the unity, linguistic and practical, of trees and wood. In fact, it would appear as if this passage in the wider symbolic task of transference from humans to holy houses was, at this point, 'deintellectualised', and handed over to the empirical world, where the barrier between living kinds can be crossed by means of a number of techniques, the most obvious and necessary of which is killing and which in this case is the transforming of trees into planks.

The passage from people to trees was possible in the mind because it is premised on the unity of the domain of living kinds. On the other hand, the unity and specificity of the domain makes the necessary passage from living kind to artefact difficult if it occurs purely in the mind. It therefore, requires for its operation the use of material symbols which themselves can make the jump. Of course, this is not to say that the process of transformation from living kinds to artefact cannot be cognised. That would be ridiculous.

But perhaps the kind of effortless slippage from one living kind to another, such as the passage from humans to trees, is not so easy or symbolically satisfactory if it involves passing from one domain to another, because it then follows conceptual connections of a more secondary character, established at a later stage of cognitive development characterised by definitions rather than characteristics. This lack of ease in demonstration of a proposition which, like all symbolical ritual propositions is a-logical and largely evocative, may explain why it requires external help in the form of material symbols at critical moments where the mind seems to recognise boundaries.

Speculating so far from one largely anecdotal case might seem barely legitimate, but in fact this case is far from an isolated instance. Much religious symbolism seems concerned with the transformation of parallels into substitutions, of living kinds into artefacts and sometimes back again. Thus African sacrifice provides us with another example. There, the sacrificial animal is at first a metaphorical parallel with the person for whom the sacrifice is being carried out, and this parallel depends on the fact that humans and cattle are living kinds. Then, as the ritual proceeds, the parallel is turned into a substitution (Evans-Pritchard 1965: ch. 10). Finally, the cattle which has substituted for the person for whom the sacrifice is being carried out, is transformed through killing, butchering and cooking into an artefact: meat.

The parallel between African sacrifice and Zafimaniry wood and tree symbolism is not accidental and can easily be repeated all over the world. The reason is that all religious symbolism is about the dialectics of life, growth, decline, reproduction, eating and excreting and about the re-representation of these processes in more or less paradoxical forms. But having said this, the cognitive processes underpinning these re-representations still remain to be explored.

Notes

1. Although Atran talks of the evidence for the specificity for a domain for living kinds in general, the evidence he adduces, as well as the subsequent work, actually only relates to animals and not plants.

2. Research among the Zafimaniry was first carried out in 1971 thanks to a grant from the Economic and Social Science Research Council and in 1988–9 thanks to a grant from the Spencer Foundation.

3. The proverb occurs in a number of variants but the meaning is constant. The version mentioned here is the simplest one.

4. The Malagasy word *tany* has a very similar range of meanings to the English word 'land'.

5. The normal Malagasy word for 'people', *olonbelona*, literally means 'living people' but I have kept the rather pedantic form in full as it seems to me the most revealing. R. Dubois, partly rightly and partly wrongly, makes a great song and dance about this point (Dubois 1978).

References

Atran, S. 1987. Ordinary constraints on the semantics of living kinds: a common-sense alternative to recent treatments of natural-object terms. *Mind and Language* 2: 27–63.

_____. 1990. *Cognitive foundations of natural history: towards an anthropology of science,* Cambridge: Cambridge University Press.

_____. 1993. Whither 'ethnoscience'? In P. Boyer (ed.), *Cognitive aspects of religious symbolism,* Cambridge: Cambridge University Press.

Berlin, B., D. Breedlove & P. Raven 1973. General principles of classification and nomenclature in folk biology. *American Anthropologist* 75: 214–42.

Carey, S. 1978. The child as word learner. In M. Halle & G. A. Miller (eds.), *Linguistic theory and psychological reality,* Cambridge, MA: MIT Press.

Dubois R. 1978. *Olombelona; essai sur l'existence personnelle et collective à Madagascar,* Paris: L'Harmattan.

Evans-Pritchard, E. E. 1965. *Theories of primitive religion,* Oxford: Clarendon.

Fentriss, J. C. 1984. The development of coordination. *Journal of Motor Behaviour* 16: 99–134.

Fernandez, J. 1977. The performance of ritual metaphors. In J. D. Sapir & J. C. Crocker (eds.) *The social use of metaphor,* Philadelphia: University of Pennsylvania Press.

Fodor, J. A. 1983. *The modularity of mind: an essay on faculty psychology,* Cambridge, MA: MIT Press.

Keil, F. C. & N. Batterman 1984. A characteristic-to-defining shift in the development of word meaning. *Journal of Verbal Learning and Verbal Behaviour* 23: 221–36.

Mandler, M. & P. Bauer 1989. The cradle of categorisation: is the basic level basic? *Cognitive Development* 4: 247–64.

Rey, P. 1983. Concepts and stereotypes. *Cognition* 15: 237–62.

Rosch, E. 1978. Principles of categorization. In E. Rosch & B. B. Lloyd (eds.) *Cognition and categorization.* Hillsdale, NJ: Lawrence Erlbaum.

Smith, L. B., M. Sera & B. Gattuso 1988. The development of thinking. In E. E. Smith (ed.) *The psychology of human thouht,* Cambridge: Cambridge University Press.

Sperber, D. 1985. Anthropology and psychology: towards an epidemiology of representations. *Man* 20: 73–89.

Part Two

Memory

Chapter Five

Internal and External Memory: Different Ways of Being in History

The text of this chapter was originally a lecture given in Finland in memory of Edward Westermarck. In it I argue that concepts of the person are closely tied to ideas about kinship because these often concern the way a social being is created. I contrast African and European representations, on the one hand, with Southeast Asian representations, on the other. Furthermore, what kind of phenomenon a person is believed to be affects the way history is understood and the way the individual relates to history. Such concerns, which are traditional ones in social anthropology, should, it is argued here, be taken into account by psychologists, who tend to forget about the cultural element when considering their subjects.

> Il y a . . . aussi de l'histoire dans les sociétés unilinéaires. Cependant, chez elles, la descendance, autrement dit les liens généalogiques, ne sont pas des moyens au service de la création historique. Celle-ci se produit du dehors—par l'effet des guerres, épidémies, migrations, disettes, etc.—plutôt que du dedans. En ce sens le cognatisme quand il apparaît, offre à la société le moyen d'intérioriser l'histoire . . . (Lévi-Strauss 1984 p. 222)

*   *   *

I am very honoured to have been asked to give this lecture in memory of Edward Westermarck, particularly because it gives me the opportunity to recreate the line of contact between Finnish anthropology and anthropology at the London School of Economics which he embodied. The continuation of that relationship is one thing he would have wanted to be remembered by.

It is common in anthropology, psychology, and history to see the study of long term semantic memory as a privileged area for the examination of the link between the individual and the social. This point was made by Bartlett (1932), Vigotsky (Wertsch 1985) and Luria (1976) three psychologists who were unusual for their time in their desire to link the individual and the social. Subsequently Sperber, in a recent article considering the links between psychology and anthropology, (Sperber 1985) has seen memory as the key area for the study of the articulation between public and private representations. Finally, and more specifically in psychology, there has been a general new tendency to move the study of memory out of the laboratory into the real world. This tendency originates in its modern formulation in the work of Neisser (1978) and is well manifested in such texts books as Baddeley's *The Psychology of Memory* (1976) and Cohen's *Memory in the Real World* (1990). However once psychologists have crossed the boundary between the laboratory and the outside they find themselves in an environment where there is no longer a defined frontier limiting what they should be concerned with and they plunge headlong into a consideration of how people in the world retain the past, not only as individuals but also as members of groups who then employ supra individual mnemonic systems and devices such as little poems and material objects. In other words psychologists stumble, almost by accident, but in a way which in principle should be very laudable, into territory normally occupied by anthropologists and historians.

Yet in spite of the general feeling that in the study of memory we have an area where psychology, with its concern with individual representations, and subjects such as anthropology or history, which traditionally deal with shared representations, might join up, the actual theoretical link between the disciplines is in reality plainly absent.

Psychologists give a nod in the direction of the fact that some aspects of memory become public representation, but, in reality, except perhaps for Bartlett, this does not fundamentally affect their approach to memory, while anthropologists and historians acknowledge that remembering and recalling are first of all individual activities, a fact they note by, for example, a mention of Bartlett and Luria in their early chapters, (usually ignoring subsequent psychological work), only to forget the psychological aspect completely when they get down to business.

In this lecture, in order to clear the ground whereby a more genuine and fruitful theoretical and empirical connection might be made, I shall criticise the way the psychologists have approached the more social aspects of memory. A criticism of the anthropologists and historians from the point of view of the psychologists is equally necessary though this will have to be considered elsewhere.

The problem with psychologists' approach to memory in the real world comes, I believe, from their failure to grasp the full complexity of the engagement of the mind in culture and history and, in particular, their failure to understand that culture and history are not just something created by people but that they are, to a certain extent, that which creates persons.

Both psychologists and some anthropologists take a largely technological approach to memory. Thus Baddeley and Cohen first consider the neural processes which might make memory possible, then they consider how this 'faculty' is used to coordinate action, next they consider the character of long term memory and what are its limitations and finally they turn to mnemonic objects and social practices which they visualise as being merely "the extension of the brain". For them the socially instituted practices of memory are merely a primitive form of artificial intelligence in that they simply concern two processes, first, the process of making of individual representations into public representations and, secondly, the process of storing of these public representations. For such writers mnemonics are external extensions of the brain in much the same way that tools and weapons are extensions of the arm.

This approach is again evident in many recent studies of literacy, most particularly in the work of Goody (1977) and Olson (1977). There, literacy is merely seen as a particularly effective mnemonic device i.e. an artificial memory with an infinite storage potential which does not deteriorate.

Such writers, then, first try to understand the workings of the mind/brain in a historical and cultural vacuum and then, following an acknowledged or unacknowledged evolutionary programme, try to see how social and cultural institutions, as they have evolved, have extended the biological potential of the individual.

This is much too simple. First of all, technological potential never explains the uses to which a technology is put. Secondly, the phenomenological maintenance or otherwise of past states is, in real circumstances, largely determined by history and people's view of themselves in history and hence, via notions of persons and places and various views of ethics and intentions (Bloch 1989a). If we want to move from concerns with potentials to concerns with the culture of the actual engagement of people in history, as the movement from the present to the public requires, then we must return to the varied context-specific ways in which people see themselves in the real world and how their abilities are engaged in the context of their own theories, purposes and conditions.

It is for this reason that I want to concern in this lecture folk theories of memory in what amounts to much the same, folk theories of the sources of knowledge and freedom. First of all, I wish to do this to show how these folk theories are of a different kind to the theories of psychologists because they never consider potentialities without also taking into account moral purposes, the very subject of one of Westermarck's most important works. Secondly, I want to show that, while psychologists tend to consider the actor, the external world and the relation between the two as unproblematic, the people I shall discuss think of themselves, their body, their mind, their knowledge and their material culture as part of a history which began before they were born and will continue after their death.

Perhaps, at the very least, the point in discussing these folk theories of the place of the "person in history" would be to show precisely the difference in ways of approaching the matter between psychologists and the people about whom I am talking, but I would argue there might also be other advantages. First of all, these people may well have something to teach the psychologists. Secondly, even if ordinary people are wrong to see things in such subtle ways, and psychologists are right in seeing matters so simply, people's own evaluation and theories of knowledge and memory affect how they treat and value these matters and must, therefore, be of relevance to those who study them.

*   *   *

I begin the examination of folk theories of memory and of the place of the person in history by going back to two familiar writers for whom the divorce of morals from the question of remembering would not even be considered.

In a recently published wide ranging book Janet Coleman *Ancient and Medieval Memories, Studies in the Reconstruction of the Past* (1992), a historian of ideas, contrasts with remarkable clarity Plato's and Aristotle's theories of memory.

Plato was above all concerned with the absolute transcendental truth of what has been called the "forms". For him nothing new of importance was ever learnt during life. Humans, because they are humans, know everything of significance from the first. Unfortunately they forget and their original knowledge becomes vitiated by events and time so they need to learn anew, but in fact, what they are really doing when they think they are learning, is remembering in the sense of recalling what they already knew. Thus when we learn something significant we are merely recalling original and unchanging truth which, because it is absolutely true, must originate beyond human experience, time bound as this must be.

Aristotle on the other hand believed that people were largely created by what they learnt, their minds were matured by new knowledge which shaped it as they remembered it and used what they remembered. The mind for him was like wax which became permanently imprinted with new information but which was represented there according to the mind's own capacity to represent sensual experience. According to him, when a person is trying to remember, what they do is merely search for the imprint of past information or events which may be unfortunately overlaid by more recent memories and information thus making it difficult to find.

These two theories are linked to many other aspects of the philosophy of the two thinkers but clearly, as Coleman shows, the difference has implication for their respective views of history. The Platonist sees particular events as swirling unimportantly around the person while the duty of that person is, above all, that he/she should retain this human identity and protect the true knowledge it implies from the injuries of events. The Aristotelian on the other hand cannot consider him or herself ultimately aloof from history. They should be actively seeking to deliberate and make choices about good events and knowledge so as to be continually created and recreated, made and remade through practical reasoning in the process of history. The Aristotelian is in a permanent transformational dialectic with the world and others. Practical wisdom is not absolute and finite for them but is being continually renegotiated through enlightening experience. For the Aristotelian living should not be a matter of holding oneself back since the very physical being is inevitably continually shaped by the response to events in a way which will remain in the mind as permanent imprints.

These two types of theories of memory are therefore inseparably linked to differing concepts of the person, of the cosmos, of morality. In this placing of memory in a wider context the philosophers are very like the ordinary people whom anthropologists study and to whom I shall shortly turn, since ordinary people and philosophers together approach the matter one way, while modern psychologists take a very different path when they forget the more encompassing totality which gives the very concept of memory its significance. However, in stressing this resemblance between the works of philosophers and the thought of ordinary people as studied by anthropologists one should not also forget that there are great differences. In particular ordinary people's knowledge is a complex mixture of implicit and explicit knowledge which is very different from the totally explicit theories of such philosophers as Plato and Aristotle. For the purpose of this lecture, however, I shall ignore this distinction since it does not compromise the kinds of arguments I shall be making.

And so I now turn to the ethnographic examples which I have promised and I start with two deliberately contrasting examples for which I rely on the analyses and documentation found in two recently completed theses in the anthropology department of the London School of Economics.

The first is a study by Gabrielle vom Bruck of the historical and contemporary place of the descendants of the Prophet Mohammed the Sadah, in northern Yemen. We should note, however, that many of the aspects stressed by vom Bruck would also be valid for similar groups in the Arab world, indeed for the Arab world as a whole.

According to the generally accepted history of Yemen, and in a way that is somewhat reminiscent of the history of Morocco discussed by Westermarck, the Sadah, one of these groups of the descendants of the Prophet Mohammed established themselves among the tribes in the ninth century

A.D. first as peacemakers and then, under the leadership of their head, the Imam, as rulers of what became the Yemeni Imamate.

As descendants of the Prophet the Sadah are privileged vessels of divine and legal knowledge by the very fact of their ancestry. But, as vom Bruck shows, the idea of a descent group who are distinguished by their sacred wisdom carries within itself a contradiction. Put simply the problem in such a conception is that wisdom is something which is learnt and holiness is something which is practised and therefore these qualities do not necessarily imply a particular descent affiliation. For example, one might be wise and holy and not a member of the Sadah or one might be a descendant of the prophet but lazy and so ignorant.

The potential contradiction in the two aspects of this elite is apparent to all, but for members of the Sadah and for believers in their pre-eminence in religious matters it is implicitly avoided in the following way. Descendants of the Prophet, because of his original contact with God, have by that fact something in their inherited potential which makes them, in normal circumstances, develop holiness and wisdom more than other lesser people. The belief in such a potential and the theory of mind it implies, is somewhat similar to the belief in innate abilities of the Platonists or more recently of those psychologists who, largely following Chomsky, stress the innate potentialities of persons to develop particular types of knowledge. Such knowledge will not develop without being given a chance but, if a member of the Sadah is properly taught in a good environment, then, they will most probably become that divine paragon that their holy ancestry innately disposes them to becoming.

There are many facets to such a belief. Inevitably, who one's parents are is critical for the Sadah. Only if one's father is a descendant of the prophet will one be a member of the Sadah and therefore have the special potential for holy wisdom. Indeed even paternity may not be quite enough, and so, to make doubly sure it is even better if one's mother is also a member of the Sadah. Thus, implied in the psychological theory of holy predisposition, is a theory about the nature and character of kinship and conception. This theory is quite specific and is based on the presumption of the determining potential of birth and more particularly of the preeminent, though not exclusive, relevance of paternity. These notions are, of course, common to all the Arab world and indeed of many societies with descent groups but they are used as the grounding of the more specific formulation of identity used by the Sadah.

There are however yet further implications to all this. Linked with this theory of the mind and descent is a theory about learning and the nature of such mnemonic devices as writing.

In a study subtitled "Islamic education and its social reproduction" which, although not based on Yemen would certainly apply to it, Eickelman (1978) stresses three characteristic features of learning in the Muslim world; the emphasis on learning by rote, its rigorous discipline and its lack of explanation. The reason for these characteristics is that for Muslims the truth is found in the words of God which the text fixes and that, therefore, the purpose of learning is, above all, the preservation of the presence of the divine message among Muslims through time. The purpose is to achieve what in Islamic theory is called "mnemonic domination" (Eickelman 1978: 489). The mind of the pupils is infinitely inferior to the mind that created the Quran because of the immeasurable distance that exists between God and humans. It is therefore important to place the holy message in these inferior minds, not so that the pupils will "make it their own", as our educationalist would say, but so that the text will make the mind of the pupils its own: and thereby make the pupils people of Islam. The learning has to conquer the recalcitrant self, not the other way round. This also explains the importance of memorising the text and not merely reading it. In such a system writing is not to be seen as a substitute to internalisation, as Goody would have it, rather it is merely one device which facilitates the internalisation, or rather the moulding, of the recipient. A similar point was made recently with great clarity by Mary Carruthers (1990) dealing with the somewhat similar notions of Europe Medieval literacy.

Now, of course, in the case of the descendants of the prophet learning in a Quranic school has a further twist to what it had in the medieval Christian world or, for that matter, for Muslims who are not descendants of the prophet. For the Sadah learning Islamic wisdom is less of a struggle since it is being implanted in ground which already awaits it. Learning Muslim wisdom by the Sadah represents the meeting of the externally unchanged scripture, maintained through the device of writing, with the internally unchanged potential for knowing it, transmitted to them through the biology of reproduction and descent. What is learnt by the Sadah is learnt particularly deeply and significantly since they are taking into themselves what is already in themselves as a potential. Madelung writing about them quotes Muslim writers saying that for them "knowledge grows in the breast of the prophet's descendants as rain causes the fruit to grow" (Madelung 1965: 48). For the Sadah there is, therefore, nothing in the process of learning or of bodily growth and reproduction which creates anew what was not already potentially there. The creation of Islamic learning has occurred once and for all and many Muslims believe that all possible future and past knowledge is found in the Quran. Learning and producing children are processes of maintenance of the divine so that what has been, is, and will not decay. The idea that the knowledge and truth are being continually created as the result of a creative and ongoing dialectic would be a terrible sacrilege.

It is because of this idea that the conceptualisation of the presence of the Sadah in history becomes fascinating. History in Yemen, just as much as anywhere else, has been a continual turmoil of events. In particular the Sadah have been buffeted by the twentieth century. Until the middle of this century Yemen, under the rule of the Sadah and the Imam, was quite isolated from the rest of the world. However, even then, the outside world impinged. New ideas, especially new pan-Arab and socialist ideas from progressive centres such as Egypt were having an effect, at least on a small intelligentsia. Secondly the fact of having to deal with external powers made the Iman behave ever more like a political leader and less as a religious one and he therefore lost legitimacy in the process. Both these factors and others combined in the events of the 1962 revolution which overthrew the Imamate and led to strong and to a certain extent continuing persecution of the Sadah.

The Sadah's reaction to this difficult situation is sensitively documented by vom Bruck and she identifies a dual response. On the one hand, the Sadah had to adapt to oppressive force and compromise. But they also tried to maintain themselves unchanged as best they could; largely through various practices such as endogamy or, in some cases, partial or total immigration. This was their duty.

They, the unchanging continuation of the chosen vessel of God, the upholders of ultimate truth, know that governments, states, polities, intellectual fashions come and go but they do and should remain. Their presence, strengthened by the learning which has naturally found a home in them, is ultimately beyond historical accident, they will always be required, if not temporarily by humans, at least by God. Truth for them, as Plato would have agreed, is always beyond events and the concept of an ahistorical truth seems the corner stone of Islam. Like truth, or as a part of it, the Sadah exist beyond history, like God. They have been here since the prophet and in their essentials they remain. Events swirl around them but they are a fixed content which must be continually rediscovered so that the wisdom of God can recreate society as the learnt Quran should construct the minds of the pupils. They are both in history and out of it, or rather they are in other people's history while they remain unchanged. To them, therefore, the particular events of history are external.

Now let me turn to a very different ethnographic example; that of a group of poor peasants and urban dwellers in a part of central Philippines, Bicol, recently analyzed by Fenella Cannell. As was the case for my discussion of the Sadah of Yemen in relation to the rest of the Arab world, many of the characteristics Cannell stresses for the Bicolanos are common to other Christian lowland (i.e. non-tribal) Filipinos.

Cannell stresses how the Bicolano poor represent themselves as people "who have nothing". They describe themselves, not entirely inaccurately, as people who have been, and are, at the mercy of more powerful others: rich landowners, powerful government officials but also at the mercy of outside colonial powers: Spain and America. This image is also consistent with their view of the supernatural world since they similarly see saints and spirits as powerful others who they have to accommodate and modify. The reaction of the ordinary Bicolanos to events brought about by these powerful others, whether earthly or supenatural, whether in the past or now, is not to hold themselves aloof, but to allow these events continually to mould them, though in the process of adapting, they will also, from their position of initial weakness, gradually and continually change these more powerful forces through a humble and somewhat ironic negotiation in order to create a somewhat more equitable *modus vivendi*. By contrast to the Sadah, they do not value or are not interested in an eternal irreducible essential in themselves, an essence which will ultimately reassert itself unchanged after the vagaries of the moment have passed. The ordinary Bicolano do not construct an imaginary pre-colonial, pre-compromise state to which they want to return like nineteenth century European romantics or Muslim fundamentalists; rather they represent their role in history as having been willing to let powerful outsiders transform them to the core and in the process having also somewhat modified those who thought they were merely conquerors. In this way they are Catholic because they accepted Spanish Catholicism though in their acceptance they created, in a way that they do not choose to stress, something new. Similarly, they watch foreign television programmes in order to adapt and mould themselves to these models as best they might. They particularly value beauty contests of all kinds because, as Cannell shows with delightful empathy, these give them a chance to appear, even if only for a sharply delineated moment, like these foreign and powerful models which they can control by their somewhat ironic participation.

In many ways this willing adaptation to foreign or urban models seems, to the Bicolanos at least, a response caused by their weakness in the historical process which they feel, perhaps rightly, is increasing. Cannell argues that this idiom of increasing powerlessness is also reflected in their relation to the supernatural and she stresses how they talk, for example in their discussion of the changes in the nature of spirit mediumship, of their growing lack of control but all this however is only a first step.

Cannell goes on to stress the significance of the idea of "negotiation" as being central to their view of how to deal with these more powerful others. The actor starts in a position of inferiority and oppression but with time and patience he/she engages the superior in a negotiation which becomes a relationship of exchange, if always unequal exchange. One transforms oneself to accommodate the superior in oneself but as this occurs one engages their pity and so one gradually builds oneself up through the accumulation of accepted experiences. As a result the negotiation from weakness becomes the basis for becoming a subject in one's own right through creative adaptive transformation.

In many ways the Bicolano emphasis on the value of becoming and on metamorphosis has a similar place to the emphasis on an absolute eternal truth in the Muslim societies discussed above. Though of course it could not be more different in terms of content. In the Philippines it is as though nothing is fixed forever, events will bring new imprints on the wax that is people and so form them in something which did not exist before, but then, the imprints of the past will be gradually covered and partially obscured by other imprints as the person is continually and gradually transformed in history from one state to another as they construct meaning through selective recollection. One could say of the Filipinos, then, that they are Aristotelians to the Yemenis Platonists.

For them the distant past is a week and fading memory gradually replaced by newer constituting events. Unlike the Sadah "they" were not there in the past and "they" will not be there in the future. Rather, for them, there were people in the past who became them, and as a result of events, the descendants they will produce will become gradually different through the effect of events and time.

With this type of ideas we would not expect the kind of mnemonic objects which must be preserved unchanged such as the religious texts of Islam which ensure the continuing moulding of the present exactly to the pattern of the past. Indeed there is a striking absence of a conservationist spirit about the lowland Philippines which makes their villages and towns poor tourist attractions. In the area where Cannell worked however there was an object which at first sight seemed to be of this kind. This was a statue of a saint (actually of Christ) which was the focus of pilgrimage. But, as Cannell points out, even here the idea of transformation and becoming had penetrated, since the saint was thought of as having grown up (literally the wood got bigger and more recognisable) in the recent past but by now was entering a period of decline and shrinking through old age.

The Bicolanos' own explanation of their cultural malleability is in terms of their weakness, poverty and negotiating ability and, indeed, the particular group which Cannell studied are both far from the centres of power and yet open, without protection, to all the whims and winds of external influence. However, there probably is more to the matter than what can be explained in purely political terms.

I pointed out above how the Sadah's view of the way they are in history seems to accord well with their view of kinship which we can call loosely the descent type. In such a system birth transmits essential and immutable qualities and gives potentialities which, if only given the right environment, will develop of themselves. This implies, as Fortes stressed in his discussion of unilineal descent groups (Fortes 1953), that each individual is a replacement of his forebears, or the vessel in which the eternal element is given a temporary incarnation. Of course such a type of kinship system and theory of the person and the body is very wide spread, far beyond the Mediterranean world into Africa and Asia. However, the particular form of this general cultural complex which is illustrated in the case of the Sadah is especially interesting in that it gives the classical idea of descent an extreme, and therefore particularly clear, formulation. There is therefore an elective affinity between the Sadah's view of their place in history and their theory of kinship and the same is probably true of the Bicolanos' concept of their malleable response to history and their kinship ideas. This means that although one can understand their views of the past in terms of their situation in the face of colonial powers a fuller explanation of their understanding of their place in history needs to take into account aspects of their culture which probably have a much longer history than that of the colonial Philippines.

It is my guess that a relationship exists between the particular formulation of the Filipino's relation to events and much more general Southeast Asian ideas about the body and kinship.

In a recent general statement about kinship in Southeast Asia J. Fox says "I think it is true for the Austronesian world (which includes the Philippines) that one's social identity is not given at birth. One gets the 'impression' if you read some of the old classical African monographs that a person's identity has been defined by the fact of being born into a lineage. Now my view would be that especially in the Austronesian world social identity is not fixed. You are launched . . . you are on a path". (Fox 1987: 174) Such a view would indeed fit the Merina of Madagascar to which I turn below, where I argue that kinship is created little by little throughout life and is only fixed after death in the final placing of the dead in the tomb. It will, I would guess also, largely fit for the people studied by Cannell and this is suggested in Cannell's forthcoming discussion of Bicolano marriage. Such a view of kinship created, not through birth but through a continual becoming, brought about through contact with the coexisting world, accords well with a view of one's place in history which results from a continual negotiation which ultimately creates permanent cumulative transformation through the taking on of new appearances which you become but which in the process you also make your own. The Filipinos' view of the past and its continuing changing imprint on them seems coherent not only with their understanding of their place in history but with their understanding of the nature of reproduction, of birth, of the character of mind and of their body. For them history is internal since events are continually changing them down to the very roots of their being since they are not defined by birth but are through life in a continual process of growing definition.

The cases of the Sadah of Yemen and of the Bicolanos of the Philippines are therefore in many ways opposites and I must admit that for the sake of a short presentation I have pushed the contrast to extremes ignoring some elements where the two are not quite to distinct. However there are systems which, even at the schematic level of this lecture, seem genuinely intermediate.

As an example of these I take a group of people living in Madagascar, the Merina (Bloch 1971, 1986). As was the case for the Yemenis in relation to the Arab world as a whole, and for the Bicolanos for the Philippines, much of what I have to say would apply to other peoples in Madagascar and possibly beyond. In fact I am much helped here by some of the ideas formulated in another recent thesis by R. Astuti concerning a quite different Malagasy group to the Merina; the Vezo, fishing peoples of the west coast of Madagascar (Astuti 1991).

The Merina are a group of people who were the subjects of a kingdom which developed in the eighteenth century by incorporating various other groups and political entities.

In many ways their kinship system corresponds well to the Austronesian pattern as characterised by Fox in that birth does not determine the person. The Merina stress how the new born child is all soft, its kinship alignments are relatively open . . . for example, as is the case with the Vezo whether she will be linked to her father's side of the family is a matter which remains open for negotiation. Adoption is always possible and common and very often leads to the original parentage being forgotten.

Accompanying this view of the nature of kinship is an attitude to history which has many similarities with that of the Bicolanos. The Merina have been very willing recipients of foreign ways of doing things. They became Christians enthusiastically long before colonisation. They adopted foreign dress, types of houses and hairstyles remarkably easily. They were very willing to emigrate to parts of Madagascar outside Imerina and very soon to France where they have for long formed an active and relatively prosperous community. The Merina, a little like the Filipines, are normally above all interested in transformation and appearance, in the transformation brought about by growth, the transformation of the growing unity of families brought about by marriage, the transformations brought about in their identity by events. For them transformation, movement, unencumbered enjoyment of the possibilities of present situations and being alive are two sides of the same coin. In this respect they are Aristotelians.

But unlike the Filipinos discussed by Cannell there is another aspect to their representation of their experience of history. Talking of the Vezo, Astuti says that for them one belongs to a descent group only after death and this would, with modifications, be true of most Malagasy. Among the Merina the monumental tombs represent the immortalisation of the descent group, its unchanging permanence through time, but also its immobile localisation in a piece of territory with which it has been and will always be placed for ever, Merina tombs are megalithic structures intended to last forever. These tombs are not just containers, in fact they conceptually merge the stone container with the content: the dry parts of the body of the members of the group which are continually being placed there, after the living have ended the mobility implied by the fact that they are alive, and after the dry parts of their body have been separated from the wet parts through the rituals which follow death.

As dried parts of tombs the Merina thus have a permanent place in history. Their tomb and, in a sense, the fact that they were there in the past in that particular locality, as events flowed around them, ensure that they will remain there in the future so long as the new generations have their remains placed in the tomb and so long as the living maintain the material structure.

This permanence in history is, however, very different to the permanence in history of the Yemeni Sadah. It is not "as a special kind of human being" that they were there in the past, and will and should be there in the future; it is as dead dried objects which contrast dramatically with living people.

There is however for the Merina a relationship between the living mutable and mobile being, endlessly modified by the moment and the imprint these moments leave on it, and the steady object in the tomb. Throughout life (including the period immediately after life) the one type of being becomes the other. As the living person goes through life and moves towards final burial in the tomb, a journey which will only be completed after death, the steady dead being is gradually taking over the fluid living being. The process of gradual invasion is caused by a person receiving blessing since for the Merina blessing involves the living coming into contact with the tomb which in a sense, little by little, places itself in the body of the maturing individual. In this way a cycle is established so that the living become the dead and the dead become the living.

What this means is that living people are dual. The young are more "live mutable mobile beings", while the old gradually contain more of the unchanging tomb in themselves, though the final transformation of the living into the tomb object is a fairly brutal process, carried out in the ritual of secondary burial which I described in *Placing the Dead* (Bloch 1971). The gradually changing mixture which are living people is therefore, first of all, conceptualised in terms of the body, and especially the contrast between the wet and dry elements in the body, but it also has many other aspects. For example, it is also manifested in terms of a dualism in ways of speaking between ordinary speech and the ancestral oratory of the old.

Above all it is a dualism of knowledge and mind. On the one hand there is knowledge concerning day-to-day practical matters, which should be dealt with the maximum ingenuity and flexibility of thought, and on the other hand, there is knowledge consisting of immobile ancestral traditions which should be merely repeated but not changed. This contrast is actually made explicit by the Merina themselves as well as by other Malagasy people (Beaujard 1991) who contrast in every possible way tales, which are intended to entertain, amuse and provoke thought, which they say are not about truth but about "lying", and what is called *Tantara* which is ancestral knowledge and which is categorically true.

This emphasis on truth immediately reminds us of the Sadah and for that matter of Plato and we can see that a notion of truth integral with certain types or aspects of being inevitably determines whether history is inside oneself or outside. As truth bearers, or as future dried ancestral bones in and merged with the localised tomb, the Merina, like the stones of the tomb itself, should be unaffected by the swirl of events. In this way, for them history is external. However they are not really like the Sadah. The Sadah in their lives are, and should be vessels of immutable holy wisdom. In their person they are permanently true because of their birth which has given them the potential truly to learn and know holy scriptures. As "living people" therefore the Sadah are only in history in the way a rock is in the middle of a stream. This is not true of the Merina. As "living people" they are like the Bicolanos, made by events, it is only fully as dead people that they will become that transcendental permanence that is the stones of the tomb. But then it will not be *them* but something which has grown in them as they have became more mature, older and which, after death, will finally dominate as the final remains of their live selves, when the wet elements are completely removed. The Merina tomb is therefore not a memorial of the dead, it is a memorial of the way the living have been abolished by transcendental stone.

This may all sound very abstract but it takes many very concrete forms. For example, the Merina who live in France seem apparently and easily totally French in their culture, their values and their aspiration. But there is one great difference, they all, at amazingly great expense, will arrange for their corpses to be flown back to Madagascar so that, in the end, they will be back as part of permanent stone structures in the soil of their ancestral land. The Merina living in France are, therefore, in a particularly dramatic way, which nonetheless is common to all Merina, participating in two different ways in two kinds of histories at once. One is a history in France where like Aristotelians they learn and are internally transformed by the flow of events and the other is a history in Madagascar which remains external, since irrespective of what happens they are still in the same place where they always have been and in a substance, stone, which, like Platonic truth, is absolute and unchanging. But in fact they do not participate in this static existence in Madagascar as live wet beings but as dead dry lithic beings, since for them being alive is about movement change and sensual pleasure (Bloch 1989b).

*   *   *

What do these three examples show? First of all that there is no one way of relating to the past and the future and therefore of being in history. There is, therefore, no one way by which one wants to inscribe memory in the public world. For example if we consider things which could be called mnemonic objects: the Quran of the Sadah, the saint of the Bicolanos and the tombs of the Merina we can see that their purpose and their character-istics are completely different. There is no point in trying to understand what such objects can do as markers of the past if we consider them as sim-ply memory devices, without also considering the more general contexts given above. There is not a generalised need of human beings to remember the past. And, in any case, as Bartlett stressed long ago, the devices which select from the past what is to be remembered also inevitably involve select-ing what of the past is to be obliterated, for example the soft parts of the body of the Merina. When we consider the social actor's attitude to the dis-tant past it becomes clear that one's effort involves not simply finding ways of remembering better, as is the aim of the psychologists' imaginary actor, but also, and equally, finding ways to forget it.

One fundamental problem in linking together the concepts of memory of, on the one hand, most psychologists, and, on the other, most anthropol-ogists and historians, therefore seems to lie with the psychologists' much too simple notion of person. Psychologists, and others like them, tend to imagine as unproblematic that entity which acts on the external or simply and passively responds to the external. When a psychologist is looking at short term memory, or at working memory, she can get away with it. The totally unconscious use of memory involved in carrying out practical tasks may probably be satisfactorily studied without taking into account the cul-tural and historical specificities which construct the actor. However as soon as we move to long term memories such as autobiographic memory and the long term semantic memory of a historical past, a memorising which ex-tends memory well beyond the lives of the individual, the problem of the nature of the subject must come to the fore.

Such recalling defines the person in relation to time by invoking, or not in-voking, notions of a past interaction with an external world which contains truth and falsehoods, permanent and impermanent elements, which is, or is not, in a state of continual creative dialectical flux. These ways of remem-bering the past not only create the imagined external world but they create the imagined nature of the actor in the past which, in so far as this actor is seen as a predecessor, refers also to those living in the present. As the mem-ber of the Sadah chooses to fix wisdom which has come from the past in his receptive body, he is defining the kind of person he really was in the past. He is constructing the kind of person he will be in the future. And sandwiched in between these two, as a filling of infinitely small depth, he is defining him-self as a permanent unchanging person in history. When the Bicolano imag-ine themselves sandwiched between their malleable forebears in the colonial past and consequently their malleable successors in the future they are constructing themselves in the present as a completely different filling to the sandwich than do the Sadah, and again the same is true of the Merina except that they, perhaps, see themselves as a single filling shared by two different sandwiches. These different definitions of the self mean that we cannot assume *a priori* that we know what the person is, irrespective of cultural or historical context. I am not arguing, however, as would a cultural relativist, that there is nothing else to actors than these historically constructed self definitions, indeed the relation of these definitions to aspects of the person which are not so fundamentally determined by specific histories is precisely an area of potential cooperation between psychologists, anthropologists and historians, but this kind of joint project cannot begin if we do not take on board the relevance of these self definitions for constructing the actor. The three examples I have given here of culturally defined actors are not anything like the hypothesised generalised and unspecific actor of psychology manuals, who is envisaged merely as an accumulator and maximiser of unproblematic memories, irrespective of content. Indeed we may suspect that this image even, may itself not be as scientific and culture free as psychologists implicitly assume since it too may have something to do with the culture in which it was produced, in this case the image of the individual as fundamentally and economic maximiser.

No human scientist can therefore ignore how people represent themselves to themselves in history because it is, to a certain extent, in terms of these representations, that they will react to revolutions, migration or colonial conquests as we have seen it to be in the case for the examples I have discussed here.

Clearly the problem of linking up the notion of memory of psychologists on the one hand, and, on the other, anthropologists and historians is therefore difficult but also thought provoking. There are two problems. The first, I have discussed here, the second I have not.

If psychologists concerned themselves merely with working and short term memory they might get away with their rather simple notion of actors, but they do not so limit themselves and they want to, and do, move on from there to discussions of long term memory which involves them in the move from private representations to public representations. If they do this, as I have to tried to show, then they must take into account the kind of matters discussed here.

However, before the anthropologists and historians become too pleased with themselves in having taught the psychologists a lesson, they should remember the second problem which I have not discussed here and which might temper their self-satisfaction. If historians and anthropologists confined themselves merely to public "representations" of the past they perhaps could ignore what psychologists have been showing concerning the place of memory in practical action, but they don't, they want to understand the mental character of what people remember and the significance this has for the form and perhaps the content of what is remembered, they want to see how the mental presence of the past affects what people do, and in this aspect of their work they will have to learn many lessons from the psychologists. I have not discussed this side of things, and in many ways the debate has been admirably opened by Sperber (1975).

In other words the study of memory may well be a privileged area for seeing how public, historically created, cultural representations join private representations but before we can go forward in this joint enterprise with much success, much preliminary but essential theoretical groundwork needs be done. I have attempted to do a little of this here.

Acknowledgements

I would like to acknowledge the help of Dr. F. Cannell, Dr. J. Coleman and Dr. G. vom Bruck for reading and commenting in a very useful manner on earlier drafts. My account of their work is however my own and the reader who really wants to know what they say should turn to their texts.

References

Astuti, R. 1991. *Learning to be Vezo: the Construction of the Person among Fishing People of Western Madagascar.* Unpublished Thesis London University.

Baddeley, A.J. 1976. *The Psychology of Memory.* London: Harper and Row.

Bartlett, F.C. 1932. *Remembering: a Study of Experimental and Social Psychology.* Cambridge: Cambridge University Press.

Beaujard, P. 1991. *Mythe et Société à Madagascar.* (Tanala de l'Ikongo) Paris: L'Harmattan.

Bloch, M. 1971. *Placing the Dead: Tombs, Ancestral Villages and Social organisation among the Merina of Madagascar.* London: Seminar Press.

_____. 1986. From Blessing to Violence: History and ideology in the circumcision ritual of the Merina of Madagascar. Cambridge: Cambridge University Press.

_____. 1989a. "Literacy and Enlightenment". In: M. Trolle-Larsen and K. Sousboe (eds.) *Literacy and Society.* Publications of the Centre for Research in the Humanities, Copenhagen.

_____. 1989b. "The symbolism of money in Imerina". In: M. Bloch and J. Parry (eds.) *Money and the Morality of Exchange,* CUP.

Bruck, G. vom, 1991. *Descent and Religious Knowledge: 'Houses of Learning' in modern Sana'a.* Unpublished Thesis London University.

Cannell, F. 1992. *Catholicism, Spirit Mediumship and the ideal of Beauty in a Bicolano. Community: Philippines.*

Carruthers, M. 1990. *The book of memory: A study of Memory in Medieval Culture.* Cambridge: Cambridge University Press.

Cohen, G. 1990. *Memory in the Real World.* Hove and London: Lawrence Erlbaum Associates.

Coleman, J. 1992. *Ancient and Medieval Memories: Studies in the reconstruction of the past*. Cambridge: Cambridge University Press.

Eickelman, D.F. 1978. "The art of memory: Islamic education and social reproduction." *Comparative Studies in Society and History* 20: 485–516.

Fortes, M. 1953. "The Structure of Unilineal Descent Groups" *American Anthropologist* 55: 17–41.

Fox, J. 1987. "The House as a type of social Organisation on the Island of Roti, Indonesia". In: C. MacDonald (ed.) *De la Hutte au Palais*. Paris: C.N.R.S.

Goody, J. 1977. *The Domestication of the Savage Mind*. Cambridge: Cambridge University Press.

Lévi-Strauss, C. 1984. *Paroles Données*. Paris: Plon.

Luria, A.R. 1976. *Cognitive Development: its structural and Social Foundations*. Cambridge, Mass.: Harvard University Press.

Madelung, W. 1965. *Der Imam al Oasim. Ibn Ibrahim und die Glaubenslehre der Zaiditen*. Berlin: de Gruyter.

Neisser, U. 1978. "Memory, What are the important questions?". In: M.M. Gruneberg, P.E. Morris and R.N. Sykes (eds.) *Practical Aspects of Memory*. London: Academic Press.

Olson, D.R. 1977. "From Utterance to text: The bias of language, in speech and writing". *Harvard Educational Review* 47: 257–281.

Sperber, D. 1975. "Anthropology and Psychology: Towards an Epidimiology of Representations". *Man* 20: 73–89.

Wertsch, J.V. 1985. *Vigotsky and the Social Formation of Mind*. Cambridge, Mass.: Harvard University Press.

Chapter Six

The Resurrection of the House Amongst the Zafimaniry of Madagascar

In this chapter I discuss how the terrible colonial war of 1947 is remembered some 40 years later in Madagascar in general and in a small forest village in particular. The village was burnt down by the French, and the inhabitants were forced to hide without proper food for almost two years. The narrative that is the main focus here recounts the traumatic return to the destroyed village. This story can only be understood, it is argued, when the central spiritual and social significance of houses is taken into account. Also of importance here is the Christian idiom, which has come to this part of Madagascar with the conversion of the inhabitants to Catholicism.

*   *   *

The Zafimaniry are a group of Malagasy swidden cultivators living in high-altitude montane forest. In terms of general culture they are fairly close to the neighbouring Betsileo or even the Merina. Their political history has been characterized by their determined attempts to avoid various forms of centralized government, attempts which on the whole have been fairly successful.

The only period when the Zafimaniry suffered tight government control followed the Madagascar-wide anti-colonial revolt of 1947 when the French army probably killed at least 80,000 people. The best detailed study of this revolt remains Jacques Tronchon's *L'Insurrection Malgache de 1947* (1974), but it would not be appropriate for the purposes of this chapter to give a general account of the events here.

The revolt affected the Zafimaniry particularly badly. This is largely because of their geographic position. The largest contingent of the rebel army had grouped on the coast to the east of them and then marched up to the central plateau in order to attack the larger towns in the centre of Madagascar. They chose to do this through the least accessible parts of the east coast forest in order to avoid detection and that meant through Zafimaniry country. The rebels and what they had to say was mostly well received by the Zafimaniry although I think very few Zafimaniry actually joined them. Nonetheless it is significant that to this day no Zafimaniry I know ever refers to the rebels of 1947 by the normal Malagasy word for 'rebel', which in their dialect has negative connotations, but they use instead another term with positive connotations.[1]

It was not the passage of the rebels through their villages which had such terrible effects on the Zafimaniry but the revenge of the French as they regained control of the situation and pushed the defeated Malagasy back the way they had come.

Because the village where I recently did field work, like most other Zafimaniry villages, had welcomed the rebels, the administration of the time deemed it should be punished. For this purpose, the French attempted to take the whole population to one of a number of concentration camps. In fact most of the villagers managed to escape in the forest leaving only three sick or crippled persons behind. The army force-marched these remaining captives to the concentration camp five miles away with such brutality that all three died before getting there.

The French then burnt the village so that nothing was left above ground and the villagers stayed in hiding in the forest for two and a half years,[2] living in low grass shelters, and eating by hunting and gathering and by rescuing what crops they could from their abandoned swiddens. Even after the withdrawal of the troops they were afraid to return, in part because the initial repression was succeeded by a bout of the recurrent colonial enthusiasm for ecology which, as usual, had the declared aim of preserving the forest from slash and burn agriculture but which was also intended to keep the people in the concentration camps, now renamed 'new villages'. However, even when this policy was abandoned, the people in the village were unsure of the government's intentions and they stayed in hiding, watching the site of their village gradually becoming engulfed by vegetation, but not daring to return.

In order to comprehend the circumstances of this return, which is what this chapter is about, it is necessary to understand Zafimaniry concepts of the house. However, even before turning to this topic something also needs to be said about Zafimaniry Catholicism since it too has a minor but significant role to play in the story.

The history of the Catholic Church in the part of Zafimaniry country with which I am concerned here goes back, as far as I can work out, to the early thirties, when, as a result of an epidemic, several closely related villages all became converted. Immediately the church sent a priest to the area, the first of a series continuing to the present day. This first priest greatly influenced certain people, especially the family with whom I shall be concerned. The influence of the church today is less than it was in 1947, but it is still very great for some people, though much less for others. However, even for those most involved in the church, Catholic belief and practice is, and has always been, only an *added* element on top of traditional religious beliefs and practices of a non-Christian character. Foremost among these traditional beliefs and practices are those concerning ancestors. These seem to remain almost totally unaffected by equally strongly held Christian beliefs.[3]

I now turn to the theme of this volume and to Zafimaniry ideas concerning the house. This is a topic that has an importance for them which cannot be exaggerated.

In considering Zafimaniry notions of the house some of the ideas of Lévi-Strauss concerning house-based societies are very helpful, although others are clearly not applicable. Firstly, grouped under the label are some very different systems so that house-based societies cannot, and probably should not, be clearly contrasted with other types of societies as Lévi-Strauss would have us do. Secondly, because the association Lévi-Strauss sees between an emphasis on the house and hierarchy is actually reversed in Madagascar (Lévi-Strauss 1979, part 2, ch.2). The Zafimaniry who are, one could say, obsessed with the house are non-stratified,[4] while the Merina who have always stressed hierarchy (Bloch 1977) have an anti-house ideology, and instead stress the tomb (Bloch 1986).[5]

For Madagascar the most valuable part of Lévi-Strauss's theory is the close association he sees between the symbolism of the house as a building and the centrality of monogamous marriage in both the symbolism and the organization of kinship. For Lévi-Strauss, in fact, the house is the 'objectification of a relationship' (1984: 195) which is marriage. As a result, he argues, in house-based societies, instead of alliance occurring *between* units, marriage actually forms the *core* of the unit, a unit which is identified with the material house. Lévi-Strauss in fact applies his theory specifically to the Merina (1984: 226) in a way which is highly perceptive but which, because of the inadequacy of his sources, is also rather confusing in its treatment of the relations between the house and the tomb. But the notion of the house as the core of the marital unit is one which if anything applies even better to the case of the Zafimaniry.

These ideas have proved particularly fruitful in Southeast Asia and Japan where we find, it seems to me, two different types of house-based societies. On the one hand, we have what used to be called stem family systems of which the Japanese *Ie* or the Iban *Bilek* are classic examples, and where one married pair alone succeeds another in the house, replacing each other with the passage of time. On the other hand we have systems where houses permanently associated with a founding couple become a ritual focus for descendants. The Northern Thai 'core house'[6] and the Zafimaniry houses are examples of this latter type.

Zafimaniry marriage and house creation are both very long-drawn-out processes, not surprisingly since the two are merely two sides of the same thing. Marriage without a house is a contradiction in terms, simply because the Zafimaniry notion which I choose to translate as 'marriage' is distinguished from other forms of sexual union precisely by the existence of a house. This is reflected in the fact that the normal way of asking the question corresponding to our 'are you married?' is phrased, literally, to mean 'Have you obtained a house with a hearth?'[7]

The process which leads to marriage begins, however, before the construction of the house. The beginning of this process is the sexual affection and intercourse which occurs between very young people indeed. The Zafimaniry seem to want to place particular stress on the chaotic, fluid and fickle character of this type of relationship, largely, I feel, to contrast it with the stability and immobility ultimately achieved by a successful union represented by the house. Ideally, out of chaotic promiscuity will emerge a more stable monogamous relationship based on mutual affection and this will lead to the partners establishing a house with a hearth.

In fact, there is often much less spontaneity than would appear in the creation of stable marriages, for the parents of the couple may have arranged a marriage between them while they were still only babies. If so, however, this agreement will be kept secret and the couple will merely be subtly encouraged towards each other by their parents, in the hope that they will begin the marriage process seemingly on their own initiative.[8] The reason why this strategy is often successful is that the parents of such a couple go out of their way to patch up the relationship between the two when it threatens to break up, while on the other hand they may actually secretly encourage the demise of other liaisons.

The rationale behind this rather strange way of going about arranged marriages is the very great importance that the Zafimaniry attach to individual attraction in sexual relations, especially among the young. This is because sexual attraction and mutual affection are believed to be linked to the important concept of compatibility, as they understood it.

The notion of compatibility in marriage is crucial for the Zafimaniry. This is well shown by the fact that they attribute the barrenness of a couple not so much to a deficiency in the woman, as the Merina and other groups usually do, but rather to a problem in the mutual compatibility of the two spouses. We can also, I believe, get a glimpse of the Zafimaniry notion of compatibility from the fact that of the most common words used by the Zafimaniry for sexual intercourse one means 'becoming one', or 'uniting', and the other means literally 'to twin'. Zafimaniry houses are often decorated with a sculpted bird placed on the apex of the roof which is explained by them, and in contrast to the meaning of such birds in other parts of Madagascar (Beaujard 1983, ch.3), as being a sign of domestic peace since if the spouses quarrelled the birds would be frightened and fly away.

The Zafimaniry concept of compatibility does not, however, correspond to stereotypic European ideas of marital love. First of all, it is thought of as being largely due to astrological causes. Most different to the western notion, however, is the fact that compatibility is not demonstrated principally by the spouses getting on well together, it is proved above all by the fertility of the union. Two spouses, however devoted to each other, who have only one child or none at all are seen as incompatible.[9] Because this fruitful compatibility grows with the production of descendants it is something to be sought and gained, largely by trial and error, but when gradually established it leads to stability which in turn leads to fertility.

Whenever a boy and girl are clearly attracted to each other and are having intercourse more regularly with each other than with anybody else, either they or their parents (depending on the part played in the relationship by the sort of parental strategy I mentioned above) may want to transform the relationship into something more permanent, something for which the English word 'marriage' offers a loose translation.

The first step along this path is the *recognition*, by the parents of the girl, of the fact that she is having sexual intercourse with a particular boy. This recognition process usually only takes place when the Zafimaniry consider a girl to be mature, in some cases this may mean she is little more than twelve, but usually this occurs when she is around fifteen.

This recognition needs to be understood partly in terms of the very strong taboo which forbids adjacent generations from having knowledge of each others' sexual activity, especially if the representatives of these adjacent generations are of different sexes.

The first stage in this revelation occurs when the mother of the boy tells the mother of the girl of their children's liaison and when, in turn, the mother of the girl tells the father. This process is called *tapa sofina*, or the breaking of the ear, because first the girl's mother and then the girl's father have their ears 'broken' by having to take cognisance of their daughter's sexual activity and thereby break the taboo.

After the 'breaking of the ear' the girl may, from time to time, spend the night at her husband's house and need not any more take too elaborate precautions of secrecy.

After the *tapa sofina* comes the *tapa maso* which means the breaking of the eyes. This involves a major ritual where the family of the boy visits the family of the girl and acts on his behalf. It seems the only absolutely essential ritual of marriage. The central part of the ritual is when the bride and groom appear together shamefaced in front of her parents, thereby making public, especially to her father, their sexual relation. In return for the break-ing of the taboo (another word for *tapa maso* is *ala fady:*[10] the removal of the taboo) the groom gives a small sum of money to the girl's parents. Then the parents of the girl will bless the boy and the parents of the boy will bless the girl. After that the girl may have sexual relations in her own house. The 'appearance' of the couple together will then be repeated in a minor way when the new spouses together visit the houses of a variety of senior rela-tives of both the groom and bride.

Ideally the *tapa maso* should be followed by yet another ritual called the *fananbarana* or 'making evident'. In many ways this ought to be the most important marriage ritual; it should involve many people and requires a big feast. However, precisely because of this it is almost never done nowadays and I have never seen it. It should occur at the house of the bride and in-volves the husband giving a formal acknowledgement of his sonhood to his parents-in-law and later the bride doing the same for her parents-in-law at their house.[11] The *fananbarana* involves a declaration by both sides of their familial taboos so that both spouses will know what not to do so as not to endanger each other, by, for example, the wife using a pot in which a food tabooed to the husband has been cooked, or by the husband bringing into the house an animal tabooed to the wife.

Most important, however, is the fact that the ritual should end with the bride being given cooking and eating implements by her parents. She will then take these implements back to her husband's village. Her *trousseau* thus consists essentially of the cooking implements which will furnish the hearth of her marital home. The most important items of this *trousseau* are a cooking pot, a wooden plate and a large stirring spoon.

I think it is clear from the names of the rituals as well as from the way that they are carried out that underlying them is the idea of the union emerging into view. This is also what we see when we look at the house as a building. Before the *tapa maso* or immediately after it the young man will have started to build a house, or rather the framework for a house. The house will be situated near his parents' house, though in an inferior posi-tion, which usually means to the south and lower. It will be a very simple house, but it will have a hearth consisting of three stones in a wooden frame and three posts. One is the central post. This is the so-called 'hot post' because it is near the hearth and it will be the largest piece of wood in the house and will consist of a particular hardwood said to be the hardest of all woods. There will also be two 'cold posts', at either end of the house, which, like the hot post, support the ridge pole. These two should be some-what less massive than the 'hot post' and made of the next hardest wood. At this stage, for the most part the house will be made of flimsy, woven, flattened-out bamboos and reed mats which let in light and sound. It will probably have doors and windows also made of flimsy material.[12]

Before the house can be lived in, and that especially means cooking and having sex in it, it will have to be blessed in an important ritual of blessing carried out by the elders of the families of both the parents of the groom and the bride.

The ritual of blessing the new house starts with cooking second-year taro on the hearth. This will be the first occasion that the cooking and eating implements brought by the bride are used and also the first time that a fire is lit in the hearth. Once the taro has been thoroughly cooked it is distributed to everyone present and used for the blessing. This blessing takes the form of the most senior elder present rubbing the cooked taro on the three posts in turn and, while doing this, calling on God and the ancestors to bring children, crops, wealth and money to the family that will live in the house.

To understand the significance of this action it is necessary to turn to Zafimaniry ideas concerning taro. Taro has central importance to them because they rightly stress that it is the food that one can always rely on, because it is not attacked by pests or bad weather like other crops. It can even be relied on in years when, for political or climatic reasons, it has not been possible to plant. This is because it stays in the ground for a long time, up to six years, and it even multiplies of its own accord underground, like naturalizing daffodils. Taro is, and is recognized to be, a guarantee of survival, a fact spelled out by the elder in his prayer as he rubs taro on the posts. Indeed the Zafimaniry repeatedly told me that, were it not for taro, they could not have survived when they were hiding from the French, and I believe them. So the rubbing of second-year taro on to the central posts ensures the continuity and successful survival of the future inhabitants of the house.

But there is more to the action of rubbing the taro on the posts. In a way that is so obvious that it only rarely gets mentioned, the house posts are associated with the man of the couple. They are what he must put up, and the man's place in the house is traditionally sitting leaning against the central hot post. The woman, on the other hand, is associated with the activity of the hearth and the furniture of the hearth, the cooking pot, the serving plate and the big stirring spoon. As we saw, a marriage is 'made clear' by the bringing of these items by the woman to the house built by the man. Therefore the consummation of the marriage, not sexually but (in the fullest and most literal sense) domestically, is the conjunction of cooking pot and house post brought about by a life-sustaining vegetable: taro.

However, neither the marriage nor the house is completed by the ritual of the inauguration of the house. A marriage of compatible people needs children and so the practices surrounding childbirth are the continuation of the process. Here I only note those aspects related to the house.

The birth of the first child in a way strengthens the marriage and in a way weakens it. It strengthens the marriage in that, as a direct result, the spouses become terminologically related through teknonymy. This links the two parents since henceforth they have the name of their child in common.

The marriage is weakened, however, by the movements of the mother. When a woman who is pregnant for the first time is approaching the time to give birth, she will leave her husband's parents' house (or her husband's house if the couple already lives independently) and go back to her natal house, whether this be in another village or in her own village. After the birth she will remain for a number of months in what might be called a hyper-house, that is a house within a house, built on the bed where she has the child. The child will be associated with the mother's parents' house because the normal birth ritual, which is done a few days after birth, will be held there. The central section of this ritual makes a crucial material association between the child and the house, and does this in two ways: firstly, by putting some of the soot of the hearth of the house on the forehead of the child and secondly by burying the placenta, thought of as a twin as in other Southeast Asian cultures, between the 'hot post' and the hearth.

In theory at least, after a few months the mother will return to her husband's house, but in fact this never happens smoothly. For her to do that she has to be courted again not only by her husband but also by her husband's family in a repeat of the *fananbarana* in order to convince her to go home. If this is successful she will probably obtain quite a few new clothes and renewed promises to be treated with great consideration by the family of her husband. Very often, however, the husband will not be successful in getting his wife and child back at this stage.

Exactly the same performance will be repeated after the birth of the second child. It is usually only after the birth of the third child that the process is reversed in that the mother remains in her house and the mother's mother comes to the house of the couple. Then the child is marked on the forehead with the soot of its own parents' hearth and its 'twin' is buried there.

Only when children are born into it are the initial stages of marriage or of house creation complete—the two ways of putting the matter merely refer to two aspects of the same process. However, it is not merely the fact that the house is producing descendants which matters, but the fact that the couple of the house can nurture and nourish these children and grandchildren, which marks fruitfulness. As a result the agricultural work of the parents, something that they do together in a way that is often rhetorically stressed and which supplies basic starch foods for the upkeep of the family, is also seen as part of the necessary process for the successful growth of the marriage.

But the house is also changing materially as a result of a different but linked form of conjugal work. When first built, the house is highly permeable to the outside. This permeability means that one can see in when one looks through the roughly woven bamboo, and neighbours are continually looking in; one can also speak from the outside to people in the house as though no partition existed. However, this flimsy permeability diminishes with time. The Zafimaniry say that the house will then be gradually acquiring 'bones'. This refers to the massive wooden planks that will, little by little, replace the woven bamboo. Ultimately the house will look a little like a Canadian log cabin, except that the wood is vertical.

The work of getting this wood and preparing it for the house is typically a task that a man does with his wife's brother's help. The wife's brother is in Zafimaniry kinship terminology called *vady lahy* by male *ego*. This term literally means 'male wife'. The act of building up the house, 'hardening it with bones', as the Zafimaniry say, therefore also involves a semi-ritualized cooperation of a quasi-marital pair. The continuing building is thus also a joint enterprise of spouses.

Two aspects of this 'house hardening' give us further insights in to the Zafimaniry understanding of marriage. First of all the wood that is used in such house building is not only particularly hard, it must also have what the Zafimaniry call *teza*. This refers to the darker, impacted, inner core of some woods which gradually appears in older trees and which ultimately forms the greater part of it. For the Zafimaniry the *teza* of trees is like the bones of humans, but a bone which continues to grow and thereby transcends the mortality of the bodies of people. The word *teza* also forms the root of the Malagasy verb for 'to remain'. Thus the marriage, by being made with the *teza* of wood, is made to last, and last beyond the mortality of its human initiators. Secondly, the hardening of the house also involves the beginning of the decorative low-relief carving which the Zafimaniry put everywhere on the hardwoods which constitute the house, but especially on doors, windows and, above all, on the central posts. What these decorations are about, according to my informants, is 'giving honour to the *teza* of the wood'.[13] This process of decorative carving, which has made the Zafimaniry famous throughout Madagascar and beyond, will continue as the house continues to harden. Zafimaniry houses therefore seem a perfect example of how the aesthetics and architecture of house building become the objectification and fetishization of a social relation in the way postulated by Lévi-Strauss.

With time, therefore, the house hardens and becomes more and more beautifully decorated. When this process has really advanced, and if everything has gone well, the children of the couple will themselves have begun the process of marriage and the family will be enlarging. The girls will, to a certain extent, have left, but, as we saw, only to a certain extent since they will return to have their children in their parents' house. More importantly, they will return with their husbands and children to seek blessing for any major enterprise from the woman's parents.

The sons, on the other hand, will be building their own houses near that of their parents but they, with their wives and children, will, like the daughters, also seek blessings from their parents.

What this means is that, at certain times, grown-up sons and daughters still consider the house of their parents as their own. They will behave there just as though they had never left and they will share in the tasks that maintain the house. In particular they, together with their spouses (including their male spouses) will contribute to the hardening and decorating of the parental house. The same will be true of grandchildren, great-grandchildren and so on.

I think it is therefore right to consider these further stages of house construction as the continuation of the process of marriage, a process which began weakly with the 'breaking of the ear' but which now stands evident and beautiful in the form of a proud building.

As the parents get older and less able to work, the marriage pattern of the children changes slightly. The last son, as he marries, instead of moving out of his parents' house, will instead divide it with a partition so that the parents can live to the north and his own family to the south. With time, this young family will look after the parents more and more until their death. When that occurs the family of the younger son will take over the house completely.

To say this, though, is somewhat misleading in that the couple who takes over the house are, in theory, only caretakers of the house of the original founders, whose marriage house it is and remains. However when this founding couple dies, their descendants gradually come to feel that they are present as the conjoined house itself rather than as two individual people. It is at this point that the house will increasingly be referred to as a 'holy house'.

A holy house is a house where one goes for blessing from God and the ancestors. This is the answer that I would be given every time I asked: 'What is a holy house?' And when I asked 'How do you know which holy house you go to to ask for a blessing'? the answer was: 'It is the house of one's forebears which has successfully produced offspring.'

Holy houses are the growing fulfilment of the marriages of one's forebears which have been fruitful. The Zafimaniry do not think of this process of marriage and house growth as ending with the death of the original couple, so long as the children of the couple, and their children and so on, continue to reproduce and multiply, so that the original marriage continues to grow and harden. Or rather, it is the holy house which grows and hardens as descendants and their affines continue to make it of ever harder wood, more and more decorated, and as they replace any bits that might have been damaged or rotted. A person who is acting morally will only build up a holy house and will never diminish it. It is for this reason that no one who needs to repair a holy house in a way which requires some preliminary dismantlement of damaged parts can do so without offering a sacrifice of atonement to the original founding couple, even though the intention of the work is clearly to strengthen and beautify the house.

As the anthropology textbooks used to say: marriage is a process, but this process continues much longer among the Zafimaniry than the books envisaged, since it continues long after the death of the pair. A marriage, that is a house, is still growing perhaps a hundred years after it started.[14]

The image of being descended from a successful marriage which has hardened into a holy house is perhaps nowhere more vivid than in the phrase that the Zafimaniry use to describe everything they inherit from forebears, whether it be rights to clear land in a particular territory, recipes for medicines, or direct inheritance of beehives and reed beds. The term is *loha lambo* which literally means 'the head of a wild boar' but which actually refers to the apex of the house. In this phrase we seem to have the blessings of the ancestors descending onto the descendants from the apex of their house.

The source of this blessing is said to be the success of the process begun by the original marriage; obtaining a house with a hearth, joining the central post and the implements of the hearth, hardening the house, and then producing, feeding and nurturing the numerous descendants who come to the original house for blessing. Being blessed in a holy house, therefore, is putting oneself under the protection of that fertile compatibility of the spouses which still flows there.

This is made clear at all the meetings and blessings which take place in the holy house. At each of these occasions, speeches and requests are addressed to the central post, and a meal cooked on the hearth with the original pot, spoon and dish must be prepared and eaten. All parts of the holy house, but especially the central post and an ancestral cooking pot and stirring spoon, must be treated with great reverence and are surrounded by many taboos. Any breach of these taboos is seen as an attack against the body of the founding couple, as is often said quite explicitly during such requests for blessing.[15] It is through these blessings that the original fruitful marriage in its hardened form as the conjoined house post and furniture of the hearth, through its continuing fetishized life,[16] still produces its descendants, still nurtures and guides them, still feeds them.

In theory, of course, any one person has a whole set of holy houses, since one holds them both on one's own side and on that of one's spouse, besides belonging to all the houses of one's parents, grand-parents and more distant ancestors.

In fact the operative holy houses from which one gets blessing are much more restricted because usually one has only two lines of ascendants as a result of the preferential moiety exchange marriage system of the Zafimaniry[17] and because one usually only concerns oneself with two houses in either line.

One set of these is the houses of one's own parents and parents-in-law and these are visualized more in terms of people rather than buildings; at least while this parental generation is still alive, one speaks in terms of getting blessing from them as people, and not from their houses.

The other set of holy houses is the houses of the founders of the lines of one's own family and of that of one's spouse in a particular locality. This means that these holy houses are the foundation houses of villages, since a village is best seen as the result of one or two marriages/houses which have produced many children/marriages/houses.

These holy houses of founders of communities are the ritual centres of their villages. In fact, symbolically they can be said to encompass the village in many ways, and one goes to such houses before any major enterprise to get blessing. They are also the place where all family rituals will take place and where the descendants will meet to discuss important matters and settle disputes. They are the source of blessing of the village.

*   *   *

So when, in 1947, the French burnt down the village they were not just burning the wooden cabins which the foreign soldiers saw, they were burning all the holy houses of the village and the founding holy house in particular; they were burning down the blessing which came from that original marital compatibility. And the villagers who could not stop the desecration were failing their ancestors by their weakness.[18]

As a result the fear of returning to the village was not only a fear of what the government might do, but also a fear of the ancestors' punishment for the destruction of the house which they should have been continuing to build and beautify.

But they did return, and this is how, more or less in the words in which, with great emotion, I was told the story.

*   *   *

While the villagers were still hiding, uncertain whether to return, the father of the head of the village, died in hiding on a Friday. This was wrong because one should, if at all possible, die in the holy house or, if not, be brought back there.[19] Furthermore, although a devout Catholic, he died without being able to say any prayers. And so his children did not know what to do. They tied the corpse up, as is usually done, and finally on the Sunday with great hesitation they decided to take it back to the grass spot where the founders' holy house once stood and they placed his body on the place of the hot post. As soon as they did this he revived for a moment, said a 'Hail Mary' and then finally died and was buried.

The villagers felt that this meant that they could return and they began to drift back and to rebuild the houses, but they kept on falling ill, in particular the only and newborn son of the man who had brought back the corpse. His father went from diviner to diviner but none could find a medicine to cure him. Finally, he went to a spirit medium who asked him to come back the next morning. The next morning, he asked him to come back on the morning after that when the same happened once again. Then the spirit medium told him that in a dream that he had seen the man's father, the one who had died in the forest, and that he had told him to tell his son that he should cook a mixture of three leaves on the hearth of the holy house and then pour some of the broth where the posts had been and feed it to the baby.

They did so. The baby recovered and so did the whole village. The original marriage was reconstructed, the ritual of house foundation had been alluded to and almost repeated, and the holy house had been resurrected. The village was rebuilt.

Notes

1. The term they use is *Belefona, lit.* 'the many spears'. The avoided term is the normal term for rebel, *fahavalo,* which means, literally, the eighth people. The number eight has strongly negative connotations for the Zafimaniry.

2. I cannot be completely sure exactly the length of this period since the accounts I was given varied somewhat.

3. An exception to this are the beliefs concerning standing stones.

4. This statement is only true if we forget about the existence of a group of descendants of slaves whom the Zafimaniry consider 'beyond the pale', and therefore not an organic part of society.

5. One could argue that the only 'real' symbolic house among the Merina is the royal palace while the tomb gradually replaces the house the lower one goes down in the social hierarchy (Bloch 1981).

6. See Turton 1972.

7. *Efa Nahazo Toko trano ve?*

8. Spouses are chosen for children on the basis of Zafimaniry calculations of compatibility, which are quite complex. I hope to discuss these and other aspects of arranged marriage in more detail in future publications.

9. In fact the Zafimaniry find it very odd that spouses without living children can continue to get on well together. When this happens, as was the case for a couple in my village, this becomes a subject of puzzled speculation.

10. The term *ala fady* is usually explained in the ethnography of Madagascar as the removal of the incest relation which might exist between the spouses (Rakoto 1965). This is probably right in many cases but the Zafimaniry emphatically denied that the phrase had this meaning for them.

11. The double affiliation of both spouses to each other's parents is similar to what I discussed in Bloch 1978.

12. The wood of the hot post should be Nato (*Imbricaria Madagascariensis*). The wood of the cold posts should be Tamboneka (*Hediocaryopsis Madagascariensis*). For descriptions of the structure of Zafimaniry houses see Vérin 1964 and Couland 1973.

13. *Omena vonahitra amin' ny teza ny hazo.* The concept of *Teza* is further discussed in Bloch 1993 and 1995.

14. The expansion of the bilateral group of descendants is severely restricted by the fact that marriages tend to be exchanges between two moieties. This is a subject I discuss to some extent in Bloch (1975), and which I also hope to address in future publications.

15. At a meeting where a youth was accused of hitting the central post with a bottle he was told: 'This is not wood but the old gentleman (*Rangahy*).'

16. Zafimaniry blessings often occur at dawn so that the rays of the sun can enter through the eastern windows of the house and shine on the descendants sitting to the west. The new light coming through the house in this way seems to represent this continuing life of the house although I was never told so explicitly. It is for this blessing that Zafimaniry houses have windows to the east while most Malagasy houses do not.

17. This moiety system is mainly operated by a strong preference for pairs of cross-sex siblings marrying other pairs of cross-sex siblings rather than by a rule of cross-cousin marriage, though the result is similar.

18. When one rebuilds a holy house one should make a sacrifice to ask for forgiveness for the inevitable harm one does to the old structure.

19. The fact that many people, especially elders, have died there makes the house more holy.

References

Beaujard, P. 1983. *Princes et paysans: les Tanala de l'Ikongo,* Paris: L'Harmattan.

Bloch, M. 1975. 'Property and the end of affinity', in M. Bloch (ed.), *Marxist Analyses and Social Anthropology,* London: Malaby Press.

_____. 1977. 'The disconnection between rank and power as a process: an outline of the development of kingdoms in central Madagascar', in J. Friedman and M. Rowlands (eds.), *The Evolution of Social Systems,* London: Duckworth.

_____. 1978. 'Marriage amongst equals: an analysis of Merina marriage rituals', *Man* 13(1): 21–33.

_____. 1981. 'Tombs and states', in S. C. Humphries and H. King (eds.), *Mortality and Immortality: The Anthropology of Death,* London and New York: Academic Press.

_____. 1986. *From Blessing to Violence: History and Ideology in the Circumcision Ritual of the Merina of Madagascar,* Cambridge: Cambridge University Press.

_____. 1993. 'Domain specificity, living kinds and symbolism', in P. Boyer (ed.), *Cognitive Aspects of Religious Symbolism,* Cambridge: Cambridge University Press.

_____. 1995. 'People into places: Zafimaniry concepts of clarity', in E. Hirsch and O'Hanlon (eds.), *The Anthropology of Landscape,* Oxford: Oxford University Press.

Coulaud, D. 1973. *Les Zafimaniry: un groupe ethnique de Madagascar à la poursuite de la forêt,* Tananarive: Fonontan-Boky.

Lévi-Strauss, C. 1979. *La voie des masques,* Paris: Plon.

_____. 1984. *Paroles données,* Paris: Plon.

Rakoto, I. 1965. *Le Fafy est-il une simple levée d'empêchement au marriage,* Cahier du Centre des Études des Coutumes, Université de Madagascar.

Tronchon, J. 1974. *L'Insurrection Malgache de 1947*, Paris: Maspéro.
Turton, A. 1972. 'Matrilineal descent groups and spirit cults of the Thai-Yuan in Northern Thailand', *Journal of the Siam Society* 60(2): 217–56.
Vérin, P. 1964. 'Les Zafimaniry et leur art. Un groupe forestier continuateur d'une tradition ésthétique malgache méconnue', *Revue de Madagascar* 27: 1–16.

Chapter Seven

Time, Narratives and the Multiplicity of Representations of the Past

In this chapter I consider critically the relation of the narrative discussed in Chapter 6 with the many other ways the events of 1947 are remembered by the inhabitants of the village concerned. The main thrust of the argument is that memory is stored in ways that are different in kind from the expressive possibility of any one, or even all, of the narratives about the past, and that what is said can never be equated with memory. It is argued that when anthropologists or historians talk of memory, they should pay attention to the work of cognitive psychologists; otherwise, their assertions about such a central issue as representations of the past are doomed to muddle and imprecision. The chapter criticises a number of recent studies on the topic.

*   *   *

This paper is intended to consider a loose theoretical position which has recently been again gaining in popularity in anthropology, history and in other social sciences. It is a theory which manifests itself in the work of writers who would sometimes consider themselves to be theoretically very different but who seem none the less to be joined by its implications.

Put at its simplest it goes something like this.

The world we live is a world we tell stories to ourselves about, that is how we make sense of things. It therefore follows that the world is constructed for ourselves in terms of the narrative characteristics of these stories. The representation of time and space, for example, is so constructed, and as a result, the lived in past and the lived in present are to be discovered in an examination of the nature of texts or narratives. There is nothing beyond the reality created in the narratives since any other past or any other present is simply invisible. This is the starting point.

Then we move to point two. If people act within their own history, constructed within their own narratives, any other history is irrelevant to their action, and who are we, professional historians or anthropologists, to understand their actions and their past in any other way than in the terms of their narratives. In doing so we are merely substituting our types of narratives for theirs and in this way carrying out a kind of intellectual imperialism. Or to put the matter in a more anthropological form, what right have we to impose our own rationality on others.

The roots of such an approach, in its most recent formulation, is to be found in the German hermeneutics tradition, to be seen perhaps at its clearest form in the works of such as Gadamer. Its influence among social scientists however is largely mediated by the French theologian\philosopher Ricoeur. For example Ricoeur says of the conceptualisation of time "Time becomes human time only in so far as it is constructed in a narrative and at the same time a story is significant in so far as it accords with the experience of living in time." (Ricoeur 1983–1985).

In such a formulation the argument, in spite of its apparent complexity, is actually taking on a relatively familiar, not to say old fashioned form, for anthropologists who recognise it as recurring with predictable regularity every few years. The argument for the primacy of narratives has become the old argument for cultural relativism and in its most radical form an argument for cognitive relativism.

The way such an argument repeats itself is particularly striking to British anthropologists who remember the largely unfortunate foray into anthropology of another theologian\philosopher Winch whose book *The Idea of a Social Science* (1958) led to a, by now familiar, discussion on the universality or otherwise of certain forms of rationality. Winch's motives were, I suspect, very similar to those of Ricoeur, in that the attack on a universal rationality was closely linked with a desire to protect the "truths" of the Christian religion from the attacks of rationalist scientific thought and science.

It is therefore somewhat surprising to see echoes of such a position in the work of two anthropologists who would not, one would surmise, subscribe to the "higher purpose" of Winch and Ricoeur.

One of these is Lévi-Strauss (1973: ch.18) who in his discussion of the distinction he makes between hot and cold societies seems to imply that people either represent the past as being driven by events or try to neutralise events by reducing them to an aspect of an unchanging pattern. According to him, at least in cold societies, people live in a world entirely constructed by their coherent and exhaustive historical narratives which not only affect their representations but consequently their actions.

The other is Sahlins. In a chapter entitled "Other times other customs: the anthropology of history" of his *Islands of History* (1985: ch.2) he argues most strongly that different peoples narrate history differently and therefore experience the passage of time differentially. In his own words "different cultural orders have their own modes of historical orders, consciousness and determination." (p.34). In fact he seems to suggest that there are two kinds of history, one associated with divine kinship and such places as ancient Hawaii and Fiji, in which history is experienced as determined by single heroes or gods, and the other kind, which is found in post nineteenth century western thought and, rather bizarrely, among the Ilongots of the Philippines, where history is seen as the cumulative result of a multitude of individual actions. Sahlins seems very close to Ricoeur in his confident assertion that the basis of cognition can be discovered in the analysis of the style and contents of narratives which are the limits of the actors world.

I have to say immediately that I find myself in total disagreement with the strong theoretical implications of such a position, though I can appreciate the value of the analysis and understanding of narratives such as is found in a number of splendid recent studies such as that of L. Abu-Lughod's *Veiled Sentiments* (1986) or Ileto's *Pasyon and Revolution* (1979). There is of course nothing new in such an approach as is witnessed by the "ethnography of speaking" school, or the flowering of the biographical autobiographical style of anthropological writing characteristic of the sixties. What I find totally unacceptable is the notion that cognition of time and other fundamental categories is constructed through narratives and that consequently an examination of narratives will reveal directly a particular group of peoples' concepts of the world they inhabit.

The position of Ricoeur, Lévi-Strauss or Sahlins can also be found in a variety of formulations in the work of a number of contemporary anthropologists, and these are very little different from those of Geertz in 'Time, Person and Conduct in Bali' which I criticised some time ago (Bloch 1977), for reasons which, although I would not now phrase them in the same way, still seem to me equally valid, and which at their most fundamental have never been directly challenged.

Here I want to argue my opposition to such a position in a different way to the way I did it then. I want to use some recent ethnographic work to demonstrate the untenable nature of such sweeping assertions.

*   *   *

Let me start with an evocation of the situation I found myself in last summer when I returned for a short stay to the remote forest village in Madagascar where I have been conducting field work, on and off, for almost twenty years. I was returning after three years absence and my return was quite difficult.

I was quite unannounced and I was dropped off some way away from the village at the end of the motorable road by a vehicle which had given me a lift. This place was a village where a weekly market is held and where I hoped to meet villagers who would accompany me for the final part of the journey which had to be done on foot. Unfortunately I arrived later than I wanted and by then the only people left at the market were the few odd drunks who remain at markets when everybody has gone home. I needed people to take me to my village and help me carry the luggage I was bringing ... in the end I convinced two unprepossessing drunken youth to come with me. I hate drunks, at least when I am sober myself and they are especially difficult companions on the difficult mountain paths along which we had to proceed. What made the journey worse was that by the time I had reached the village I was by then very tired anyway and it was very cold and raining. When I got to the village I was freezing and in a very bad temper.

To make matters worse, when I got there there was nobody of my "family" in the village and I had to wait to be let in to my house. During this wait in the rain with my feet deep in mud large numbers of people began to gather round and ask me a whole tumble of questions about how I had come, what I had been doing since I left, how much my ticket had cost etc.. . . . I have to admit that I was very rude and hardly answered anything as a way of stopping myself coming out with anything worse. The whole situation was chaotic.

Soon however, my adoptive family came back from the swiddens where they had been working and they rapidly took in the whole situation and dealt with it. What they did was take me into the house and close all the doors and windows, a public sign that nobody is in, or at least that the people inside want to be thought not to be in. They then lit a fire which got me and my clothes dried, they unpacked and organised my things, fed me and then, little by little, began to try to ask for information about my absence and the details of what my journey had been like.

Then they prepared the main room of the house by spreading clean mats on the floor and the wall and got me to sit to the south of the room surrounded by the other important members of my adoptive family who by now had sneaked into the house. We placed ourselves in a row according to our different ages and statuses and we took up the polite postures suitable for hosts. Then, and only then, did we open the windows and doors and all the people of the village young and old female and male came one by one or in small groups to visit and hear my news. The whole process lasted a couple of days though all the visits were similar in form.

Each visit began with the long half sung formal exchange of greetings which the Zafimaniry consider as one of the most significant aspects of their culture.[1] Then I was asked a question about my journey and my news. To this I was expected to give a fairly long account. Then the proper thing to do is for the person who has asked, that is the visitor, to thank the new returnee for the information and actually repeat what he has been told and then give his news and that of the village. In fact the whole proper process is more complicated in that certain polite interruptions should be made as for example a death is mentioned the hearer should interrupt the speaker to say how sad he or she is. Finally the returnee should make a small present to the visitor, two or three tiny sweets for example. I know roughly how such an account should be given but I am not an expert. And so at first I stumbled over my lines but this did not matter because the other members of my family took over from me and answered for me. Indeed since the whole process was repeated so often in some cases I did not say a word since one or other of our group would take it upon himself or herself to play my part.

The expected information given from my side concerned what I had done since I was away, whether any members of my family in England had been ill or died, what news there was of other people who they knew, the itinerary and reasons for my journey. From their side I was told who had died and who had been ill, what the harvests had been like and a very few other notable facts.

What was very obvious to me as a participant was how the endless repetition of the interchange involved the building up of a received narrative account of my absence and return. On the occasion of the first visits I tried to answer the question about my doings in a variety of ways partly so as not to bore the people of my family with the same story and partly not to bore myself. This was totally inappropriate. When I answered appropriately I was allowed to talk but if I began to elaborate my story or talk of things which had not previously been discussed in the dark with my family I was interrupted and a senior member of our house took over and answered for me. At every repetition what I could say and could not say became clearer and clearer, when I could answer or when I had to leave other senior members of our household answer for me became fixed. Rapidly we became experts at this performance and every thing went extremely smoothly.

Clearly during these endless repetitions a narrative had been built up, that is if a very formalised dialogue can be considered a narrative, since what was organised was above all the articulation of two temporal sequences—what had happened in the village and what had happened to me outside the village. In many ways it was a peculiarly uninformative double narrative. The narrative consisted of two stereotypic separate sequences of people and places evoked in past space and time, so that they could join together in the perfected present orchestration of voices, bodies and clean house which took place at every visit. The dominant impression of "rejoining" was particularly well created by the explanation of my coming that we all built up together. This transformed the total arbitrariness of my coming at this particular time and in this way into an apparently inevitable and morally appropriate sequence. I could not come sooner because the university had been saving up money in order to be able to afford the fare; the year before, when I had intended to come, my parents had asked me not to come because they knew that there had been riots in the capital of Madagascar and because they had felt ill . . . and so on.

The narrative was very poor on information but very strong on the reestablishment of order, by making my journey predictable it made the account acceptable. It could be said, in the loose way in which anthropologist are wont to talk, that the construction of the narrative abolished the specificity of time by reordering and making the past follow a predefined pattern, that, it did this by dissolving the specificity of events into a prototypical present or in the more elegant phrasing of de Certeau an author to whom I shall return and whose position is similar to that of the others I criticise, in this type of history the march of time does not need to be marked or certified by the distancing and separating of the "past". In Lévi-Strauss's terms the whole sequence of visits and the creation of an approved narrative of my absence could be seen as a typical case of a cold society abolishing eventuality.

What had happened on the occasion of my coming was in no way exceptional. The people of my family had organised things so that they followed a familiar pattern. The arrangement of receiving all callers who squat near the door to the north into an ordered house, where the clean mats have been spread, where the returnee is surrounded by his kin sitting to the south is typical of what happens to all Zafimaniry when they come back to their village after a long absence. For example, I have seen exactly the same performance taking place when young men who have gone away to do wage work as lumbermen for some months come back to the village. Significantly it is not just the ritual of return which is similar in these cases but it is also the content of the narrative of the absence which is built up by the endless stream of visits. Surely nothing could show better how such a performance abolishes specificity than the fact that the account of the absence of a young woodcutter employed by an Indian entrepreneur on the West coast of Madagascar can be almost identical to the account of a three year absence of an anthropologist who in the meantime had left the country to teach in a British university.

But the question I want to consider in the lecture is more than the simple observation that this kind of narrative event can be said to abolish eventuality and create a type of history and an image of the past. Such a point is an easy one to make and a quasi literary analysis of what was said would be very satisfactory to the reader of an ethnography since she could see for herself how the conclusions flow from the data which would be all there for her to read on the page. However, the nature of the claim which lies behind such an interpretive analysis would be very unclear in its implications. If our analysis of the narrative leads us to the conclusion that it represents time as static or rather as non cumulative we must then say who holds the kind of view of the past which our description has revealed. Presumably Ricoeur would deduce that such a narrative constructs the Zafimaniry's conceptualisation of time but would I be right in following him in saying that what happened when I returned is that the Zafimaniry's memory of my coming and of the dribs and drabs of information which I had given them as I was standing outside in the rain, the arbitrariness of the whole event had been transformed by the repetitions and organisation of the formal visiting so that any other versions of these events had been obliterated? Would it be right to say that the villagers interest in what I had been up to since I had left had been fully satisfied by the standardised question and answer of the ritual of homecoming which had taken place?

It is not difficult for me to answer both these questions in the negative. What I said when I was standing in the rain was brought up, again often somewhat embarrassingly in informal conversations. Indeed this may well have been the point of the intensity of this "inappropriate" questioning. All sorts of other questions and matters concerning what I had been up to when away, and concerning the details of my journey were asked and discussed and often laughed over in informal contexts during the whole period of my stay. Indeed I often felt that my co-villagers had an insatiable thirst for detail and specifics which I sometimes found irritating. Now all these questions would have been totally inappropriate in the formal context of visiting. Similarly I was given much more detailed information about what had gone on in the village while I had been away. All this formed parts of other types of narratives appropriate for other contexts than the ones I have just described. However, the significance of these different types of narrative events must it seems to me, also be taken into account before we pronounce grandly, à la Sahlins or à la Ricoeur about a particular group of peoples, view of their past or cognition of time.

In order to consider this point further I want to turn to an illustration which might be thought more significant than the somewhat personal anecdote I have just discussed.

I have been for a long time now interested how the Zafimaniry remember the dramatic events of the anti-colonial revolt of 1947 when approximately 80,000 people were killed. This revolt affected the Zafimaniry of my village particularly badly as the village is situated in the area where some of the main events took place because, as a result of their sympathy for the rebels, the French burnt down the village and several people killed.

In 1989 I recorded an account of these events which I had heard several times before and which, although a private account in that it concerns only the village, is seen in many ways as the authoritative account of what happened and is told to children as a solemn memory, often on ritual occasions. This account is very moving and will form the basis of a paper which, although completed two years ago is awaiting publication as a part of an edited volume.

I will not go into details about the story except to note that this account performs the same narrative feat that I just described for the construction of my absence in the process of visiting, though of course for a matter of infinitely greater significance. It reduces the arbitrariness of specific events in time to a well honed cultural pattern where the cultural institutions of the village, whether linguistic, material, such as the holy houses of the village, or social, such as the kinship arrangements, are used as tools to reorder the events of the past so that they accord with timeless values and beliefs. I suppose through a stylistic analysis of the narrative one could construct a "Zafimaniry view of time and eventuality" such as Ricoeur and others would have us do.

However an event which occurred during my most recent period in the village brought home to me just how misleading this would be.

One day I got caught by heavy rain with my adoptive village father when we were crossing some fields which overlooked a well swiddened valley and we took refuge in a little field hut. It continued to pour and we stayed there for several hours chatting and warming ourselves by a fire we had made. We talked of many things but in the end we started to talk about the rebellion and I was then given an account of what had happened totally different in style and content to the account I had previously been given and which is the subject matter of my article.

This account was a very detailed factual account, a very event focused account where the movements of troops and rebels were described graphically and were attached to the topography which lay before us. In fact the spot where we were had much to do with it since from the entrance to the hut we could see a whole landscape where particular events had taken place. Hence, the story I was told was prompted and organised by the topography which lay before us. This account would be best compared to good journalism in that it was not in the least moralistic and was merely concerned with evoking the presence, movement and events concerning people long departed which had taken place in the space at which we were looking while we were talking.

Any analysis of this narrative would have revealed totally different principles governing the correlation of time and space than the "official" account I knew. Similarly, significance attributed to unique events was quite at variance with that implied in the other account. Sahlins would have believed himself to be "in another place and another time" but in fact the two accounts came from the same place the same time and from the mouth of the same people. We might be tempted therefore to ask which of the two accounts is the best guide to the Zafimaniry's view of the past and the passage of time. However, choosing between the two would be clearly quite misleading and, equally, it is wrong to consider these two accounts as in some way contradictory. The point is that they are both suitable narratives for different contexts. One for the formal ritual context in which it is expressed the other for the informal *ad hoc* context of the field hut and the speculative conversation of two friends with time on their hands.

As soon as we recognise in this way that Zafimaniry culture is actually providing two different types of narratives which evoke the same past in contrasting ways, we might want to go further and see what other ways there are for Zafimaniry of talking about the past. But even formulating the question in this way immediately brings us up against the enormity of such a task. We might want to begin by defining types of verbal narratives concerning the past. I have already discussed two such types but there are others. During my recent short stay I noted quite a list which can be grouped for the purposes this lecture under the following headings.

First of all there is the distinction made throughout Madagascar between *Tantara* and *Anganon*.[2] *Tantara* a term which has been roughly translated as history, and of which my "official" account of what happened in 1947 would be an example. The account of my absence and return which was becoming fixed through the visiting process was also on the way to becoming *Tantara* or at least it manifests many of its formal features. This type of story about the past tends to reduce events to exemplary tales where the moral structures of the society win against the requirement of transmitting information. *Tantara* does not abolish time but in it the passage of time is not cumulative, it does not lead to a succession of new unique events, rather in *Tantara* the past is seen as precedent. What the Malagasy stress most about *Tantara* is its categorical "truth" which also conveys its moral value, and this contrasts most with another type of narratives about the past which are called *Anganon*, a word which can be roughly translated as "tales" or "myth".

These *Anganon* form a second type of narrative. They refer to events which take place in an unspecified past and concern fantastic beings as well as normal people. These tales are often funny stories the truth of which (in the sense defined above) is systematically denied by the phrase which always either precedes them or ends them and which is "Don't blame me for these lies, I am only repeating what was said by previous generations."

Besides these two recognised narrative forms there are the types of narratives of which the story about 1947 told me in the hut under the rain are characteristic. Such narratives make a claim to truth, in our sense of the word, but the accounts do not have the character of moral truth which partly characterises *Tantara*. These narratives are true if you evaluate the speaker as being sincere but whether this is so is continually being monitored and often challenged, something which is ruled out by the elaborate context of *Tantara*. The Zafimaniry have no name for this type of evocation of the past because it does not involve any self-conscious stylistic definition. Because of this, and other similar manifestations in other places, anthropologists have tended to ignore this type of narrative when they consider the very general topic of the relation of narrative to cognition. However, it would surely be highly misleading to forget the existence of this type of narrative in our discussion since among the Zafimaniry they are, in fact, the most common linguistic evocations of the past. These are highly event driven accounts, stressing the arbitrariness of outcomes brought about successive moments and volitions. For Lévi-Strauss they would characterise hot societies. In their form these correspond quite closely to some aspects of modern historiography.

Among this type of narratives I would include accounts of past price fluctuations of various goods which form a continual subject of conversation in the village, also what would best be called gossip, as well as other factual accounts of events either from the distant or the recent past. Perhaps it is misleading to call these narratives a single type since on closer examination we might want to distinguish among them in ways which might not be exclusive nonetheless their importance cannot be underestimated.

So far I have only mentioned evocations of the past occurring in verbal narratives. To stop there would however be totally misleading. In this respect the Zafimaniry themselves taught me a lesson. I was discussing with some young women the patterns they weave on their hats, patterns which vary significantly from village to village, and I had asked what the significance of these differences was. I was immediately answered by being told that these patterns were "*vakon*" *drazana* literally "pearls from the ancestors". This is a phrase which the Zafimaniry use to describe all valuable things passed on from previous generation most notably *Tantara*. What these women were saying therefore was as they sat there making their hats they too were evoking the past and continuing it in the present. This is, I believe, of great importance because the presence of the past is felt to a lesser or a greater degree in nearly all aspects of life in that activities are always consciously or unconsciously evaluated as following or departing from the ancestors way of doing things. In other words beyond the verbal narratives there are at least some and perhaps many evocations of the past in the most mundane of actions.[3]

For example the Zafimaniry live in houses which are, in their material aspect the product and celebration of the marriages which brought them about and which generated both the building and its inhabitants. Every act in these houses is consciously framed and organised by a past of which all are conscious. A consciousness which manifests itself verbally but is, I am sure also present when not commented upon. There is a sense in which almost every aspect of practical living in such houses is a kind of stronger or weaker evocation of past times and peoples (Bloch 1992).

*   *   *

The general point I want to make is simple. When we consider such people as the Zafimaniry we find that they have a variety of narrative ways of evoking the past and of representing the passage of time, some are oral and some are non-oral. One image may dominate in one context and another in another context. But because of the multiplicity of these types of narratives it is not legitimate to assume that any can be equated with the Zafimaniry cognition of the past and of the passage of time. Furthermore the multiplicity of these narratives means that the cognition of the passage of time and our knowledge of the past must exist outside any one type of narrative since there is no suggestion that one type of narrative dominates the others as far as thought is concerned. Concepts of duration, causality or person are neither constructed nor contained in any one type of narrative. Instead narratives are used to present a certain representation of a world which must be known in a way neither constructed nor transparently or completely reflected by narratives.

And indeed there is a sense in which proving that cognition of the passage of time is not reflected in any particular narrative by pointing to their multiplicity is actually unnecessary. This is because what we know of the construction of the cognition of time and duration from developmental psychologists makes the hermeneutic point of view adopted by Ricoeur or Sahlins totally unlikely.

It is clear from all the work on cognitive development that the most fundamental cognitive categories are established in the child long before she can speak or be aware of any of the types of manifestations which I have discussed so far and that the basis of these categories is neither linguistic nor even logic-sentential. Indeed all the psychological evidence is that the conceptualisation of time at its most fundamental develops in the child as a result of genetically programmed potentialities which are identical in all humans, indeed in all primates. Furthermore it is also clear that the development and establishment of such potentialities result from the child's very early interaction with the environment, approximately in the first four months of life, in other words at a stage where cross-cultural psychologists can detect no trace of cultural specificity in the cognitive process of the child.

Narratives and texts of the kind discussed here cannot therefore be the source of the fundamentals of cognition. Adult humans construct a multiplicity of narratives of different types appropriate to different contexts and this very multiplicity ensures that their knowledge is not bounded by the narrative characteristics of any one of them. Narratives talk in different ways about what is known. They are not knowledge itself.

If we go back to what happened when I returned to the village I think we will see well what this means. In the period in the preparatory time in the dark, when the windows and doors were shut, a *representation* was being prepared, the stage was being set, clean mats were being laid out, the staircase was being swept and, as occurs in any theatre before the curtain goes up, the actors took up their position, though in this case it was not a curtain which went up but shutters which were opened. What was to happen in this painstakingly constructed setting, very reminiscent of a theatre representation occurring behind a proscenium arch, was therefore carefully parenthesised. True, an image of the past was to be created, but the parenthesising meant that everyone was being made aware that this was not all there was to it, that this was merely one way, a very important and reassuring way of looking at something which existed beyond that particular representation. It is not surprising that in other contexts and at other times other representations of the known world could be produced but knowledge of the world always remained prior to any such performances. A song is just a song . . . a narrative is just a narrative.

In saying all this I cannot but feel that I am saying the obvious, but, if this is so, we may well wonder why a different view can be entertained, why we can have the arguments of such as Sahlins and Ricoeur, not to mention de Certeau. Before we can answer these questions I think it is important to note the kind of data with which such writers work and in relation to which they have developed their theories. The writers mentioned are people working on literature, philosophers or theologians working on ancient texts and also historians. Sometimes anthropologists also adopt their theoretical position but then they are anthropologists working as historians and basing themselves on literary sources. This is very much the case with Sahlins who, in the article to which I referred to above and where he argues the point about different types of history most fiercely, is discussing 18th or 19th century Hawaii or Fiji and is again basing himself on very few texts all of the same sort.

Now it is not surprising that those who only have texts as the basis for the construction of their representation of the culture they study should stress the importance of the verbal and the narrative. Quite simply they have nothing else to guide them. There is however another reason.

If we take Madagascar again as example it is most informative to look at what happened when literacy was introduced in the nineteenth century among the Merina and in the twentieth century among the Zafimaniry. Basically literacy was used at first partly for the writing down of *Tantara* and partly for letters writing (Bloch 1989). Now Malagasy letters are very peculiar to Europeans because of the small amount of information they contain. After a few formalities they often repeat entirely the text of the letter they are answering. Then they go on to give information in such a way that this information is merely a list of events and places summarily leading to the present in an inevitable sequence. This pattern I hope will already be familiar to you. It is the pattern of the interchanges which characterise the formal visiting which I described in the first part of this lecture. Indeed Malagasy letters are exactly in this style and are clearly just an attempt to recreate this kind of event at a distance and in writing.

In a situation such as this therefore, only one type of narrative gets written down while the others do not. In the Malagasy case only *Tantara* and the closely associated formal exchanges typical of visiting are preserved in written form. Now it is possible to imagine a historian using such documents a hundred years from now and trying to understand the cognitive character of Zafimaniry culture. Not only would such a historian be inevitably focusing on texts but they would only have one kind of narrative. This would mean that the narratives would present a quite misleading impression of coherence in the representations of the past which it would be very tempting to present as the Zafimaniry notions of time and the past. Indeed this is not such hypothetical case. De Certeau a philosopher *cum* historian whose position is very similar to that of Ricoeur did precisely this. In the introduction to his book on the writing of history he contrasts the modern concept of time and of the past with a "non occidental" view of the past for which he uses as one of his prime example a study of a published corpus of Merina *Tantara* by Délivré which satisfies him as a source for Merina cognition of time (de Certeau 1975: 11).

Clearly an anthropologist dealing with living people whose knowledge is implicit not only in what they say but also in what they do, who is faced by a multiplicity of narratives occurring in a variety of different contexts would normally reject such an unlikely and simple view of knowledge based on such restricted evidence.

However some anthropologists, perhaps overwhelmed by the complexity of their task, are tempted by the writings of scholars such as philosophers, historians or literatures, who do not have as the base of their theorising the richness and complexity of real life and who can therefore afford to propose simpler and more engaging positions, seem willing to sell their inheritance (the observation and participation in real life) for a mess of quasi literary thin pottage.

Notes

This chapter was originally formulated as a response to an unpublished article by F. Hartog and G. Lenclud presented at the "Colloque Anthropologie contemporaine et anthropologie historique" held in Marseilles in 1992. I am very grateful to these two authors for the stimulation supplied by their original paper.

1. These are called *Sokela*.

2. For a good discussion of this distinction for a nearby Malagasy group see Beaujard (1991).

3. A similar point has been made in a most stimulating way by March (1983).

References

Abu-Lughod, L. 1986. *Veiled Sentiments*. Berkeley: University of California Press.

Beaujard, P. 1991. *Mythe et Société á Madagascar*. Paris: L'Harmattan.

Bloch, Maurice 1977. The Past and the Present in the Present. *Man* n.s. 13: 21–33.

_____. 1989. Literacy and Enlightenment. In *Literacy and Society*. M. Trolle-Larsen and K. Sousboe, eds. Publications of the Centre for Research in the Humanities, Copenhagen.

_____. 1992. What Goes without Saying: the Conceptualisation of Zafimaniry Society. In *Conceptualising Society*. A. Kuper, ed. London: Routledge.

_____. 1995. The Resurrection of the House. In *About the House: Building Groups and Categories in Holistic Perspectives*. J. Carsten and S. Hugh-Jones, eds. Cambridge: Cambridge University Press.

de Certeau, M. 1975. *L'écriture de L'histoire*. Paris: Galimard.

Geertz, C. 1973. Person, Time and Conduct in Bali. Reprinted in *The Interpretation of Culture*. New York: Basic books.

Ileto, R. 1979. *Pasyon and Revolution: Popular Movements in the Philippines, 1840–1910*. Manila: Ateneo de Manila University Press.

Lévi-Strauss, C. 1973. *Anthropologie Structurale Deux*. Paris: Plon.

March, K. 1983. Weaving Writing and Gender. *Man* (n.s.) pp. 729–44.

Ricoeur, P. 1983–1985. *Temps et Recits*. Paris: Seuil.

Sahlins, M. 1985. *Islands of History*. Chicago: Chicago University Press.

Winch, P. 1958. *The Idea of a Social Science*. London: Routledge and Kegan Paul.

Chapter Eight

Autobiographical Memory and the Historical Memory of the More Distant Past

This chapter continues the argument of Chapter 7 in considering whether it is possible for nonlinguistic memory to be transmitted from generation to generation. The example of the same Zafimaniry village is used to show how visits to historical sites can make descendants of those who participated in the original events reexperience what happened to their forebears and thus "remember" the distant past as though its events were events in their own lives. Again, this chapter combines theories from social anthropology with others originating from cognitive psychology.

*   *   *

Nowadays everybody seems to be talking about memory in disciplines such as anthropology, sociology, and history. Memory, however, used to be more a field of enquiry in psychology. Are we therefore witnessing, in contrast to what seems to be happening elsewhere, a coming together of the social sciences with a subject which, in some of its manifestations at least, is a semi-hard science?

Such a hopeful enquiry is likely to very rapidly lead to serious disappointment when we look more carefully at what the practitioners of these disciplines are actually writing about when they talk of memory. They would seem to share nothing in common but the use of a word which can indicate almost anything and to ignore almost totally what each side says on the subject.

Historians, anthropologists, and sociologists are concerned with the representations of the past which are, or are believed to be, transmitted from generation to generation. They may also be concerned with the ways by which this transmission is achieved: oral tradition, literacy, ritual, or material culture. Psychologists, on the other hand, are interested in the mechanisms by which storage and recovery of information is achieved by individuals, but not in the nature of this stored knowledge or how it is transmitted from person to person. And if this lack of correspondence were not enough, we find that ninety percent of the work of psychologists, as Ulrich Neisser pointed out in an influential article which deplored the lack of contact between the disciplines (Neisser 1978), concerns memories which last less than a minute and are therefore quite irrelevant to what concerns social scientists or ordinary people interested in the subject.

Neisser's purpose in stressing this fact was to call for more cooperation from the two sides, and to a certain extent he has been successful in that psychological concern with long-term memory "in the real world" (Cohen 1990) has recently greatly increased and there is a genuine desire from both sides for a coming together.

Good intentions, however, are seldom enough. We now have psychology books such as those of Neisser himself and more recently of Baddeley (1990) and Cohen, to name only a few, which include references to the work of social scientists and historians. Similarly we have the works of sociologists such as Paul Connerton (1989), anthropologists such as Dorothy Holland and Naomi Quinn (1987) or Whitehouse (1992), and historians such as Carruthers (1990) which refer to some of the psychological work on long-term memory, but they often seem to go little beyond the "getting acquainted" stage; it appears there is much difficulty in going beyond such polite preliminaries.

This chapter is part of an attempt to go beyond this initial stage. In an earlier paper (Bloch 1992) I argue that the realisation by such psychologists as Nigro and Neiser (1983) of the role of memory in the construction of the person meant that they had to take into account anthropologists' more general work on cultural specificity of the notion of the individual in history. Here I want to argue for a reverse flow, that anthropologists and sociologists will benefit from quite technical psychological work if they want to understand, as is clearly one of their central tasks, the complexity of the presence of the cognised past in the present. In this I join a number of other anthropologists, such as Dan Sperber (1985), who have similarly drawn the attention of their colleagues to work in psychology though their points were different though not incompatible with mine.

Autobiographical and Semantic Memory

I also want to argue for something which at first sight might seem paradoxical: that the characteristic of the individual's memory of what she has experienced during her lifetime—her autobiographical memory—is not all that different from her knowledge of more distant historical events which she cannot possibly have lived through. I am therefore making use of the distinction spelt out clearly in psychology by E. Tulving (1972) between autobiographical, or episodic, memory and semantic memory, if only, later, to stress their similarity. Autobiographical memory is concerned with memories of events that have happened to the individual concerned: for example, when he learnt to swim. Semantic memory concerns facts that one has learnt from others such as the name of the capital of New Hampshire. Semantic memory includes memory of facts about the past, and a subset of semantic memory can therefore be called semantic historical memory or simply historical memory.

Autobiographical and semantic memory are treated very differently in the psychological literature. Psychologists have been very interested in the character of what is recalled in autobiographical memory and also of its relation to the sense of self. In particular, when considering it, they have stressed the contrast between remembering and recalling. People recall the past, either in the presence of others or in the imagined presence of others, in heard or silent soliloquies. However, people remember much more of what they have experienced than they recall, indeed much more than they are aware, as the story of Proust's Madeleine makes clear, or more mundanely as is witnessed by the fact that we can soon recognise that we have read a book as soon as we begin it, although we had previously thought we had no recollection of its content. This is so to the extent that several psychologists argue that nothing is ever completely forgotten that, under certain circumstances, cannot be recalled; and much experimental work has shown how memories which individuals did not know they had can be brought to the surface by, for example, inducing certain emotional states. As a result, autobiographical memory is both all-pervading and extremely difficult to pin down.

The psychological work on semantic memory, on the other hand, has apart from a few exceptions (some of which are discussed below) rarely been concerned with the nature of its content or its relation to concepts of personhood or identity. Rather, the questions which have been asked have been almost exclusively about the mechanisms of retention and forgetting.

This contrast is interestingly similar to that commonly made by historians between memory and history. When historians talk of memory they are concerned with what individuals remember of what happened during their lifetime, and since they are interested in what this tells them about the past, they are acutely aware of its labile and multifaceted character—which they may consider a problem (Courtois 1993) or a source of richness (Todorov 1995). When they turn to the more distant past they lose interest in the problems of the incarnation of knowledge and become purely interested in how efficient and accurate the mechanisms of transmission—oral history or documents—are.

Here, however, I am interested in history as a social fact in the lives of people, and just as I intend to show that in this perspective the difference between autobiographical and semantic historical memory is much less than we might believe, similarly I want to ultimately question whether the difference between history and memory is as sharp as it has been made out to be.

In taking such a position I am both approaching and distancing myself from the great and multifaceted works on memory of Maurice Halbwachs (1925, 1950). Halbwachs's main concern was similar to mine, that is, to convey the subtlety, the irreducibility, the multiplicity of aspects, both implicit and explicit, of the past in the present, and this he does superbly. He also wanted to quite rightly stress the social character of memory because recalling involves communication with others, and that since individual memory is continually being transformed and reworked as this communication occurs, so it loses its independent isolated individual character. In this way it becomes possible, according to Halbwachs and as we shall see below, for memories referring to periods much before the life of the recaller to share much of the characteristics of autobiographical memory.

However, perhaps because of the influence of Durkheim and because he fails to make clearly the distinction between recalling and remembering, Halbwachs wants to go so much further in his argument so as to deny any epistemological role to the mechanisms of the individual brain. Such a stance leads him to make patently false assertions such as that memories which are not shared are soon forgotten. For him, therefore, there is absolutely no difference between autobiographical memory and collective memory since autobiographical memory is also the product of social contact. This merging of the two types of memory leads him also to contrast absolutely memory, which for him is subjective, though collectively subjective; and history, which is objective and apparently independent of the social context in which it is produced or consumed. Worst of all, the elusion of the individual mind as an active factor in the transmission of the past makes him leave the whole process and even the character of memory strangely unspecified and vague for a work which made this its aim.

In what follows I want to show, in the light of a specific case study, that we can retain and advance the very great insights of Halbwachs but that we can do this by losing his Durkheimian antipathy to cognitive psychology. Only then we can begin to understand the very social processes he sought to explain very much more clearly.

Remembering the 1947 Rebellion in Madagascar

To illustrate the fruitfulness of bringing together considerations from cognitive psychology to bear on the typical social phenomena which interest social scientists, I want to return to an example from Madagascar which I have already used in previous articles to make somewhat different points.

It concerns a village of shifting cultivators in the eastern forest of Madagascar which I have been studying for almost twenty-five years now. In 1947 the village was burnt down by French troops in retaliation against the supposed support given by the inhabitants to the anticolonial rebellion of that year. This brutality was followed by a period of terrible hardship of more than two years when the villagers hid in the forest from the French fearing being captured.

In a first article (Bloch 1995a) I considered what might be called the official account of this traumatic period, especially the story of the villagers' fearful return to the village. This was a standardised account which wove in a seamless fabric traditional symbolic themes as well as Catholic ideas in what might be called the received version. The decision to tell me that account was taken after great deliberation by three elders of the village who knew I wanted to find out what had happened but who had, until then, been reluctant to tell a European about this. In fact the elders often recount this story to their compatriots on such occasions as wakes, where I have since heard it spoken almost word for word on several occasions.

The second article (Bloch 1993) was occasioned by my return to the village after the first paper had been completed and sent to be published. Then, as a result of being blocked for several hours in a field hut with one of the survivors of the period of the rebellion who had been the elder who had told me the received version originally, I was suddenly given a totally different kind of account of what had happened, although it did not actually conflict with the received version. This other account was much more factual and lacked the timeless mythological quality of the first. It was largely prompted by the fact that from the field hut we could see a valley where important events from the time of the rebellion had occurred. The person seemed to be able to see again in his mind's eye what had happened in these terrible days as he looked onto the topography in front of him.

The theoretical conclusion I drew from this event was that we should not confound one narrative version of what had happened with the memory that participants retained. An account was an account of that memory, but people could consult their memory "in their mind's eye" to construct other accounts when stimulated by social—and in this case, visual—contexts. Memory was not encapsulated in any one account, or for that matter all accounts; it was stored in forms which probably did not resemble any particular linguistic account, and its content was indeterminate even for those concerned. Thus the man who was recounting the details in the field hut seemed to be discovering ever more detail as time went on.

In a sense the experience demonstrated only too well that recalling is not the same as remembering. The anthropological significance of such a fact is very great since it means that the presence of the past in the present is much more complex, much less explicit but perhaps much more powerful than the presence of explicit narratives would ever make us believe. It suggests that individuals may not be aware of what they remember, as in this case, and that they, therefore, may be unaware of how significant it is for them as psychoanalysis would have us believe. But in fact much less problematic work in cognitive psychology, backed by considerable experimental work, shows individuals' ability to recall an extraordinarily rich variety of memories. Of particular interest to social scientists is that certain memories which appeared to be totally lost can be retrieved when the person concerned reenters the emotional state they were in when the original event occurred (Baddeley 1990: chaps. 12 & 15). This means that the past is an ever-changing resource according to the situations or moods in which the persons find themselves, situations and moods which will often be due to organised social contexts (Gilligan and Bower 1984)[1].

From Autobiographical Memory to Historical Memory

Although the significance of psychological considerations might be granted in the case of autobiographical memory, it might be argued that nonetheless this type of data has only limited implications. After all, the distinction between recalling and remembering on which it rests would seem to only apply to memory of events that happened to oneself, since for evocation of a more remote past the participants/informants have to rely simply on accounts they have heard from others, which lack the multifaceted character of memories of events in which one was involved. In other words, when dealing with this type of historical memories we seem to be simply dealing with semantic memory, and the only relevant psychological considerations would relate to the efficiency, or otherwise, of different mnemonic devices for the already constructed narratives which informants have heard from others.

Such a conclusion—although apparently commonsensical—is, I believe, wrong, and in order to show why this is so, I, first of all, turn to what happened to me during yet another return to the same village which had been the subject of the other two articles.

In September 1995 I was taken by a group of villagers to the site where the villagers had hidden in 1947. Among my companions were the person who had been my main informant for the memories which were the subject matter of my previous articles as well as about ten members of his family, including several of his grandchildren and even one of his great-grandchildren. Being on the site was the occasion of going over much of the stories that I had already been told and having much added, prompted in part by the topography and by a few traces we discovered. He, of course, was the main source of information, telling me in detail what their houses had been like, how they had managed to cook, where they hid their meager supplies, how they kept watch on the army unseen, and so on. However, what was perhaps more surprising was the fact that all the members of the family, including the children, were showing me what they did then, where they had stayed, and what it had been like, although, of course, they had not been alive in 1947. Indeed the atmosphere created by being in such a situated place was the occasion for a general conversation and rehearsal of what was known where all seemed to take part, apparently not simply to inform me, but also to tell and elaborate what each knew.

There was nothing really all that mysterious about this. What had happened was that all the members of the family had often been told many things concerning these events and had probably been on the site many times; they therefore knew what it was like. When talking about this period, young and old were using a "we" pronoun. The imprecision which this allowed is significant. It could mean that they had been there or simply that "our family" had been there. I believe that the rhetoric implied that this choice had not been made, though if questioned, they probably would agree that they had not been physically present. Actually my informants used not the exclusive Malagasy "we," which excludes the person being addressed, but the inclusive "we," which includes the person being addressed—in this case, me. In doing this the speakers did not suppose that I had been there, any more than the young children had been there; but they were indicating by this use of the pronoun my inclusion in the family, something which Malagasy do often, in part because exclusion is often an impolite form but also to show the continuity which exists between people who are morally linked. These people would easily have understood the implications of John Donne's question: "Ask not for whom the bell tolls." If there is nothing very unexpected in such a situation, this fact makes its occurrence all the more significant because it shows how common such situations are.

It shows among other things the role played in such transmission by material objects. The topography infused with history is, as here, particularly significant in that it facilitates this re-experiencing as though one was there. The role of a historically saturated landscape is something which historians, sociologists, and anthropologists have often discussed (Lowenthal 1985, Connerton 1989, Nora 1984, Bloch 1995b). It has also been pointed out by, for example, Schmitt (1978), studying a local tradition about a sacred wood, how the attachment of story to place ensures a strangely accurate long-term transmission. Our understanding of the power of imagery attached to objects and places has often been demonstrated by those psychologists interested in mnemonic devices (Baddeley 1990: ch.5), and it shows that it is no accident that long-term evocative social memory makes such great use of visits to sites hallowed by what is believed to have occurred there.

However, the main significance for me of the way everyone, young and old, recalled what the place of hiding had been like was that it showed so well how the presence of a past—which one did not experience oneself, either because it occurred before one was born or because one was not there—can nonetheless exist in the present, as much more than simply the memory of narratives one has been told. The children who were showing me around the site of the village, and myself for that matter, were imagining the past, but this past was attached to direct emotional and empirical experiences of the same type as if we had been there. What was being stored in our mind was therefore a mental model containing both imagery and emotion and which could therefore subsequently be "searched" in the same way as autobiographical memories.

This, of course, is not to say that the information retained by the children was the same as that of the people who had lived through the traumatic events of 1947. This is very unlikely, but also it was not entirely different, since any too fanciful version of these events would be monitored by the continuing contact between the generations in the way so stressed by Halbwachs. Above all, it was also for them a "lived" experience. Their memory of the period of hiding was therefore not of a fundamentally different *kind* to that of those who had lived then.

The full significance of such an observation only appears when we consider what it means for the long-term transmission of the past. If we think of the children who were with me on the site we can see that they will be able to pass on the memory of the revolt in ways which are similar to the way it was passed on to them—that is, not by reciting once again what they had been told, but by reimagining the events which they both did and did not experience and constructing narratives based on the information stored in their memories in the ways we are beginning to understand such traces of the past can exist in the brain (Johnson-Laird 1983: ch. 15). Such recalling will take place in a variety of ways and places, most probably especially often on that very site where we were together in the presence of others who will then be able to repeat the process of passing on a distant, yet autobiographical-like, experience.

Oral Tradition as Autobiographical Memory

Such a mechanism as we have seen operating when memory is evoked in a particular locality is not limited to such situated transmission but, I believe, also occurs when the memory evoked is only being carried by oral and written tradition.

It might be thought that if we are dealing with transmission through narratives, the element of autobiographical memory which we saw existed in the case of the transmission of the events of 1947 cannot take place. In such cases, the only relevant questions may be merely how well individuals remember the stories which they have been told and how traditional storytellers achieve the kind of feats of memory which have often been recorded (Parry and Lord 1954). Similarly, most psychologically inspired studies of semantic memory, however different the theoretical underpinnings of these studies might be, also are mainly concerned with retention and its absence. Thus David Rubin has studied the cognitive psychology of oral traditions in what is the most detailed study of the subject, but here again the questions asked are the classical ones about recall of semantic information. Although he considers extensively the significance of the evocation of visual imagery for the memorisation of narratives, he sees this merely as a cueing device for the text; he does not ask questions about how the presence of such visual memory acts as an *alternative* to the memorisation of texts or how it relates to autobiographical memory, or how it affects the texts themselves (Rubin 1995).

There are, however, certain exceptions to this lack of interest in the content of semantic memory. For example, Dan Sperber argues that which narratives are remembered is determined, in part at least, by innate predispositions of the human mind which act in time as a sorting device for humanly appropriate stories and in this way explain the presence of certain contents rather than others. Any demonstration of such a bold theory seems however still a long way off.

An almost opposite, though not incompatible, approach which goes back to the Cambridge psychologist Frederick Bartlett in his book *Remembering* (1932) does, however, suggest that the mechanisms of retention of narratives is much more like that for autobiographical episodes than might seem at first. Bartlett was concerned with the remembering of narratives and consequently with the storage of such knowledge. He used anthropological material to shown how the remembering of an Amerindian myth by Cambridge undergraduates was only easy when they had so transformed it that it accorded with their culture, or to use the term Bartlett introduced, the *schema* of their culture. What is particularly important for the argument of this article is that according to the implications of Bartlett's theory it is not the actual narrative which is stored but a representation in some sort of mental coding which is unexplicit, but memorable, of the events that the narrative recounts.

What this means is that certain aspect of the stories are not stored in linguistic narrative forms but in terms of imaginations of "what it was like". Further confirmation that narratives are not stored as narratives is provided by the amusing experiments carried out by Ulrich Neisser and John Hupsey (1974) on the memory of Sherlock Holmes fans who form societies, one important aspect of which is to test each other's memory of the stories. What the authors found was that cueing by, for example, bits of text or names was much less effective than cueing by often insignificant bits of plot. Such a study again suggests that a narrative is not stored as a narrative but as a complex re-representation of a sequence of events like the sequence of events that happen to oneself.

There is, however, a key element of autobiographical memory which we might still consider to be fundamentally different than the memory involved in oral tradition—the fact, discussed above, that recall of individual experience is almost infinite in the way the empirical content of experience is infinite. As noted above, ever-different aspects of what happened can be recalled by the activation of such memory through different forms of cueing. In the case of memory of an event evoked by a narrative it might be thought that the information available was inevitably so much poorer, since only a single and schematic point of view can be conveyed in a narrative. This is no doubt true in the case of much information about the nonautobiographical past, but it might not be so for the more highly charged past contained in such stories as what happened during the rebellion.

The conclusion drawn from the study of the memories of stories of Sherlock Holmes was that what happened in the story was stored; it was not the narrative itself being stored. A more elaborate theory encompassing such observation is the notion of mental models developed by Johnson-Laird (1983) which itself can be seen as a development of Bartlett's schema theory. The author argues and shows, with a good deal of experimental data, that normally to remember a story is to construct a coherent mental model which enables one to imagine what is happening as though one was witnessing it; it is this imagined event and not the text that is remembered. Furthermore, this "effort towards meaning", to use Bartlett's terminology once again, means that elements not included in the text have to be inferred to make understanding at all possible. This idea is argued for most strongly by Sperber and Wilson in their book on the comprehension of language (Sperber and Wilson 1986) and is further developed in a criticism by Sperber of Johnson-Laird when he points out the insufficient way in which the latter specifies the rules according to which such inference will take place and how much more extensive, far-reaching, and fundamental inference is to any form of comprehension (Sperber and Wilson 1986).

This, I believe, is most important for our understanding of the nature of historical narratives which are highly relevant to the identity and moral life of people concerned, such as those discussed here. Because of their significance, it is likely that the inferential fleshing out of a heard narrative in the mind of those who will retain it in their memory is very great indeed, so great that the inevitable empirical thinness of a narrative is replaced by an experience that is as "all around" as one which has been lived through. It thus becomes possible for individuals to "recall" aspects of the past which they learned about in a story that did not contain any such information, but which they have inferred in order to make sense. This means that in spite of the poverty of the original input they can, when remembering, search an almost unlimited and vivid memory of the events contained in the story in exactly the way that an individual can do this when recalling autobiographical memories. In this way the difference in the nature, if not the content, of historical and autobiographical memory for narratives of events of great importance for those concerned disappears completely.

Autobiographical Memory as Historical Memory

If there is a sense in which memory from narratives can take the form of autobiographical memory, there is also some evidence that the recalling of autobiographical memory of distant experiences can become more like the recalling of events that happened to others which one has only been told about.

Studies of autobiographical memory suggest that as people recall events which they themselves have witnessed or participated in long ago, they remember these events as though they had been external to them. Thus Nigro and Neisser found that individuals felt that their memories of distant events were experienced from the outside, as though they had not been really involved and were mere onlookers (Nigro and Neisser 1983). Such an impression means that certain autobiographical memories are rather like historical memories where people have learnt what happened only from a third party.

Another aspect of autobiographical memories is that on the occasion of their recall it is possible, and even likely, that the speaker is remembering not the event itself but the last time she recounted the story of that event. Thus in the case of the story which I analyzed in the first of my three articles on the Zafimaniry, it is most probable that the elders who told it to me had told it often before and were thus only partly reexperiencing the past but mainly remembering similar situations when they had told the stories before. In such a case there is practically no difference between oral history as it is normally understood and the telling of such an "autobiographical" memory. In the case of the evocation of 1947, in the second article this is unlikely, as I believe the man who told it to me had never told it before and I could almost see the memories appear before his "mind's eye". There the difference with semantic memory was clear in that its personal character meant that experiential, empirical, and emotional aspects could be recovered almost indefinitely. In most cases, however, we are dealing with something a little in between, but this is precisely the point; as we begin to examine memory in the real world, autobiographical and historical memory merge into each other.

Literacy and Memory

So far I have argued that the transmission of the past in the present, through the historical charge given to objects or localities and through oral

transmission, relativizes the distinction between autobiographical and semantic memory. But what about the introduction of literacy?

With literacy it might appear that the separation between an account of
the past and individual experience is absolute since the mechanism of storage is no longer a form of human memory. When the past is stored in explicit form in documents, books, or other artifacts, the element of imagination and nonlinguistic organisation of knowledge is ruled out. This point,
however, needs qualifying. We must not forget that for writing to become
history it needs to be read and then, most probably, be written about again.
There is no reason to believe that the process of storing in the brain a narrative one has become acquainted with through reading is in any way different to storing a narrative one has become acquainted with through listening, and therefore the same psychological processes are at work.

It is worth noting that the study of Sherlock Holmes fans, discussed
above, actually concerned a text which is written, but it was nevertheless
stored in the memory of the readers in ways which involve their imagination of the events, perhaps, to a certain extent, as though they had been
present. The fact that the fans got to know the stories through reading and
not through hearing is irrelevant, though of course this is not to deny that
this has significance for the long-term stability of the content. It is therefore
quite possible for a story learnt from written documents to create mental
models in which inference also has a necessary role in order to create understanding and storage in memory. Indeed, that this might be the case is
given from one of the most orthodox groups of people who normally see
their task as creating stories which rely on, and only on, almost exclusively
written documentary material: historians. Thus George Duby, the medieval
historian, writing about the soldiers who fought in the battle of Bouvines in
the thirteenth century says "Je les observais comme Margaret Mead avait
observé les Manus. Aussi dèsarmé qu'elle, mais pas plus" ("I was watching
them in the same way as Margaret Mead was able to observe the Manus")
(Duby 1991: 156).

What seems to happen in the case of a written historical tradition of sufficient importance to people to be stored in their memory is a continual
processual flow where the mental models of the past, perhaps constructed
in part from documents but having the richness of quasi-autobiographical
evocations, become the source of further written narratives. These are, in
turn, characterised by their explicitness but also by their evocative thinness,
which in their turn will become an element in the construction of mental
models liberally completed by inferences from individuals. It therefore
seems likely that for ordinary people—and not only for professional historians, who might be expected to guard themselves against such things—
episodes of the distant past are "remembered" in ways which are strikingly
similar to those which people have experienced within their lifetime.

Conclusion

I have argued that the past in the present cannot be understood simply as the transmission of "oral history" but needs to include an understanding of how individuals are affected by their own episodic memory. Because of this, the work of cognitive scientists has proved of great value and cannot be ignored by social scientists. Memory of the past is no mere "collective representation". Those who would have us see matters in this way are led inexorably to the typical anthropological position which rightly stresses social recalling (Bohannan 1952, Kilani 1992) but forgets that what is not expressed need not be forgotten and have social significance thereby since it is a stored resource for future social representations. This having been said, however, we should not also forget Halbwachs' point: Memory is also social; that is how it is transmitted. We saw this in the case of the return to the place of hiding for the Malagasy village. However, we also saw that such transmission requires to be understood, and that these are the very individual psychological processes which Halbwach sought to exclude.

Notes

1. Similar points have recently been made by a number of writers interested in recent history who have pointed out the highly situated character but infinitely rich character of such things as French accounts of the German occupation by people who have lived through it (Todorov 1995), where again memory seems almost infinite.

References

Baddeley, A. 1990. *Human Memory: Theory and Practice*. Hove: Lawrence Erlbaum Associates.

Bartlett, F. 1932. *Remembering*. Cambridge: Cambridge University Press.

Bloch, M. 1992. "Internal and External Memory: Different Ways of Being in History." *Suomen Antropologi* 1992.

_____. 1993. "Time Narratives and the Multiplicity of Representations of the Past." *Bulletin of the Institute of Ethnology* Academica Sinica n. 75.

_____. 1995a. "The Resurrection of the House" in J. Carsten and S. Hugh-Jones (eds.), *About the House*. Cambridge: Cambridge University Press.

_____. 1995b. "People into Places: Zafimaniry Concepts of Clarity" in E. Hirsch and M. O'Hanlon, *The Anthropology of Landscape*. Oxford: Oxford University Press.

Bohannan, L. 1952. "A Genealogical Charter." *Africa* 22.

Carruthers, M. 1990. *The Book of Memory: A Study of Memory in Medievial Culture*. Cambridge: Cambridge University Press.

Cohen, G. 1990. *Memory in the Real World*. Hove: Lawrence Erlbaum Associates.

Connerton, P. 1989. *How Societies Remember*. Cambridge: Cambridge University Press.

Courtois, S. 1993. "Archives du communisme: mort d'une mémoire, naissance d'une histoire." *Le Débat* n. 77.

Duby, G. 1991. *L'histoire Continue.* Paris: Odile Jacob.

Gillingham, S. G. and Bower, G. H. 1984. "Cognitive Consequences of Emotional Arousal" in C. Izard et al. (eds.), *Emotions, Cognition and Behaviour.* Cambridge: Cambridge University Press.

Halbwachs, M. 1925. *Les Cadres Sociaux de la Mémoire.* Paris: Presse Universitaire de France.

_____. 1950. *La Mémoire Collective.* Paris: Presse Universitaire de France.

Holland, D. and Quinn, N. 1987. *Cultural Models in Language and Thought.* Cambridge: Cambridge University Press.

Johnson-Laird, P. N. 1983. *Mental Models.* Cambridge: Cambridge University Press.

Kilani, M. 1992. *La Construction de la Mémoire.* Geneva: Labor and Fides.

Lowenthal, D. 1985. *The Past Is a Foreign Country.* Cambridge: Cambridge University Press.

Neisser, U. 1978. "Memory: What Are the Important Questions?" in M. M. Gruneberg et al., *Practical Aspects of Memory.* London: Academic Press.

Neisser, U. and Hupsey, J. 1974. "A Sherlockian Experiment." *Cognition* vol. 3.

Nigro, G. and Neisser, U. 1983. "Points of View in Personal Memory." *Cognitive Psychology* vol. 15.

Nora, P. (ed.) 1984. *Les Lieux de Mémoire.* Paris: Gallimard.

Parry, M. and Lord, A.B. (eds.) 1954. *Serbocroatian Heroic Songs,* Vol. 1. Cambridge, Mass.: Harvard University Press.

Rubin, D. 1995. *Memory in Oral Traditions.* Oxford: Oxford University Press.

Schmitt, J-C. 1978. *Le Saint lévrier Guinefort: Guérisseur d'enfant au XIII ième siècle.* Paris: Flamarion.

Sperber, D. 1985. "Anthropology and Psychology: Towards an Epidemiology of Representations." *Man* n.s. vol. 20.

Sperber, D. and Wilson, D. 1986. *Relevance.* Oxford: Blackwell.

Todorov, T. 1995. "La Mémoire Devant L'histoire." *Terrain* n. 25.

Tulving, E. 1972. "Episodic and Semantic Memory" in E. Tulving and W. Donaldson (eds.), *The Organisation of Memory.* New York: Academic Press.

Whitehouse, H. 1994. "Memorable Religions: Transmissions, Codifications and Change in Divergent Melanesian Contexts." *Man* n.s. vol. 27.

Part Three

Literacy

Chapter Nine

Astrology and Writing in Madagascar

This chapter was written a long time ago, but its concerns are fundamentally the same as those of the others in this book. Goody, among others, had then outlined a thesis that has continued to gain in importance since then: that the introduction of literacy changed fundamentally the nature of culture. The argument here goes against that thesis by using the example of written astrology, which has been present in Madagascar for several centuries but which seems to have had only superficial effects on Malagasy understandings of the world. The chapter is also a criticism of the type of ethnography that takes well-formed, explicit schemes as fundamental frameworks of cognition—ethnography that, in other words, does not recognise that there are different types of knowledge in society. Astrology in Madagascar, it is argued here, is an add-on and needs to be treated as such.

*   *   *

The Malagasy word for 'written thing' is *Sora,* a word which comes straight from the Arabic. This is in itself an indication of where writing in Madagascar first came from.

The history and the nature of the influence of Arabic culture, and more especially of Islam, in Madagascar help us to understand certain aspects of present-day Malagasy culture. At present two groups of people claim close contact with Islam. A number of tribes claiming to be *Silama* (Islam) live in the extreme north-west and another group of tribes in the south-east of the island. The former are acquainted with part of the Qur'ān and Arabic cabalistic and magical lore. They follow certain of the Muslim laws. The vocabulary of their language, though basically Malagasy, contains many Swahili and Arabic words. They owe their Arabic culture to a string of trading posts along the north and west coasts of the island, the ruins of which can still be seen. Contact with the Arabs on this coast probably goes back to the tenth century (Grandidier 1908: 4–7). These trading posts were linked, up to the seventeenth century, with the Comoro Islands, which to this day are peopled largely with Swahili speakers, dominated by an Arabic ruling class. In medieval times the Comoro Islands and the Malagasy ports were probably linked to the East African port of Kilwa (Freeman-Grenville 1962: 85). At all events, the Arabic trading posts in the Indian Ocean were in contact with one another, and have remained so, to varying extents, to this day. In fact the renewed contacts between the Comoro and Madagascar have recently caused a resurgence of Islamic culture in the area.

These remnants of Arabic civilizations in Madagascar are well known, but objects of Malagasy origin have been found all along the east coast of Africa, and also along the trade routes known to lead to the Arab ports, for example, along the route leading to Zimbabwe (personal communication from P. Verin).

In Madagascar, however, the power of the Arabs was broken by the Portuguese, especially by Tristan da Cunha and his sailors, who burnt Arab towns all along the coast and exterminated the Muslim trading population with notorious brutality. The sixteenth-century sailor Ludovico Barthema wrote of Madagascar: 'I believe it belongs to the King of Portugal because the Portuguese have already pillaged two towns and burnt them' (Ferrand 1891:52). Even more far-reaching than direct attacks was the fact that first the Portuguese, then other European nations, ruined the Arab trade in the Indian Ocean. Madagascar, one of the most remote outposts of the chain of Arab trading posts that existed in the Indian Ocean, became isolated from the rest of Muslim East Africa. It seems likely that the Arabs and Swahili themselves left Madagascar or were killed, and that the present *Silama* are descendants of converts made among the Malagasy.

This may explain the surprising fact that although the north-west of the island, the part to which I have been referring above, is the area where the closest contact with Islam and the Arabs existed, it is not the area where Arabic writing survived.

Writing is found in another area of Muslim influence, on the south-east coast of Madagascar near the present-day towns of Mananjary and Manakara (see Map 9.1). In this area two tribes, the Antambahaoka and the Antaimoro, claim to be partly of Arabic origin (Flacourt 1658: 47). A similar claim is advanced by certain groups among the neighbouring peoples, including the Tanala studied by Linton. The closest contact with Arabic culture is seen near the old village of Matitanana and the modern town of Vohipeno, where the aristocratic sections of the Antaimoro live.

The exact nature of the contact between these people and Arabic culture is still unclear. We know from independent sources, mainly Portuguese missionaries like Father Luis Mariano, that Arabic culture was already well established in the sixteenth and seventeenth centuries. It does seem that at this time these peoples were much closer to Islam than they are now. Some could understand Arabic and they seem to have kept Ramadan, even

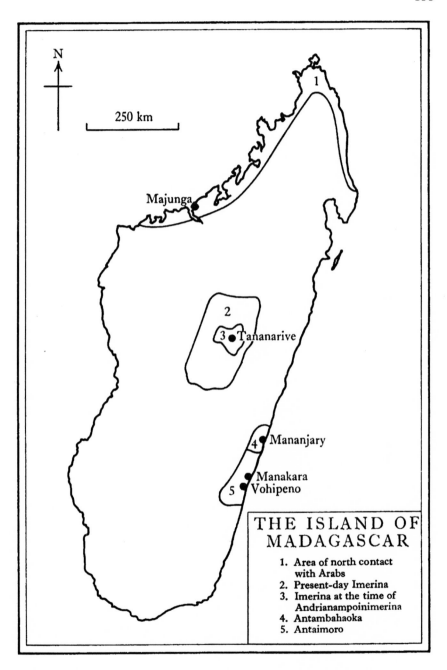

N

250 km

Majunga

2

3 ● Tananarive

4 ● Mananjary

● Manakara
5 Vohipeno

THE ISLAND OF
MADAGASCAR

1. Area of north contact
   with Arabs
2. Present-day Imerina
3. Imerina at the time of
   Andrianampoinimerina
4. Antambahaoka
5. Antaimoro

though it appears that their Muslim forebears had already been there for a considerable time. According to their written records they came at various times from the north, and this indeed seems likely. Also, according to these records, they were at the time of their arrival in touch with the Muslim centres of the north-west. By the time of our earliest independent records, however, they had already lost touch both with the Muslims of northern Madagascar, and the Muslim world as a whole. At present these 'Arab' tribes are physically indistinguishable from other Malagasy (Deschamps and Vianes 1959: 39) and it is clear that, of their ancestors, only a small proportion could have been Arabs or non-Malagasy. Their history remains uncertain to this day. According to their own traditions, they came from Mecca (*Imaka*) by way of a number of places, in particular a town which has been sometimes identified with the Indian port of Mangalore, sometimes (and more credibly) with the East African port of Mogadishu.

Whatever the precise nature of the contact, or the itinerary taken, there can be no doubt that some of the ancestors of the Antaimoro and Antambahaoka were bearers of an Arabic culture and are culturally and also possibly genetically linked with the Arabian peninsula. Archaeological evidence makes it clear that they must have originated in trading communities, probably governed by non-Malagasy but with a large non-Arabic element in their population (Deschamps and Vianes 1959: 10). This is a type of community with which we are familiar all along the east coast of Africa. Apart from archaeological evidence a certain amount of documentary evidence reveals the extensive nature of the Arabic colonization (Freeman-Grenville 1962: 133). Details of the Arabic contacts in the south-east are not known, however, and much of the speculation on this subject has only been made on the flimsiest evidence.

I am not qualified to judge which of the many theories concerning the origin of the Antaimoro and the Antambahaoka is the most acceptable, but one point is worth making: the geographical location of these groups makes them an even more remote outpost of the network of Arabic ports than the Islamized peoples of the north-west of Madagascar. This means that the cultural ancestors of the Antaimoro and the Antambahaoka would be even more affected by the breakdown of Arab trade which followed European intrusion into the Indian Ocean than their northern equivalents. This fact would explain the rather ambiguous (at the present day) relation to Islam of the Antaimoro and the Antambahaoka.

Even if they describe themselves as Muslims, the Antaimoro and Antambahaoka are only Muslims to a limited extent.[1] They perform hardly any of the Muslim rituals and have only the scantiest knowledge of Muslim theology. The Qur'ān is practically unknown, although some of the scribes remember odd, uncomprehended verses. Muslim prayers are not known, and feasts such as Ramadan are not kept. No Antaimoro or Antambahaoka makes the pilgrimage to Mecca. They have only a few practices of Arabic or Muslim origin: a special respect for Fridays, a taboo on pork (Deschamps and Vianes 1959: 70, 71), the occasional use of pious Arabic expressions (Ferrand 1905: 20), and, among the aristocratic group, the Anakara, certain short Muslim prayers, mostly in Malagasy (Ferrand 1905: 21). To this list must be added the use by a few ritual specialists of uncomprehended magical and astrological formulae, in what was once Arabic (Deschamps and Vianes 1959: 43). The Antaimoro and Antambahaoka combine with this incomplete version of Islam other beliefs which are in fact often incompatible with the theory of the Muslim religion. Nowadays, the majority consider themselves to be Christians, and a good many of them attend Protestant or Catholic churches regularly. They also all follow magico-religious practices common throughout Madagascar which are neither Christian nor Muslim in origin.

The most significant features in the heritage of Arabic culture possessed by the Antaimoro and the Antambahaoka, however, are the art of writing in Arabic script and manuscripts. The effect of these manuscripts is that Arabic practices are not solely maintained by tradition, but can be continually reaffirmed by reference to written records.

The long-standing existence of writing in a particularly remote part of what was until the nineteenth century an otherwise preliterate country has been the subject of much comment by European writers, from the earliest to those of the present day. So we are particularly well informed on this subject. We know that Arabic script was already in use in the sixteenth century. For example, at the very beginning of the seventeenth century a Portuguese sailor reports how he made a treaty with an Antaimoro ruler and how this treaty was written down in Arabic script in the Malagasy language (Grandidier 1908: 437–8).

The fullest early account of the place of writing in the Antaimoro country is given to us by the seventeenth-century French governor of a short-lived French colony sited around the town of Fort Dauphin. I give below a translation of what he says, including translations of the Malagasy words that he uses.

> There are two kinds of witch doctors, the witch doctor writers and the witch doctor diviners. The witch doctor writers are highly skilled at writing in Arabic. They have several books which include a few chapters of the Qur'ān. For the most part they understand Arabic, which they learn to write in the same way as Latin and Greek are learnt in Europe . . . They heal the sick. They make *Hiridzi, Talizmans, Massarabes* and other writings which they sell to those in high positions and to the rich to protect them from a thousand possible accidents and diseases, from lightning, from fire, from their enemies and even from death, in spite of the fact that they cannot even protect themselves from it. In these ways these tricksters obtain cattle, gold, silver, cloth and a thousand other different commodities by means of their writings which they raise up

unto heaven. These witch doctors are extremely feared, not only by the people, who believe them to be sorcerers, but also by their leaders who employed them against the French . . . These (sorcerers) sent to the fort of the French basketfuls of papers covered in writing, eggs laid on Fridays covered with figures and writing, unbaked mud jars covered in writing (etc.) . . . These witch doctors have been taught by those of Matitanana where there are schools which teach the young [Flacourt 1658: 171–2].

Flacourt then goes on to describe Antaimoro astrology, which he makes clear by implication is connected with the Arabic books which he lists. He gives the impression that the writers and astrologer diviners are two different sets of people, a division which, even if it did exist in the past, does not exist today. Having told us something of writers, he goes on to analyse in more detail their actual technique:

The script which the witch doctors use is like that used by the Arabs, written from right to left, but for some letters the pronunciation is different from what it would be in the Arabic language . . . The use of writing was brought to these parts two hundred years ago by certain Arabs who came from the Red Sea and who said they were sent to the island by the Caliph of Mecca. They appeared in their boats at Matitanana and married there. They taught and teach the Arabic language and the Qur'ān to those who wish to learn and run schools . . . [Flacourt 1658: 185–6].

This account is interesting from many points of view. It suggests that there existed then a much closer link with Arabic culture and language than at present, but it also makes clear that links with the Arabs had already been broken, and that the script had already been fully adapted to Malagasy. It emphasizes a feature which is still important today, that is, the power, religious, magical, astrological and medicinal, of the written word, both for those possessing the art and those without it, and it shows how the services of those who controlled writing were sought by neighbouring peoples.

This emphasis on the virtue and power of the writing of special texts is a common feature of Islamic cultures. In Madagascar, however, the emphasis is different in many ways from what we should expect to find in other, more orthodox Muslim countries.

The first point to notice is that the script has been separated from the actual Arabic language. It seems from Flacourt that Arabic was still used in his time, although already the script had been adapted for Malagasy. However, since the nineteenth century at least, Malagasy only has been written, and it seems that this must have been the case for a long time as no full-length Arabic texts written in Madagascar have been found, in spite of the fact that we possess quite a number of old manuscripts (Anon 1960: 113).

The adaptation of Arabic script for Malagasy has presented a certain number of problems which make it very difficult to read—in particular, the vowel signs sometimes added to the main line of the Arabic script have become attached to consonants, and often mislead Arabic scholars. Also, other signs have been introduced and the phonetic value of each is naturally different from what it is in Arabic. Because of these modifications, Arabic scholars have described the Antaimoro script as being a kind of picture puzzle. This is, in fact, completely unwarranted, and some people can read the script with little difficulty if they are acquainted with Malagasy, and with the few dialectical variants which are commonly found in that part of Madagascar. The task of adapting a foreign script to a previously unwritten language is formidable but we do not know when or by whom this was achieved.

The second most significant difference between the south-east of Madagascar and any orthodox Muslim country, from the point of view of literacy, is that in Madagascar the Qur'ān is not of great significance. This point is related to the absence of the Arabic language. Since one cannot have Islam without the Qur'ān, and one should not have the Qur'ān without Arabic, an orthodox community cannot divorce the language from the Book. The lack of importance attached by the Malagasy to the Qur'ān removes the link between writing and Arabic. The Qur'ān is replaced by a series of sacred manuscripts called *Sorabe,* or 'great writings'. This a series of books kept and copied by the scribe aristocracy of the Antaimoro and Antambahaoka. These books have often been described (Julien 1929 and 1933; Deschamps and Vianes 1959). Some are old, although their precise date is uncertain; others are more recent. There are two kinds of works. First are contemporary chronicles and historical works dealing with the mythical origins of 'Arabic' peoples of the south-east. It is these *Sorabe* which have been studied most often (e.g. Ferrand 1891; Julien 1929 and 1933). Second, and equally common, are works on the related subjects of medicine, geomancy, divination and astrology. These latter are of particular significance here because these sciences are what gave the possessors of writing such prestige in all pre-colonial Madagascar. I intend to discuss the nature of this knowledge later, but I shall just mention here that these works are (like most *Sorabe*), translations or adaptations of earlier Arabic works on these subjects.[2] A study of one of these astrological manuscripts by the orientalist G. Ferrand (1905) has shown quite conclusively the Arabic origin of Malagasy astrology, and links it up with some of the early Muslim writers (Ferrand 1936). Also of great interest are certain manuscripts manufactured in Egypt and Syria which had been kept in the Bibliothèque Nationale with Malagasy manuscripts. Closer examination revealed that they were not Malagasy, but this does not prove that they did not come from Madagascar. It seems probable that these are manuscripts which were in the hands of the Antaimoro, as they correspond with the *Sorabe* in many points, and that they were placed with Malagasy books because they had been brought back with such books from Madagascar. If this is true, they would complete the chain between Malagasy and Middle Eastern astrology, a chain which we know must have existed (Grandidier 1908: 636).[3]

The existence of a scribe aristocracy among the Antaimoro and Antambahaoka is important not only for our understanding of the society and culture of these people, but for our understanding of the society and culture of the whole of Madagascar. The prestige and power of writing, and the magico-religious information that goes with it, are spread throughout Madagascar. It is clear from the passage by Flacourt quoted above that Antaimoro scribes and medicine men were employed by other Malagasy peoples. Other evidence of this includes the testimony of an eighteenth-century French traveller who noted how Antaimoro were used near Tamatave to record transfers of land and genealogies. Scribes from the south-east travelled throughout Madagascar and sometimes settled among other tribes, practising the arts of medicine, magic and divination. Indirect evidence of this contact is provided by the fact that astrological and divinatory knowledge recorded throughout Madagascar accords closely with what we find in the *Sorabe*. A comparison of the account of Betsileo astrology given by Dubois (1938: 949) or of Merina astrology given for the early nineteenth century by Ellis (1838: 156) with the *Sorabe* translated by Ferrand (1905) shows this clearly.

We possess, however, direct evidence of the influence of Antaimoro astrologers on other tribes during the reign of the Merina king Andrianampoinimerina. This king, whose probable dates are 1787 to 1810, began his famous reign by uniting the many small chiefdoms of what was to become Imerina, and then went further still, incorporating non-Merina peoples in a very large kingdom. This kingdom was greatly enlarged by his son, Radama (as he is called by writers on Madagascar), or Lehidama (as the Malagasy themselves call him). He set up an elaborate centralized state employing specialized judges, local representatives of the central government, messengers and other full or part-time government officials. We are fortunate in that we have detailed knowledge about the administrative organization set up by Radama, an organization which was responsible for the subsequent stability of the kingdom (Julien 1908).

One of the first acts of Andrianampoinimerina when his state became an important power in central Madagascar was to send for a number of Antaimoro astrologer-diviners whom he asked to settle at his court, which they did. This shows that Antaimoro astrologers must have been in contact with the Merina before, since the king was clearly aware of their reputation.

We are particularly well informed about the Antaimoro who came to the court at this time, since one of them wrote an account of the activities of their delegation (Ferrand 1891: 101 ff.). It is clear that the role of these Antaimoro at the king's court was to advise on astrology and other magical matters. They accompanied the king on his campaigns, advising him of propitious times for attacks and other dangerous actions requiring a specific time. They supplied the king with charms, some of which became the objects of major cults (e.g. Rakelimalaza). These charms were later to be a major object of missionary hostility and were to end by being burnt at the time of the queen's conversion. These Antaimoro were also doctors, making use of the recipes for medicines that are found in the *Sorabe,* and they used the mode of divination called *Sikidy,* for which they were renowned. Indeed to this day Antaimoro astrologer-diviners are still employed by the Merina for the same purposes.

I shall return to the effect of these magico-religious activities, but first let us consider a rather lesser known aspect of these astrologers' influence, which is nevertheless of the greatest significance.

At the end of the reign of Andrianampoinimerina a number of Merina officials could write Arabic script, and it would seem that the astrologers had set up a school in Tananarive. There is much evidence to suggest that the Antaimoro at the court trained Merina astrologers and magicians, but they must also have taught writing so that it could be used for administrative purposes. James Hastie, a British diplomat sent from Mauritius in 1817, reports that in Imerina only the king, the eldest prince and three other men could write (Berthier 1953: 2). However, Berthier points out that, although 'it is likely that the number of natives who had learnt to write Arabico-Malagasy was fairly limited', it was 'certainly much less so than James Hastie states in his journal' (1953: 3). Berthier gives some evidence to support this statement and points out that many Arabico-Malagasy texts must have been burnt with other 'idols' when Radama's successor was converted to Christianity.

Our most direct evidence for the use of Arabic script in Imerina is the school book of the son and successor of Andrianampoinimerina, Radama. It is known that this king could write well and easily, and later wrote letters. The so-called 'school book' contains quite a variety of materials. A section was used by Radama for learning French words from a French envoy named Robin; there is also information on financial and military matters and even a section on astrology which serves to remind us who the teachers of Radama were.

There is sufficient evidence to say that before the coming of the British missionaries and the introduction of European script, a certain amount of the business of government was carried out in writing in Arabic script, either by administrators who were themselves literate, or by ones who used Antaimoro scribes. These scribes had the dual roles of diviner-astrologers and secretaries. The importance of these Antaimoros should not be ignored in understanding how the Merina were able to hold together and administer a kingdom considerably larger than the British Isles.[4]

Arabic script has only a fairly small place in the history of Imerina because, as soon as it started to spread, it was replaced by European script. If
we may hazard a guess at the date of the establishment of the Antaimoro
school in Tananarive, it would be probably around 1800; by 1820, however, two missionaries of the London Missionary Society, David Jones and
David Griffiths, with the co-operation of a Frenchman called Robin, produced an adaptation of the Roman script for Malagasy. According to Deschamps (1961: 161), who unfortunately does not give us the source of his
information, by 1827 there were more than 4,000 people who could read
and write in Imerina and new laws and edicts were pinned up at the Palace
gate. By 1868, a compendium of Merina law had actually been printed and
it is quite clear that writing was very widespread. I do not wish to follow
through the development of writing as such after this date, but its adoption
and spread were fantastically rapid. It seems possible that the Antaimoro
astrologers had prepared the way for this advance by familiarizing the Merina with the concept of writing, probably for centuries before the coming
of the missionaries. It is worth noting that today Imerina is probably the
area of the 'third world' with the highest literacy rate.

There is one point about which we can be more definite. From the details
of the present-day orthography of Malagasy in Roman script it is certain
that this adaptation followed the earlier adaptation to Arabic script in
many technical respects (Berthier 1953: 2). In other words, it is probable
that Griffiths, Jones, Robin and some of their informants were aware and
made use of the devices of Arabico-Malagasy writing.

In this way these Antaimoro astrologers and magicians introduced into
Imerina a tool that was also used for the secular administration of the kingdom. What, we may then ask, are the relevant factors which enabled this
secularization of writing to take place? First of all, the form of writing that
began to be adopted under Andrianampoinimerina and Radama had been
available, in all probability, for at least four centuries. It was, however, a
special kind of writing. Compared with pure Arabic script it was rather
clumsy. In its favour, however, are two important facts. First, it was fully
adapted to Malagasy (and here I should mention that the dialect spoken in
the Antaimoro country is very close indeed to that of the Merina and so
there was not yet another language barrier); secondly, it was not associated
with Islam. In fact, these two points are linked, since it is the association of
writing with the Qur'ān which maintains the association with Arabic. The
Malagasy sacred books were concerned only with history, astrology, divination and medicine. Astrology, divination and medicine are all forms of
supernatural knowledge, but they are undertaken with very immediate
practical ends in mind. It seems quite possible that this is an important factor in facilitating the adoption of writing for purely practical purposes. On
the other hand, all this does not explain why writing was taken up at the

particular point in time at which it was. Here, however, the evidence seems fairly conclusive. Writing was taken up when a large, powerful, centralized state grew up. In such a state there is a great need for writing. Some of the uses to which writing can be put in such a situation can be seen from the example offered by Imerina, first with Arabic script, then with European. These uses are:

1. credentials of government employees;
2. messages from the central government to its more remote representatives; and
3. written laws.

In this way the astrology and writing which the cultural ancestors of the Antaimoro had brought with them spread throughout the island and gave prestige to the initiates. In Imerina in the nineteenth century, however, the Antaimoro started to teach directly, bringing about two results. One was the use of writing for secular purposes, which was quickly superseded by European missionaries and their schools. This secular writing is undoubtedly the most important from the point of view of the sociology of the Merina but it belongs to a different tradition and raises such important questions that it cannot be followed up here. The other result of the Antaimoro teaching was the use of writing and astrology as a source of prestige to a few specialists. This, too, has stayed and astrologers, the heirs of Antaimoro astrology, are still important in the Merina countryside. I want now to turn to an examination of the astrologers, their knowledge and writing, and show how the historical background to their science helps us to understand some of its features today.

In spite of the secular uses to which writing was put, there is no doubt that the Antaimoro at the court were primarily ritual specialists and their influence in this field is clearly present in modern Merina.

Some aspects of astrology, as I found it in the field in 1964–6, can be explained, even today, by the close association with writing. Before considering this, however, I must describe another symbolical system which is closely associated with astrology but is of a different origin.

Malagasy notions of direction are in terms of the points of the compass rather than in terms of distance, right and left. The points of the compass are used because of their practical value, but they are also given moral value. It is, basically, a simple system. The north-east is considered particularly good and associated with the dead and with God, whilst the opposite direction, the south-west, is considered as lacking in all virtue. Intermediate directions are considered to have varying degrees of religious and moral value (Hébert 1965). This according of different degrees of value to different orientations is manifested in a variety of ways, the most noticeable of which is the orientation of houses and tombs. In the case of a house, it means that the living room is to the north of the kitchen, while the door is to the south-west; the bed of the head of the household and his spouse is at the north-east of the living room, and children and servants sleep to the south-west of the main bed. In the north-east corner first-fruits are kept from one year to the next and 'medicines' and other articles with good supernatural associations are stored. When a group of people are together in a house, they position themselves in order of status around the walls, the most important at the north-east and the least important at the south-west. This practice is particularly noticeable on ritual occasions, such as marriages, circumcisions, and funerals, when the directional symbolic system is used to express essential aspects of the proceedings (Bloch 1967: chs. V and VI). In all these ways and in many others, this sytem of orientation influences some of the aspects of Merina life. However, for nearly all actions, only this simple scheme of orientation is relevant. By contrast, the elaborations of this scheme (which are considered below), linked as they are with astrology, are not relevant to everyday life. It should also be noted that, although the orientation system is universally known and accepted, no very great importance is attached to it. Informants with whom I discussed this matter denied that punishment would follow if a house was not built with the right orientation. It seemed to be rather a matter of etiquette, which was strongly sanctioned on ritual occasions as it was then an intrinsic part of the right way of performing the ritual in question.

Merina astrology is linked to this orientation system. It is a system of beliefs still basically close to those of the Antaimoro *Sorabe,* and consequently of the medieval Arab astrologers and cabalistic writers. Astrological systems are probably the aspect of Malagasy culture which has been most thoroughly and accurately described, probably because it is fairly easy to obtain statements of Merina astrological beliefs. One of the clearest accounts is given by J. Ruud in *Taboo* (1960). Briefly, the astrological system centres on the belief that one's destiny (*vintana*), lucky or unlucky, good or bad, dangerous to others or not so dangerous, is determined by the time of one's birth. Thus, lunar months are strong or weak, and so are the days of the month, the days of the week, and the times of the day. Astrology not only concerns itself with the time of one's birth, but also the time when one performs actions. The right time for an action is not simply a fixed matter, but is related to one's personal *vintana*. Thus, at least two variables must be taken into account if astrology is to be used as a guide for action. This system is further complicated when the actions involve more than one person, as their respective destinies interact on one another. Thus, the time of a marriage is determined by finding out at what time, day, and month the destinies of the two spouses will accord. In other words, three variables are taken into account.

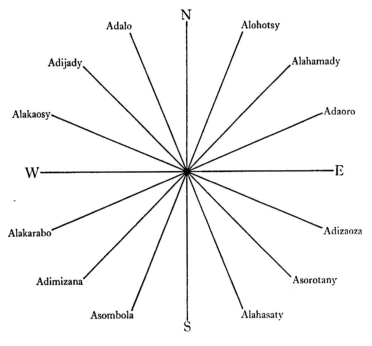

FIGURE 9.1

As such, the system is still not over-complicated, but in fact it is usually elaborated in a variety of ways. First, the basic scheme is capable of great elaboration by the simple device of dividing and subdividing the significant units of astrological time. Second, the astrology proper is often associated and merged with other information and types of knowledge. Thus, colours, various kinds of stones, etc., are said to correspond to particular astrological times. In a similar kind of way, social, ethnic and politico-geographical divisions (Danielli 1950) are associated in a single scheme of classification, reminiscent in many ways of those systems described by Durkheim and Mauss in their essay on primitive classification.

A particularly striking and well-known example is the association of the orientation system described above and the astrological system. This is done by identifying the various months and their destinies with directions, and hence with the various parts of the house (since Malagasy houses should all have the same orientation). In this way (Figure 9.1) we have the following joining of month and direction.

The month and destinies are further joined to parts of the house, so that in a traditional Merina house facing west, the various parts of the walls are

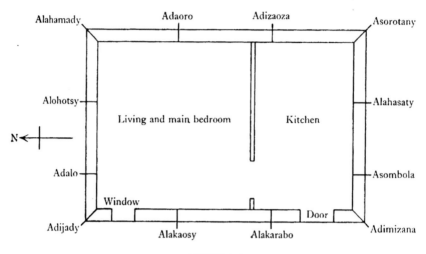

FIGURE 9.2

associated with lunar months. Thus, a normal house is divided in the way shown in Figure 9.2 and certain household articles normally stored in these parts of the house are also associated with the various destinies, as are the uses to which the articles are put.

Endless elaboration of the basically simple pattern of astrology in this way presents us with a system of classification which apparently takes in the entire universe. As such, this cosmological classification has fascinated many writers on Madagascar, in the same way as similar systems in other parts of the world have fascinated other writers. However, it is only when we see what this system is used for, and by whom, that we can evaluate its significance for the life of the Merina. I shall try to show that it would be mistaken to assume that such a complete organization of the world is necessarily the matrix which organizes the Merina's cognitive processes.

First of all, it is to be noted that astrology, to the Merina, is not only descriptive, but also predictive. The basic concept behind astrology is that it reveals a quality about people and things which, although apparently hidden, is more fundamental than the evident qualities, in that it determines these same evident qualities. In other words, *vintana*, if it were fully known, would explain everything about a person, past, present and future. The astrologer, owing to his capacity to know *vintanas*, knows the past, present and future, and of these three, the future is obviously the most interesting. The ordinary Merina, therefore, goes to the astrologer to discover what future actions he should take to fulfil his *vintana*, and to avoid the difficulties which will occur if he does not fulfil it. Thus, before a circumcision, the correct time for the operation must be discovered by the astrologer, taking into account the *vintana* of the boy concerned. In the same way, at a funeral, the time of the ceremony, and the colouring of the coats of the cattle to be eaten, are discovered by a consideration of the *vintana* of the dead, and of the mourners. The astrologer will be consulted before going on a journey, buying an expensive article, etc. In fact, whenever any danger is involved (as Malinowski would have pointed out), the astrologer has to be consulted.

This is all to be expected, but what is surprising is that when the astrologer is consulted, he does not go to great lengths to discover the exact time of birth of his client, or other astrological data about him; instead he divines the right course of action to be undertaken according to a variety of systems, some of which are of Arabic origin.

The fact that the astrologer (*mpanandro*, or 'maker of the day') is nearly always also the diviner (*mpiskidy*) and the medicine man (*ombiasy*) is at first surprising, since divination of the right course of action by means of the principles of astrology seems a contradiction in terms. Why refer to this elaborate semi-mathematical system if its logic is not to be followed anyway, and a short cut is to be taken by divining what conclusion to reach? The answer to this question is to be found when we examine the social position of the astrologer-diviner: this, in turn, helps us to evaluate his esoteric astrological knowledge.

A man or woman may become an astrologer-diviner in a number of different ways. He or she may, for example, be taught by a practitioner, and then perhaps introduced to a group of other astrologer-diviners who carry out certain regular rites to maintain their power. It is also possible to claim power as an astrologer-diviner through some mystical experience, or to do nothing more than claim the knowledge and power necessary. Being an astrologer-diviner is, like the subject matter of Merina astrology itself, a combination of the possession of complex knowledge and the possession of supernatural powers.

In practice, however, the lack of a clearly defined qualification for entry into the profession means that an extremely large number of people claim to be astrologer-diviners. What matters, therefore, is much more the ability to succeed in acquiring a large clientele than being a practitioner.

However, as soon as we look at it in this way, a very important fact begins to emerge. As regards social position, there are really two kinds of astrologer-diviners. One kind, which I shall call the professional, is extremely rare, and consists of people who make their living through divining, healing, and discovering destinies; to this day, these are often Antaimoro. The other much commoner kind are the amateurs, who practise the art for the sake of the prestige thereby acquired. These amateurs are numerous, and in the area where I worked nearly all the influential older men, apart from the *fonctionnaires*, were astrologer-diviners of one kind or another.

The reason for this is that there are now very few ascribed statuses in Merina society, and so a man who wishes to reach a position of importance or power, by, for example, being elected a *conseiller*, or by becoming the head of a family group or a village, must manoeuvre himself into that position. Naturally, there are many ways of gaining prestige, but, to be in the running at all, one must be a senior man (*raiamandreny*), which is achieved partly through age, partly through wealth, but also through the possession of knowledge, i.e. traditional knowledge, called *fomba*. The possession of this lore is demonstrated in a number of ways. Most important of all, a senior man must be a good orator, which means, apart from knowing how to express himself in the very complicated traditional speech form of the Merina, knowing also an immense number of proverbs and stories, either traditional or biblical. The more one knows of these the better, and so a suitably embellished speech may last two, three or more hours.

As well as knowing many proverbs and stories a man well versed in *fomba* is expected to have a large store of astrological knowledge and therefore, very probably, to practise divination and medicine. These important people are therefore those that one would expect to be astrologers, and this particular knowledge is thought of as part, a very important part, of their knowledge. The near identification of the roles of senior man and astrologer is demonstrated by the fact that many informants could never decide if the walking-stick made of power-giving wood (*mpanjaka be ny tany*, literally 'great king of the earth') was the symbol of office of a *raiamandreny* or of an astrologer. It seems clear that they sometimes said one thing and sometimes another, because they considered the two roles closely associated. An important man is a wise man, and a wise man is *par excellence* an astrologer.

Although the amateur astrologer is principally trying to gain political prestige, his skill is also a source of supplementary income. The family astrologer receives a small annual reward, consisting usually of a red cock and other minor commodities, and much more important major rewards when his services are required on special occasions. In the part of north Imerina where I worked, the usual payment for the services of an astrologer given in the case of a major ceremony was either a bull or the sum of about 5,000 FMG (i.e. £7. 10s.). However, receiving regular presents (which are really fees) is also part and parcel of the position of an important man, since all people of importance are regularly given presents by their inferiors, often quite substantial presents. The fact that the astrologer receives such fees is, to the ordinary Merina, yet another demonstration of his status.

Now this 'wisdom' possessed by the astrologer, if it is to be a sign which effectively marks off the *raiamandreny* élite from other more ordinary people, must be difficult to acquire. In addition, since acquiring status of this kind is very much a matter of competition, the more complicated the knowledge that a claimant has, the better. This element of competition was continually brought home to me during my field work. It was very quickly assumed that what I was trying to discover was this special esoteric knowledge in which the wisdom of the elders consists, since in many ways this is what seems to the Malagasy to be interesting in their society. As a result of this, people of importance were extremely offended when I tried to obtain information from ordinary people because, as I was told, 'they don't know'. Also, when I had been to one man of importance, and then went to another for information, the second would immediately ask me what the first had told me, and would then go on to explain and elaborate further, to the great admiration of all present. On one occasion I even witnessed a competition between two men of importance, rivals, before a wedding; they were arguing, obviously for the sake of prestige, on the nature and the ultimate significance of the rituals to be performed at the wedding. This was not for my benefit. Now, this argument, like the others I mentioned, was not to prove who was right and who wrong, but to show who knew the most elaborate version of what they were discussing. In such a situation, the occurrence of extreme elaborations of astrological theories is comprehensible. This competition for ever greater complication, not to say obscurity, seems to me to explain why the astrologer has to *divine* the solution to the problems presented to him. The astrologer, when first consulted, dazzles his client with all sorts of complicated and foreign facts about destinies, and other matters which are just as foreign and mysterious to him as to his client. Naturally, the astrologer cannot really *use* these facts for his solution, so he has to take a short cut, which is how I described divination.

One typical example of such an elaboration by a man of importance is the information reported by Mary Danielli (1950) in her article on the Merina state, information which she misleadingly presents as though it were generally known to the ordinary man. In fact, these rather fantastic schemes have often been recorded as a result of the techniques of most of the ethnographers who have worked in Madagascar and who have been satisfied with information obtained solely from the most renowned *raiamandreny*, who were most probably also astrologers.

If competition between learned men, especially in the field of astrology, explains the complexity and obscurity of some of the schemes which have been reported, this is not to say that the elaborations of these learned men are their own personal fantasies.

First, astrology is always based on the same rather simple pattern.[5] Secondly, the information which the astrologers incorporate into the astrological scheme comes from well defined sources. The astrologer uses information some of which is well known, such as the orientation of a traditional house, and shows that the orientation system is really the same scheme as the astrological one.

In the kind of scheme just described two kinds of material are juxtaposed. On the one hand, there is the strange foreign information which usually derives from written sources. As Goody and Watt have pointed out, it is no coincidence that the strange foreign information goes back to written works, for, if information in any amount keeps its foreign unexpected quality, it is likely to have been transmitted otherwise than by oral tradition since oral tradition is continually being moulded by the present conditions in which it is retold.

These written documents are available from two sources. First, the *raiamandreny* have usually at least one chap-book into which they have copied and preserved all kinds of information on many subjects, including astrology. These books are very precious, and are passed on from one head of a family to his successor. It is possible to record in them the most complicated information, long successions of proverbs, anecdotes and biblical quotations, which can then be produced at the right moment. In fact these men often look up several references before making a speech, and seem soon to remember effortlessly the most complex and esoteric information.

Not satisfied by these chap-books, however, most of these men now supplement them by small, cheaply printed books containing proverbs, anecdotes, model speeches and much astrological information or material associated with astrology. The few books (other than hymn books) normally read in remote areas are nearly all concerned with astrology. The contents of these books come from many varied sources. First, there are translations of *Sorabe;* second, missionary accounts of Merina beliefs, proverbs, etc.; third, foreign works, mainly on astrology and usually in French. Indeed, those few who can read French can supplement their astrological knowledge from the truly staggering number of French works on this subject on sale in Tananarive, and also from the columns of the many old French newspapers imported in bulk into Madagascar as wrapping paper.

The prestige of such works comes in part from their strangeness, in part from their being in written form. From the point of view of the villagers, these two qualities are really one, since they are things and statements which the villager has not made and which come to him, as it were, from an extraordinary, supernatural world, ready made. In fact, this power is thought to be present in all written things. During the period of my field work people would stare for hours at my books, especially at my dictionary. To the Merina villager, all written information was the same kind of thing, something which contributed to one's 'wisdom', the kind of knowledge of esoteric fact which marks out a *raiamandreny*.

Foreign written knowledge is particularly suited to marking out an élite since it is a scarce good, access to which is limited in four ways. First, one of the major sources of this knowledge is the chap-books which, as we saw, are passed on from one head of family to the next, unlike other property which is inherited bilaterally. Secondly, another source of foreign knowledge is books which are bought in bookshops in Tananarive and which are therefore restricted to those who are in contact with Tananarive. Thirdly, obtaining knowledge from written sources requires the ability to read with ease. Fourthly and most significantly, this 'knowledge' is so complex and difficult to acquire that it requires long study, practice, concentration and skill to master. In fact, as I suggested above, it is complicated and obscured for the sake of making it difficult to obtain—a scarce good.

The other kind of information incorporated into the astrological scheme is, by contrast, everyday. It is, as we saw, things such as the orientation of the traditional house, the moral qualities with which people are credited. In this case, the source of the prestige of the astrologer is different. It comes from the fact that he is able to reveal in his discourses and explanations connections where none were thought to exist before, and to show connections between the world of the obvious, which therefore pertains to oneself, and the strange world of foreign astrology. The astrologer is, to use Lévi-Strauss's analogy, a *bricoleur*, in that he uses materials intended for one purpose in another, completely different whole. But in this case, in contrast to the kind of scheme that Lévi-Strauss is referring to, the enhanced value of the elements comes from the fact that they are placed in *strange* relationships to one another. In other words, the order imposed by the astrological scheme is interesting to the actor because it runs counter to the classifications of everyday life: it is a scheme which appears to the actors, as it does to us, as nebulous, fantastic and supernatural, and it is because of these qualities that it is valued.

I have given this account of the nature of astrological knowledge to show the light in which the often reported descriptions of Merina astrological schemes should be viewed. There is a danger of our assuming, as Durkheim and Mauss do when discussing the Chinese 'classifications', that the astrological view of the world is a view which directs the actions of individuals. In the case I am considering here, these schemes are elaborations, even mystifications, by men competing for prestige. In confirmation, let me here quote Father Dubois, whose remarks on the astrology of the neighbouring Betsileo apply equally well to that of the Merina:

> Let us note in this matter, that in the case of astrology, like that of divination, the professionals have gone out of their way to complicate their manoeuvres in order to increase the possibilities of associations, while retaining a certain uniformity of principles and method. The divisions, subdivisions and divisions of divisions of subdivisions are built up along the same pattern and in the same initial terms, but the scheme has been multiplied for the sake of it. All this gives greater freedom in the operations and impresses more those who are not initiates, who find themselves completely lost [Dubois 1938: 953].

Astrology is best seen as a work of art which makes use of the basic categories of Merina culture, not in the normal way but by 'playing' with them. This is not to say that this whole scheme is totally divorced from social action. The very fact that it is a credential of belonging to an élite and a system of competition between leaders gives it a social function. Secondly, it incorporates systems such as the orientation system, which, as we have seen, is a feature of everyday life. Nonetheless, the fact remains that the astrological cosmology is not the cosmology of the ordinary Merina; the reason for this can be explained when we take into account the origin, mode of transmission and formulation of the knowledge of the astrologers.

Notes

I carried out field work in Madagascar in 1965–6. This was financed by the Nuffield Foundation of Great Britain, to whom I wish to express my thanks.

1. They have recently stressed their connection with Islam more strongly as a result of contact with immigrant Muslims such as the Comorians and the Indians who have settled in Madagascar.
2. Some of these manuscripts contain short passages in Arabic and, in one case, Persian (Faublée 1967: 2).
3. Many of the books listed in the bibliography discuss the *Sorabe* in detail.
4. M. Faublée mentions the discovery by M. J. Valette of an inventory of weapons dating back to this period (Faublée 1967: 2).
5. J. C. Hébert points out how the basic simple structure of astrological information serves as a mnemonic device for the astrologer while his client, not knowing the basic scheme, is all the more baffled by the information.

References

Anon. (1960). *Madagasikara. Regards vers le passé* (Etudes malgaches. Hors serié). Tananarive: Université de Madagascar.

Berthier, H. (1953). *De l'usage de l'arabico-malgache en Imerina au début du XIXe siècle: le cahier de Radama I*. Tananarive: Académie malgache (Mémoires 16).

Bloch, M. E. F. (1967). *The significance of tombs and ancestral villages for rural Merina social organisation*. Ph. D. thesis, Cambridge.

Danielli, M. (1950). The state concept of Imerina, compared with the theories found in certain Scandinavian and Chinese texts, *Folk-lore*, LXI.

Deschamps, H. (1961). *Histoire de Madagascar* (2nd ed.). Paris.

Deschamps, H. and Vianes, S. (1959). *Les Malgaches du sud-est* (Monographie d'ethnologie africaine). Paris.

Dubois, H. (1938). *Monographie des Betsiléo*. Paris: Institut d'Ethnologie (Travaux et Mémoires, XXXIV).

Ellis, W. (1838). *History of Madagascar*, I. London.

Faublée, J. (1967). Brève note sur les manuscrits malgaches en caractères arabes, *Bulletin de l'Académie Malgache*, XLII (1965).

Ferrand, G. (1891). Les Musulmans à Madagascar et aux îles Comores. *Publication de l'ècole des lettres d'Alger, Bulletin de Correspondance Africaine*, IX.

_____. (1905). Un chapitre d'astrologie arabico-malgache d'après le manuscrit 8 du fond arabico-malgache de la Bibliothèque Nationale de Paris, *Journal Asiatique.*

Flacourt, E. de (1658). *Histoire de la Grande isle de Madagascar.* Paris.

Freeman-Grenville, C. S. P. (1962). *The East African coast; select documents from the first to the earlier nineteenth century.* Oxford.

Grandidier, A. and G. (1908). Ethnographie, in A. Grandidier, *Histoire physique naturelle et politique de Madagascar.* Paris.

Hébert, J. C. (1965). La cosmographie malgache suivie de l'énumération des points cardinaux et l'importance du nord-est, *Taloha I. Annales de la faculté des lettres,* Université de Madagascar.

Julien, G. H. (1908). *Institutions politiques et sociales de Madagascar.* Paris.

_____. (1929, 1933). *Pages arabico-madécasses. Histoire, légendes et mythes* (3rd series). Paris.

Ruud, J. (1960). *Taboo: A study of Malagasy customs and beliefs.* London.

Chapter Ten

Literacy and Enlightenment

This chapter continues the argument against those who see the presence or absence of literacy as, in itself, a determining factor in culture. I show how the introduction of literacy in Madagascar has merely meant that a new and better tool became available, but that it was used to do the same things as oratory and other specialised language uses had done before. The chapter goes on to criticise the literacy thesis in a different way. Making use of fieldwork in Japan, it shows how the relationship of spoken language, writing, and thought are different with different types of writing systems. This makes impossible any broad generalisations about "literacy" in general.

*   *   *

In 1968 J. Goody edited a book, which has justly continued to exercise a strong influence on anthropological thought, called *Literacy and Traditional Society* (Goody 1968). Its first chapter was a re-publication of a joint article by J. Goody and I. Watt on the implication of literacy. With some modification the argument of this article was reproduced in a later book which ranged much more widely, *The Domestication of the Savage Mind* (Goody 1977).

The original book was itself rather problematic. The problem was that apart from the Goody and Watt chapter all the articles in the book presented evidence which contradicted the central thesis of Goody and Watt, that literacy had brought about a sharp divide in the nature of knowledge in society. The problem was partly acknowledged by Goody who in his introduction elaborated the notion of 'restricted literacy' in order to explain cases of cultures which possessed writing but had not been transformed in the way predicted by Goody. However, as pointed out by Parry, the significance of limited literacy had largely disappeared by the time the publication of *The Domestication of the Savage Mind.*

Goody's argument seems to me in retrospect to have been extremely valuable in that it raised much useful discussion. Goody was voicing in a particular way a theory which is accepted implicitly by many social thinkers and which therefore needs examining critically.

I want to argue here, however, that Goody is not justified in the theory he puts forward. This is not only because the historical evidence does not bear him out, as a variety of recent studies suggest, but because buried in his argument is an unacceptable view of knowledge and communication. This limitation has great significance in that it reveals some of the intellectual roots of anthropology which explain why an anthropologist such as Goody might look at the matter in the way Goody has done.

If we strip Goody's argument to its bare minimum it goes something like the following:

In pre-literate societies knowledge is buried in social relations. The value of what is said is not evaluated in terms of its truth but in terms of who says it. As a result criticism on the basis of reason or information is impossible without there being an attempt at revolt. Even when a revolt occurs criticism does not lead to an advance in knowledge but it leads simply to a change in political personnel. For example, knowledge about genealogies is endlessly moulded by the requirements of the changing present. Here Goody turns for support to classical functionalist studies of folk history (Bohannan 1952, Cunnison 1959). Without genuine criticism the basis of authority cannot be challenged, time cannot be appreciated as lineal and above all science, separate from the web of social relations in which it was produced, cannot emerge and develop.

Once literacy is introduced everything changes dramatically. It is then possible to challenge authorised knowledge by using documents from the past. Under literacy in the Tiv lineage, so well observed by Laura Bohannan, at the moment when the Tiv elder began to recite an altered genealogy because of different politico-economic circumstances, a voice from the back of the crowd would be heard saying "Wait a minute. This is quite inaccurate. What you said seven years ago was quite different. It is all written here in my notes." All at once the idea of scientific criticism would be there and also as a result of this challenge to obscurantist authority, democracy would be on its way. This is because in Goody's argument democracy is also seen as a result of writing. Literacy enables knowledge to be politically liberating. Indeed according to Goody it was as a result of their alphabet that the Greeks discovered democratic government.

Having reached this point in his argument Goody introduces a qualification to the effect literacy is said to have on the political. The reason why literate peoples, other than the Greeks, had not become true democrats was due to the fact that these people were unfortunately stuck with inferior types of writing. A prime example of these insufficient writing systems was ideograms. This limitation of ideograms, according to Goody, explained why democracy did not develop in countries such as China and Japan, though Gough in *Literacy and Traditional Society* casts doubt on Goody's interpretation of what happened in China.

The contrast which Goody draws sharply on either side of the "great divide" brought about by literacy echoes the theoretical changes which occurred in British anthropology at the time when structural functionalism was coming under attack. One central tenet of this is that knowledge is moulded by social conditions. This view, however, was being challenged from two different directions. On the one hand, the structuralism of Lévi-Strauss stressed how the intellectual character of knowledge gave it a specificity which meant that it could not be reduced to the mirroring of the politico-economic. On the other hand, the growing concern in anthropology with complex, large-scale, literate societies made the view that knowledge could be explained purely in terms of the social structure of the unit studied by one fieldworker, clearly implausible. For example, how could one account for Hinduism in central India purely in terms of what was happening in that particular village?

Goody's work on literacy was principally a response to this second challenge from someone who had, up to then, been fairly closely associated with structural functionalism. Goody's solution to the problem posed by complex societies is simple. He argues that for pre-literate society knowledge is indeed moulded by the politico-economic context while this was not any more so for the more complex societies towards which his colleagues and himself were turning their attention. As a result it had to follow that some magic ingredient had brought about a change in the two different kinds of societies. A change so fundamental that different types of theories were appropriate for the two types. This magic factor was literacy.

In other words the general argument seems to be this: before literacy functionalist constraints explain knowledge but afterwards it is something which looks like logical positivism. The Chinese and Japanese were partly caught in the traps of functionalism by their unsatisfactory writing system.

In order to argue against Goody's thesis I turn in this chapter to two illustrative examples. One is from Madagascar and shows that literacy of itself does not free knowledge from the kind of politico-economic constraints which the structural functionalists had shown existed. The other is from Japan and it serves to show that the way Goody conceptualises the relationship between knowledge and writing is both ethnocentric and misleading. Implicitly I contrast these two examples with what I believe is the situation in Modern Europe.

Madagascar

In 1984, I attended an international colloquium on the history of the East coast of Madagascar which took place in Tamatave or Taomasina to give it its Malagasy name. The participants consisted for the most part of Malagasy historians and students mainly from the excellent history faculty of Tananarive. There were also a number of foreign scholars, including myself. Apart from these standard attenders of academic gatherings there were a few less predictable contributors. These were people who are best described as local worthies. They included local administrators, from the town, the police and the army, the heads of large business or development agencies who were appropriately given a rough ride when they described their various activities, and most prominently of all a local intellectual and politician, Arthur Besy.

Besy has had a significant role in the history of Madagascar this century. He was prominent in the resistance to the French occupation of the country and had been imprisoned a number of times. Since independence he has represented his country abroad notably as ambassador in Algiers, where he was able to re-form his earlier contacts with anti-colonial movements from the whole world and to recollect his hectic life in relative tranquillity. As a result his ever present scholarly bent developed and he became engaged in writing history, especially the history of his natal region of Tamatave. At the conference he presented the University of Tananarive with a typescript which must have been approaching a thousand pages dealing with the history of the area. His contribution to the conference also dealt with this subject. More specifically with the origin of the name Taomasina or Tamatave.

This presentation contrasted sharply with that of the professional historians. We had all been allocated 15 minutes to talk to our paper, although nearly everybody exceeded their time. Besy, however, went on for nearly two hours. While all the historical papers were delivered in French, as is usually done in Malagasy universities, and as was done in this case partly out of politeness to the non-Malagasy speakers present, Besy insisted in speaking in a most eloquent and traditional Malagasy. Totally wedded to this use of Malagasy was his style, that of traditional Malagasy oratory: following its formal structure, which has been discussed by a number of writers, stuffed full of proverbs and scriptural illustrations, redolent with repetitions, certain passages recurring again and again rather like the chorus in a popular song. As a result, if the content of his paper had been presented in a more Cartesian manner it would probably have not taken 15 minutes to speak. As academic history its content was unconvincing to Besy's university compatriots, whose work resembles the proverbial tiny stream flowing between mountainous banks of footnotes.

Yet, these academic historians listened respectfully, if not perhaps very attentively, to this grand oratorical performance. They recognised that this was a different kind of thing to what they did themselves and, that its value too, was to be respected.

Most interestingly Besy was also aware of this difference and commented on it at various points of the conference. He clearly felt that in spite of his polite reception, the whole of the proceeding were an attack on the kind of literary activity which had occupied his life in recent years, and so he defended himself. His justifications were basically in terms of who he was. His heroic and courageous life, his age, the patience with which he had learned from elders long ago, the long years of study, of reading, of writing his manuscripts, the famous people he had known, the honour and respect he had been shown as a diplomat around the world, at the United Nations and elsewhere, all these validated his historical contribution. Indeed he delicately implied that young upstarts like the people from the university or myself, although we were doing something which he could understand had its own rationale and rigour, and which had a place within its own limited and rather unimportant context, was not really history. Our futile lives, our age and our limited experience meant that we did not have the right to speak or *write* history.

Besy was using a distinction between two kind of language uses which is fundamental to Merina culture. On the one hand there is ordinary talk which is marked by an informal style and on the other there is the formal style of oratory, which is used for important matters especially history (Keenan 1975). The style of oratory, *kabary* is the mark of a person in authority, typically an elder. Besy saw his contribution to the conference in these terms.

The two kinds of language which the Merina distinguish reflects two aspects of the person. At birth a person is believed to consist entirely of wet perishable elements which are linked to individuality. However, as a person grows older a dry elemenent begins to develop in them. This dry element is the ancestral element which will gradually take over, so that ultimately, some time after death, the person will have lost all wet individuality and will be entirely dry ancestor. Indeed I now look on Merina descent very much as a form of possession (Bloch 1985: 73), in which the ancestral gradually colonises internally the living, the ancestral is a kind of dry coral which in the end will be all that remains of people when they are finally placed in the ancestral tomb. This process of possession is evidenced in elders in part by their ability to speak in a formal oratorical manner, it shows that they have the ancestral inside them since this type of oratory is considered the words of the ancestors. Ordinary talk is merely the wet speaking, the perishable individual which there is no point in preserving.

The process of internal drying is not merely the product of maturation, for the Merina it is the product of blessing. Blessing, for the Merina, occurs when the elders who are by definition close to the ancestors transmit their contact in a number of ways. This contact through blessing therefore makes you become an ancestor and so the descent group persists. Blessing creates descendants. Now, *Kabary* is seen as a form of blessing. As a result hearing such speech, like receiving other forms of blessing, transforms you permanently, it is what causes the ancestral coral to grow inside the descendants/hearers, thus it makes of the hearers descendants of the speakers.

For Besy writing or speaking history was the sign that he was close to the ancestors that he was speaking for them. He had the right to use this style and to represent them because in the past and throughout his life he had received the blessing of the ancestors in a number of forms, prominent among which would be hearing *Kabary* from elders. This had made him to grow inwardly into a more ancestral being, and soon he would be all ancestor, all dry. Of course this role was also due to his achievements and the two aspects of being an ancestor cannot be kept apart. This role comes from the light of experience. It is the culmination of a multitude of activities, of successes, of sorrows and hardships. This kind of authoritative authorship requires a very fixed and traditional oratorical form because that is the way of the ancestors and elders. Its rhythms and form make you hear the ancestors beyond the actual speaker. Such speech is the beginning of the organisation of society which time and ultimately death will fix in an ordered eternal pattern. As a result the slow formalisation matters as much as the content (Bloch 1975).

If Besy felt that it was wrong and impossible to speak *Kabary* in French he had no such inhibitions about writing. Clearly what he had to say followed the traditional form of oratory characteristic of an elder. This, however, was not essentially oral, as he was speaking he was following a written text in French, and the great manuscript he presented to the university was in identical formal ancestral style. This manuscript was clearly for Besy the highest fruition of his historical scholarship as an elder, the highest stage of oratory. Besy's thought of himself first and foremost as a senior elder and a most important aspect of this was manifested in that he was a historical writer and a great orator, for him two activities were similar. This was because they were both marked by the style of *Kabary,* something which can persist even in translation in the written form, and which remains quite distinct from ordinary talk.

The case of Besy is significant in that it shows the irrelevance of literacy as an ideological transforming agent in such a case. His written work both in Malagasy and in French fulfils Goody's prescription for what is typical of pre-literate culture and the characteristics of his written work are with slight modifications those given by E. Keenan and myself for Malagasy oratory (Bloch 1975; Keenan 1975).

The reason is that the relation which binds the rhetoric with the social which Keenan and I discussed for oral performances holds in just the same way for literate Besy as for non literate Malagasy elders. As would be the case for any elder it was his social position which validated his knowledge and criticisms from people without his standing were irrelevant.

This apparent continuity between the written and the oral could be attributed perhaps to the fact that writing is new in Madagascar and that as a result its social effects have not yet been felt. This would be completely wrong as the history of Madagascar shows. In fact Besy is the heir of an old literate tradition which grew up in the 19th century. He is typical of a whole class of Malagasy authors.[1]

In 1968, in the book edited by Goody, I discussed the early history of Malagasy literacy. Since that time a great deal of excellent research has been carried out especially by Munthe on Malagasy manuscripts written in Arabic script (Munthe 1982) and by Ayache on the works of Raombana (Ayache 1976) by Raison-Jourde on missionary activity (Raison-Jourde 1977) and above all on the work of the many anonymous Malagasy writers whose work was compiled by Callet in the 19th c. in the book entitled *Tantaran ny Andriana* (Delivre 1974). On the whole, however, the general picture has remained unchanged. We do, however, know very much more now about what was being written especially by Malagasy historians, in the 19th century.

From approximately 1820 on, the Arabic script which had been used for astrological and later administrative purposes had been entirely replaced by Roman script. This was partly due to the influence of the London Missionary Society which not only encouraged the use of Roman script but spread literacy and even printing (Munthe 1969; Raison-Jourde 1977). By 1829 there were in Imerina almost 1,500 pupils in school who were taught to read and write (Gow 1979: 7), and since there was a yearly intake the numbers of literate Malagasy must have numbered by then several thousands. The literary activity of the Merina during the period 1820 to 1835 was principally administrative.

From approximately 1835 on, the relation of the Merina to the London Missionary Society, and for that matter to all representatives of foreign countries, changed dramatically. The missionaries were expelled, the spread of literacy was seriously restricted and the schools closed. This is the period, not discussed in my earlier article, to which I briefly turn now.

What happened to Christianity during the period of isolation from 1835 to 1862 is well known and fascinating. Christianity, which was banned and brutally persecuted, flourished and developed in a way that was far more rapid and meaningful than when it had been tolerated and when missionaries had been present organising and building a number of churches. The reason for this development has been discussed and variously interpreted. What has been rarely explicitly noted is that during this period the same sort of thing happened for literacy. It too was severely restricted, if not banned, but this was when Malagasy letters flourished.

During this period the administrative uses of literacy continued unabated, but a new phenomenon arose. A number of Merina began to produce manuscripts of a historical and ethnographic nature. Not many of these manuscripts survived though more are emerging all the time. The reasons for the disappearance of these manuscripts were many. They were destroyed during the period of Christian persecution. They were destroyed during the period of French repression when anything written in Malagasy was suspicious. They were bought by French "collectors" who usually then lost what they had obtained etc. However, enough of these are accessible to let us know what these written documents were like and why they were written in the first place. Indeed several have been published.

The missionaries from the first had introduced the Bible and devoted a large part of their efforts to establishing a written form of Malagasy into which it could be translated (Munthe 1969). The significance of the Bible is that, in a way, it is the first book in Imerina. It was enthusiastically pushed by the missionaries. Its impact cannot be exaggerated and we also know something of the reaction to it and how it was seen during the period when the missionaries were expelled and when the manuscripts were written. This can best be understood in the way the Queen viewed Christianity. For her Christianity was an attempt "to make the Malagasy worship the ancestors of the Europeans: Moses and Jesus Christ in order that they stopped worshipping my ancestors: Andriananpoinimerina and Radama". In other words Christianity and the Bible was political subversion, an attempt to make the Malagasy subjects or descendants of the whites. (In Malagasy the same word can be used for subjects and children.)

For the Malagasy the Bible was seen as part of that knowledge which not only legitimates the existence of descent groups and the authority of their elders but also, as noted above, materially transforms people into descendants of those who disseminate it. This knowledge is carefully preserved and passed on from generation to generation by elders addressing their juniors. The display and the implicit teaching and transmission of such knowledge through oratory implies political authority whether of elders or kings who were represented as super elders. The receiving of such knowledge in the form of *Kabary* causes the ancestral coral, which ultimately takes you over, to grow inside you.[2]

Of course the display of such knowledge is not sufficient in itself, it is only powerful when it is part of the multi-faceted status of being an elder. If it is not part of such a multi-faceted status it is irrelevant or ridiculous (Bloch 1971). (This was how Besy viewed the display of knowledge of the historians.) However, when it is accompanied by sufficient power as was the case for the missionaries, it is a claim to power. When such people base themselves on a different genealogy, as did the missionaries, the propagation of such knowledge is a challenge to the incumbents. This is how the Bible was seen.

What marked out the Bible as the type of powerful transformative knowledge which was previously represented by the oratory of elders was its formal authoritative style, which the translators of the Bible naturally adopted. It was written *Kabary*. The fact that it was written and printed was significant, not because this marked a different kind of knowledge to the oral knowledge of elders, but because it represented a more powerful, impressive, efficient form of the same kind of knowledge. A new technology had been harnessed for an old purpose to make a competing claim. It was rather as if the orator was using a loud-hailer.

The response to the political challenge posed by the distribution of the Bible was that the Merina who wanted to resist this spiritual colonisation wrote their own 'Bibles'. These gave their histories, their genealogies and accounts of important status legitimating events. These 'Bibles' also gave accounts of traditional practices accompanied by their 'origins' which validated them. This was the traditional subject matter of the knowledge and oratory of elders as it is the subject matter of the Bible itself. The Merina, like their queens, were fighting back against the subversive implications of Christianity and its amplified oratory, by reaffirming their traditions and customs and using the same tool. It is therefore not a paradox but a totally understandable fact that these manuscripts should date from the period when the missionaries were out of the country because of the anti-European and anti-Christian reaction.

This reaction to the Bible was exactly like the reaction of the Merina to all aspects of European culture during that period: highly pragmatic. It was a rejection of the subversive and political implication of things European, but a retention, indeed often a development, of European technology under the control of the Merina for their own ends. This is what the Merina did for metal working, and especially military technology, but also for a whole range of other techniques. They used writing in this way, principally for administrative purposes, but also for ideological purposes. They therefore used writing in their reassertion of their history and customs against the political threat of outside predators. They were using the technology of the Bible to fight it. This is what produced the manuscripts under discussion.

The written word was, and by and large still is, seen as a form of ancestral oratory. As a result it is largely treated in similar ways as oral *Kabary*. People without authority have no right to use it, and if they do they are ridiculous. What has been written once should be repeated in further writings and publications. It should be carefully transmitted from authoritative person to authoritative person. Written documents are not, any more than the words of a respected elder who uses the style of ancestral oratory, open to critical examination and evaluation. Reading written documents is exactly like listening to traditional Merina orators and what is written is by and large identical to what would have been said.

In other words Besy's writing and attitude was not a left over from an earlier preliterate age, he was not a kind of oral man who had learned to write but had not fully realised the implications of the tool he was using. In fact Besy was the heir of a century old literary tradition. He was using writing in the Malagasy way where it is a development of oratory. It is therefore not surprising that this use of literacy should share all the characteristics which Goody attributes to the oral.

This tradition is central and indeed typical of the Merina who are not only one of the most literate people I know but also one of the most literary. The number of Merina authors is quite bewildering. First of all they write little histories of their own descent groups which they have printed or typed and duplicated in the capital, then they write stories, ethnographies, novels and poems of varying quality but all of which clearly derive and are still very close to the oratorical forms which also continue to flourish. Indeed it is no accident that Malagasy authors, especially poets, have been major contributors to the French literary scene for at least the last fifty years. The Merina are certainly more literate than the English middle classes yet most of their work is like that produced by Besy, though usually shorter. Literacy has not transformed the nature of Merina knowledge—it has confirmed it.

What this Malagasy example shows is that the idea that literacy, of itself, has a liberating effect, or even leads to critical evaluative knowledge concerning the political situation, is quite wrong. What the Malagasy did in 19th century Madagascar with literacy was to use it as a tool for the kind of ideological practice which had before been oral. With writing they simply transmitted their ideology rather more efficiently. Literary knowledge did not act on its own, rather people used literacy for their own purposes. The people who were using literacy were part of a system of social relations and therefore it was in terms of that system of social relations that literacy was significant and its relation to knowledge was in terms of these uses. Literacy did not desocialize knowledge as is implied by Goody and it therefore had no political significance as a democratizing agent.

The modern situation of the history colloquium was of course not identical with that of the 19th century. When we consider the relation of Arthur Besy to the modern historians we do see different types of knowledge associated with different politico-social existences (the two types are only indirectly linked with literacy) occur side by side. This situation, however, is not one where genuine non-social knowledge confronts tainted social knowledge, where inevitably the former must defeat the latter. Rather the two types of knowledge are irrelevant to each other so long as there is no meaningful social relation between the people who are concerned with it. Besy was as irrelevant to the historians as the hypothetical man with the notebook in the back of the Tiv assembly. Similarly on his side Besy felt that the historians were complete irrelevancies and he ignored what they were saying, and indeed, as far as most Merina are concerned he is probably right.

The Enlightenment

In many ways it is strange that an anthropologist such as Goody should have made the mistake about the nature of knowledge in literate societies which is revealed by this Malagasy example. After all anthropologists are probably the social scientists who have most emphatically stressed the social constraints on knowledge. The cause of the mistake seems to lie very much in the history of ideas of the subject as was already suggested above. It is thus worth tracing this history further back, not only to put Goody's position in context, but also because it enables us to identify the second problem in Goody's formulation which will be considered in this chapter.

When Firth, in a celebrated phrase, denied that Anthropology was the bastard of colonialism but rather that it was the legitimate child of the Enlightenment, he was claiming a genealogy which was not necessarily as unproblematic as he seemed to imply. First of all when we look at the Enlightenment it appears much more as a wonderful cacophony rather than an organised intellectual mass movement. Secondly, of course, the intellectual positions taken at that time have subsequently been heavily criticised.

There was, however, one moment in the French Enlightenment when mystical, anti-rationalist Rousseau, vitalist Buffon, humanist Diderot, empiricist Voltaire, rationalist D'Alembert got together and this was when they collaborated in the writing of the Encyclopedie. Although originally intended to be merely a translation of Chambers encyclopedia the editors agreed on a much bolder enterprise outlined in the entry "Encyclopedie" of the Encyclopedie. The idea was to make all knowledge available simply and clearly to the ordinary man in one illuminating book. Furthermore, the availability of this knowledge in a fairly easily accessible book was also to be politically liberating.

This was to happen when the obscurantism of priests and politicians supporting despotic and unjust governments had been dispersed by the clear light of knowledge emanating from their publication. This is one of the main themes of the whole book, revealed in the continual metaphorical use of the contrast between darkness and light (hence the "enlightenment", a metaphor which the contributors used themselves). The image of the opposite of enlightenment: theological and political obscurantism is also well developed as might be expected in such entries as 'Copernicus' but nowhere more so than in the myriad of ethnographic entries about such primitive peoples as Hindus (see the article on Brahmins) which shows how such peoples were enslaved by obscurantism by being denied access to science and knowledge. The way these ethnographic articles were written also made clear the irony of the inevitable concluding remarks, which always added how 'lucky' the Christian French were not to be so subject to such mystification. The book was, therefore, intended and was seen to be revolutionary, and its purpose was to be achieved through freely available knowledge which was to clear the hazes and curtains obscuring the light for illiterate primitives and orientals. In this general aim all the encyclopedists were agreed. It was only when they began to discuss what the light behind the veils might be that they fell out and were never able to get together again.

It is striking how the thinking of the encyclopedists seems to be repeated in the thinking of Goody and Watt. They seem to be all agreed that primitives and orientals have no access to socially free knowledge and are therefore at the mercy of obscurantist dominators. They also seem to agree with the encyclopedists that once knowledge is made freely available, preferably in book form, this will enable the oppressed to throw off their chains. Yet the history of ideas since the Enlightenment has been marked by the harsh realisation that things are not so simple.

This realisation came early, especially in the work of Rousseau, but most clearly at the end of the nineteenth century, by which time the apparent failure of such political events as the American and French revolutions to turn citizens into limpid rationalists led to the rethinking of the whole problem in a variety of ways. Much of this rethinking has been the source of modern social science theories. If we look at the three acknowledged founders of sociological thinking Marx, Weber and Durkheim, we see all three of them struggling in different ways this fact.

Marx in his early works is fascinated by the religiosity of the U.S. in spite of its "democracy". Durkheim points out the insufficiency of theories of religion which view the phenomenon as merely poor science, because if it was merely that it would have disappeared with the rationalist Enlightenment of the revolution. Weber argues, most radically of all that not only did liberalism not lead to a pure non social, non religious knowledge but that it itself had a religious, i.e. social, origin. Thus he seeks to argue that our scientific and political notions, especially the cardinal one of rationality are the product of non rational premises.

In a variety of ways all these authors are therefore reacting to the enlightenment view of knowledge; that once the power of priests and despots have been removed pure knowledge will shine forth. They say that there is no such thing as the pure light which the encyclopedists sought to reveal outside a social construction. For Durkheim knowledge is made possible by the totality of the pattern of social interaction in society. For Marx, and to a certain extent for Weber, knowledge varies in terms of the nature of different groups or interests in society. For all, however, the answer to the question of why liberating science does not shine forth irresistibly after the apparatuses of mystification engineered by rulers and priests have been swept away, is that the nature of knowledge is inseparable from social relations.

It was as a result of the theoretical positions of such writers as these that the functionalist theory of knowledge was formed, a theory against which

Goody was later to react. It is therefore not really all that surprising that he should simply have moved back to the earlier position which Weber, Durkheim and Marx were criticising, on the well-known principle that the enemies of our enemies are our friends. Unfortunately such a reversal has taken us back to where we were and has reintroduced all the old problems. Knowledge cannot be separated from the social.

There is another fallacy which Goody has inherited from the Enlightenment. The metaphor of light standing for knowledge and of the obscuration of light standing for the lack of a suitable medium for the transfer of knowledge is also present in the work of Goody. This leads him to thinking of systems of communication purely as transmitters of something else, knowledge, from which they are totally independent. Thus for him systems of communication whether they are written, spoken, or otherwise, are merely ways of transmitting knowledge, they are quite separate from, not part of, knowledge itself. Systems of communication are therefore to be judged in terms of their transparency. This is particularly obvious in the way Goody treats different types of script. For him the less a script gets in the way the better it is. The less script is thought about for itself the more efficient it is for communication. Hence Goody's low opinion of ideograms in China and Japan.

Japan

And here we must look at our second case: Japan. The facts about Japan immediately cast doubt on the reasons for Goody's low opinion of ideograms. The first fact is that the Japanese, unlike the Chinese, have had for centuries, side by side with ideograms of Chinese origins, two perfectly efficient phonetic writing systems available to them which they use in a number of ways and contexts. One would have thought that if ideograms were as cumbersome as Goody assumes they would have disappeared long ago and have been replaced by the phonetic systems. The second fact is that most studies of Japanese society make it clear that the Japanese have now, and have had for several centuries, a much higher level of literacy than was achieved in Europe with its purely alphabetic system (Dore 1965). Thirdly, there is the fact that numerous reformers inspired by various waves of Westernisation have repeatedly attempted to replace ideograms by phonetic systems, yet these attempts at reform have always failed as ordinary Japanese have felt that the abandonment of ideograms would in many ways harm them. This is exactly the opposite to what the Goody thesis would lead us to expect, i.e. that such attempts at reform would be welcomed especially by ordinary people. Even the less ambitious attempts to merely reduce the number of ideograms in common use have only had very limited success and at the present time the number of ideograms used is, in spite of several Governmental attempts to stem the flow, growing at a healthy rate.

The reason for these facts, is that the Japanese attitude to the relationship between writing and knowledge is quite different to the western one. Our folk theory of this relationship goes something like this: Writing is a way of making the spoken permanent so that the spoken can be transmitted beyond the limits of hearing and so that the ephemeral spoken can endure. This is also how Goody views writing. The purpose of writing is to make us "read" the spoken behind it. The writing itself contains no information it merely transmits information which is elsewhere.

For the Japanese, however, almost the reverse is true in so far as writing with Chinese characters is concerned. The spoken is seen as one way of communicating knowledge whose form is in the characters, and it is a rather poor and inefficient way at that. To properly understand a spoken statement of import it should be written first. The Japanese are endlessly commenting on the inadequacies of their spoken language to express deep knowledge and they often gleefully point out how it is unfortunately full of homonyms. The significance of such remarks is that for them the characters are the base of knowledge and the spoken is a poor refraction of this base.

For the Japanese the characters themselves are the information. Thus, you will often see Japanese in serious discussion who feel that to make quite clear what one means to the other they either have to write the ideograms which correspond to what they are saying, or at least pretend to do so on their hands.

The specific nature of the reaction to the numerous attempts at simplification and diminution of the number of characters is highly revealing in this respect. The first and most furious response to the most recent attempt came from people who felt that their names were being abolished by the reform because the characters with which they were being written would not be acceptable any more. The Japanese did not think that a change in the characters being used, which would have produced exactly the same sound, would have merely been a change in the way their names were being written. The characters were the name, while the sound was merely the way the names were spoken. Hence abolishing the characters was abolishing the name. Once again the perceived relation between the spoken and the written is reversed between Japanese and European culture.

Perhaps the intrinsic value of the characters for themselves can be seen in two aspects of modern Japanese education which appear particularly strange to Europeans. The first is that the different stages of learning which a school child is achieving is typified by the number of characters he or she has learnt. The reason for this is not simply that there are a lot of characters to learn but that the characters contain inside them the knowledge which has to be assimilated. The child is not merely taught how to recognise and reproduce the character but above all to understand the knowledge they constitute. The closest parallel in Europe is the way having a wide vocabulary is thought in folk psychology to be a sign of wisdom. It is not the fact of knowing many words for themselves which is thought to be important rather it is that the mastery of the words is believed to indicate a mastery of the concepts.

The second insight which Japanese education gives into the nature of characters shows how they can convey meaning without in any way having to correspond to speech. Japanese schoolchildren are taught to "read" Chinese classics through the ideograms employed. But they have no idea nor any curiosity as to how to pronounce the text. They are not merely substituting Japanese sounds for Chinese sounds since, because Chinese syntax could not be more different from Japanese, the words occur in a totally different order. They read without having to attempt to reconstruct what the authors might have said. This is only possible because of the nature of ideograms not as units of sound but as units of knowledge.

Good literary style in Japanese is not judged by what the writing would say, were it read, but by the choice of characters with which the text is written. This means that authors choose with great care between a number of characters which when read are pronounced identically. This may lead to great obscurity as novelists for instance may choose for the sake of style little known characters which are not understood by the ordinary reader. The problem is overcome by the characters being paraphrased by others or by phonetic writing in the margin of the book. Again we can see it is not the sound which the writing produces which matters since the sound produced by reading the character and the marginal footnotes are identical.

The very Japanese word which is normally translated by the English word culture: bunka, is in Japanese made up of two characters which can be glossed 'to take the form of writing'. This is not only revealing in itself but it also illustrates how characters contain information and interpretation of knowledge which have the role of etymologies in folk learning. They reveal the true fundamental meaning of a spoken expression both in their shape as a whole and in the combination of the elements of which they may consist.

Most revealing however is the nature of Japanese calligraphy. The word calligraphy suggests to a European a careful exercise of decoration. European illuminated manuscripts were the decoration, the beautiful encasing of the word of God or of the fathers of the church with painstaking lengthy care. Indeed medieval books in their bindings resemble closely reliquaries which made their contents imperishable.

Japanese calligraphy is completely different, both in intent and in execution. First of all it should be the action of a moment on the part of the calligrapher. Random elements such as the marks left by stray hairs of the brush are particularly valued. They are the trace of the speed and the lack of retouching of the writing. For the same reason, the most valued paper for calligraphy is very much like blotting paper. It is impossible to write on it slowly without making a mess. The significance of this is that the speed required bears witness to the internalisation by long practice of the particular characters. The speed of the execution demonstrates how truly the knowledge that is the character has been learnt. It is the outward reflection of inner wisdom. What is inside one is the character, not the words, and the calligraphy is the fleeting material manifestation of this inner state. The Japanese view is that the characters in one self are the knowledge and that these can be manifested very poorly by speech and a little better by writing. While the western view is that what is in one self are thoughts which are believed to be necessarily in the form of words and that these words may take on a superior form when they are expressed through writing which is what gives them permanence and ultimate value.

For that reason the wisdom of famous men of the past, Buddhist saints for example, is not preserved by endlessly writing in ever more beautiful ways what they said, but rather in preserving their calligraphy which shows their wisdom even if what the calligraphies express are not their own writings but almost any sacred phrase. Indeed in a number of famous cases the calligraphy is of only one character.

A learned Japanese man is therefore one who has so internalised the knowledge of previous generations, that is characters, that he can produce it by semi-instinctive movement of a large part of his body without having to divert the transmission by the disruptive intermediacy of sound. The character is seen as a repository of knowledge in itself whether traditional or modern. It does not refer to information it is information.

The nature of ideograms is extremely complex but enough has been said to show that for the Japanese the relationship between the written and the oral and between the written and knowledge is completely different for the European way of looking at these things. A way which Goody assumes is universally the case. The idea that the ideograms might obscure the dissemination of meaning is absurd in the Japanese way of looking at things. It is viewed in just the same way as an attempt to enforce a reduction in the vocabulary would be viewed in Europe.[3] Any reduction in the number of ideograms is a reduction in knowledge. If the ideograms were simplified this would simply enslave in ignorance those who used such an easier script. Indeed this was very much the way that the Japanese viewed the syllabic scripts which were associated with women and which were seen both as the proof and the cause of their inferiority.

With such a view of writing as the Japanese the notion that the task of writing is to be transparent so that it does not hide knowledge becomes quite incomprehensible.[4]

Conclusion

This brief excursion into Japanese ethnography has fundamental significance for the Goody argument. It shows how culturally specific his view of writing actually is and how careful we must be when we use it for what it is intended to be: a universalist thesis.

The fact that the Japanese view the relationship between knowledge, writing and speech differently to the Europeans is not a reason why we should accept their folk view any more than we should, like Goody, accept the European folk view. Rather it should make us reconsider the theory critically, especially the relationship that we see between knowledge and the potentially material phenomena that is writing.

In this chapter we have seen three possible patterns associated with Europe, Madagascar and Japan. They reveal variation on a number of levels but there are probably many more possibilities that could be found in cultures not discussed here.

First we have the European pattern. There thought and knowledge is believed to be primarily a matter of language. These linguistic thoughts are visualised as individual creations of the moment. They are transitory, always changing and flowing, and because of this, valuable thoughts are always in danger of being lost. These thoughts/words may emerge from the individual in the form of spoken language. This is again visualised as a fluid individual phenomenon. However, thanks to writing, it is possible to fix and make permanent individual thought or language and so valuable knowledge is not lost. Written language is therefore immobile and this permanence should be marked by the care and deliberate way in which it is made. Also because writing is permanent it is not so individual as the spoken word, this is because the individual is itself perceived as fleeting and when his or her language is fossilised it becomes a common possession to be stored in libraries. The European view of writing thus ultimately rests on a European view of the person as a unique individual and his or her place in society.

Secondly we have the Malagasy pattern and this again requires an understanding of the notion of the person in cultural terms. There again thought and word are associated, but as every thing that pertains to the individual and his body these are of two radically different kinds. On the one hand there are the fluid individual thoughts linked to the wet side of the body. Like that side of the body these should have no permanence and should not be fixed, either by oratory or by that extension of oratory, writing. On the other hand there are those thoughts/words which are the manifestation of the ancestral in the self and which gain prominence as one gets older and approaches the ancestors. These have permanence because the ancestors are permanent and everlasting. They manifest themselves in a form of speech, formal oratory, which is non individual and immobilised and this may be further immobilised by writing.

Finally we have the Japanese. There what should be permanent is the ideal concept which should have been put in the head of a person by long education and practice. This ideal character is very reminiscent of a Platonic form. The outward manifestation of the learnt forms are visualised as fleeting shadows and indeed should be so. These outward manifestations are of two kinds. One, speech, is a low form and it is continually denigrated. The other is more noble, it is the material writing which, although also an outward shadow of its source, is closer to it than speech. However, it would be wrong if the outward manifestation was confused with its permanent origin and so the best writing is that which flaunts its fleetingness.

Until such ground rules of the relationship between thought, knowledge, speech and writing have been established the kind of ambitious task attempted by Goody cannot begin.

Notes

I wish to acknowledge the help I received from the National Museum of Ethnology of Japan for the short research I carried out in that country. I am particularly endebted to Dr. S. Tanabe for his help when discussing this subject.

1. Although what is said in the following sections of this paper concerns the Merina it should be remembered that Besy was a Betsimisaraka. This however has little significance for my argument since the Betsimisaraka have very similar notions of ancestorhood and blessing. Also such members of the elite as Besy have been since the 19th century merged with the Merina.

2. It is interesting to note in this respect that nothing marks out a king as much as his right to make formal speeches.

3. This comparison was suggested to me by Professor W. Goodenough.

4. Basil Hall Chamberlain writing in the late nineteenth century makes exactly the same point. "We mean that the writing here does not merely serve to transcribe words . . . the slave in fact becoming the master" and he goes on to explain why as a result there can be no question of the attempts at Romanisation succeeding (Chamberlain 1971 p. 520).

References

Ayache, Simon (1976) *Raombana l'historien. (1809–1855) Introduction a l'edition critique de son oeuvre.* Ambozontany Fianarantsoa.

Bloch, Maurice (1968) Astrology and Writing. In Jack Goody (ed.) *Literacy in Traditional Societies.* Cambridge University Press, Cambridge.

_____. (1971) Decision Making in Councils among the Merina of Madagascar. In *Councils in Action.* Cambridge papers in Social Anthropology 6, Cambridge University Press, Cambridge.

_____. (1975) Introduction. In *Political Language an Oratory in Traditional Society.* Academic Press, London and New York.

_____. (1985) *From Blessing to Violence, History an Ideology in the circumcision ritual of the Merina of Madagascar.* Cambridge University Press, Cambridge.

Bohannan, Laura (1952) A Genealogical Charter, *Africa* Vol XXII no. 4.

Callet, R. P. (1908) *Tantaran ny Andriana eto Madagascar.* Academie Malgache, Tananarive.

Chamberlain, Basil Hall (1971) *Japanese Things, Being Notes on Various Subjects connected with Japan,* reprint of 1904 original. Tuttle, Rutland and Tokio.

Cunnison, Ian (1959) *The Luapula peoples of Northern Rhodesia, Custom and History in Tribal Politics.* Manchester University Press, Manchester.

Delivre, Alain (1974) *L'Histoire des Rois D'Imerina, Interpretation d'une Tradition Orale.* Klincjsiek, Paris.

Dore, Ronald P. (1965) The Legacy of Tokugawa Education. In Marius T. Jansen (ed.), *Changing Japanese attitudes towards Modernisation.* Princeton University Press, Princeton.

Goody, J. (1968) *Literacy in Traditional Societies.* Cambridge University Press, Cambridge.

_____. (1977) *The domestication of the Savage Mind.* Cambridge University Press, Cambridge.

Gough, Kathleen (1968) Implications of Literacy in Traditional China and India, in Goody 1968.

Gow, Bonar A. (1979) *Madagascar and the Protestant Impact.* Longman and Dalhousie Press, London.

Keenan, Elinor (1974) Norm makers, Norm Breakers: Men and Women in a Malagasy Village. In R. Bauman and J. Sherzer (editors), *Explorations in the Ethnography of Speaking.* Cambridge University Press, Cambridge.

_____. (1975) A sliding Sence of Obligatoriness, in Bloch 1975.

Munthe, Ludvig (1969) *La Bible a Madagascar, Les Deux Premieres Traductions du Nouveau Testament Malgache.* Forlaget Land og Kirke, Oslo.

_____. (1982) *La Tradition Arabico-Malgache vue a travers le Manuscrit A-6 d'Oslo et d'autres Manuscrits Disponibles.* T.P.F.L.M. Antanarivo.

Raison-Jourde, Francoise (1977) L'Echange Inegal de la Langue: L'Introduction des Techniques Linguistiques dans une civilisation de l'Oral. (Imerina au XIX siècle) *Annales E.S.C.,* Paris.

Chapter Eleven

The Uses of Schooling and Literacy in a Zafimaniry Village[1]

In this chapter I again look at the uses of writing in a village where it was recently introduced. I then consider the significance of writing for the way villagers evaluate the Western type of education that, for them, is above all concerned with teaching literacy skills. This evaluation is inevitably in terms of their own folk theories about what type of knowledge is appropriate for different stages of life. As a result, what the villagers want from education seems totally at odds with the original purpose of the type of education they are given.

*   *   *

This chapter describes how schooling and literacy are used outside school, in one small and remote village in rural Madagascar. My example may perhaps seem untypical or even eccentric. Still, it is chosen in order to make a general point, since I do not believe that it is possible to discuss any of the effects of literacy or schooling usefully except within a specific context. Literacy can be used (or not used) in so many different ways that the technology it offers, taken on its own, probably has no implications at all (Bloch 1989). Since what goes on in schools is itself so varied, it is perhaps even more hazardous to attribute particular social, political or psychological effects to schooling.

    The choice of a concrete example very remote from the sort of conditions generally described by educational experts is intended to show that many of what are normally taken to be the inevitable effects of the introduction of literacy and schooling are in fact nothing of the kind, but result from the social and cultural contexts typical of western industrialised societies. Such factors normally pass unquestioned and unexamined, since most western commentators rarely have the contrast with nonwestern societies forced upon them. It is from this point of view that a Malagasy village where I have twice lived comes to seem an obvious starting-point for a discussion of schooling.

In stressing the importance of looking at real contexts, I am of course merely echoing the frequent recent demands in psychology and especially in the psychology of education for 'ecological validity'. But I believe that even those who have stressed the importance of looking at education in the world rather than in the laboratory or the school have envisaged context much too narrowly; in particular they have surely ignored implicit cultural contexts of which we become aware only when working in fundamentally 'other' cultures.

I want to demonstrate the determining influence of two connected types of contexts. There has already been a good deal of discussion of the effects of my first type, the politico-social context, on schooling and literacy, and so I shall only touch on this briefly (see for example Willis 1977).

The second type of context I discuss here, by contrast, has been generally neglected. That is the significance within a specific cultural setting which is attributed to different types of non-school knowledge, and the importance of this for the way in which ordinary people evaluate and use school-knowledge. Jean Lave in her fascinating book *Cognition in practice* (1988) has shown the small use that is made of school mathematics in everyday activity, but this leads her to an over-simple contrast between practice (regarded as non-school knowledge) and abstract theory which for her is taught in school only. This may be adequate for the United States with which she is mainly concerned but, as we shall see, when dealing with Madagascar we need to distinguish more finely, between knowledge in practice and explicated knowledge, between explicated knowledge in and out of school, between meta-theories of knowledge employed in school and those employed out of school. Furthermore we shall see how actors' theories about knowledge, whether implicit or explicit, relate to their theories of person, of gender, of the body, of maturation and of birth and death.

*   *   *

The Zafimaniry are a small group of people living in the forest of eastern Madagascar who, until recently, relied exclusively on slash and burn agriculture. Unlike their neighbours they have never been fully integrated into state structures and for most of their history they have been concerned with avoiding such integration.[2]

The small village of Mamolena[3] in Zafimaniry country where I carried out field work in 1971 and again in 1988 and 1989 is situated in a very remote part of the country which has been relatively little affected by centralising forces in Madagascar such as government administration and large-scale trading.

Until 1947 the agents of government hardly ever appeared in the village but then, following a nationwide anti-colonial revolt, the French, represented by their army, arrived in Mamolena, killed people and burnt the place down completely. For a few years following this colonial 'reconquest' the government established fairly tight administrative control which, in milder form, lasted until about 1975. Since then, as far as the inhabitants have been concerned, the state and its institutions have gradually withered away, and, at the same time, integration into the national and international economy has diminished, so that, by now, hardly any manufactured goods are to be found in the village. The intrusive contact of radio programmes has vanished with the villagers' inability to obtain batteries, and no government representative of any kind has set foot in the place for at least the last ten years.

However, the fact that the state and its apparatuses are retreating does not mean that the inhabitants, or at least the male inhabitants, of the village are completely isolated. This is because the villagers can and do make contact with the state and the wider economic system on a largely voluntary basis by occasionally seeking it out. Firstly, a significant number of young men go on labour migration to different parts of Madagascar, often passing on their way through the national capital or other major urban centres. Secondly, villagers quite often go to the nearest administrative centre, Ambohivohitra, about two hours' walk away, either to market or for contact with government agencies.

After 1947, when the French made Ambohivohitra one of the *loci* of their repressive activities, that centre became reachable by road from the town of Ambositra for at least half the year. Since that time it has contained government offices and a fairly well-run government school where pupils were, until recently at least, taught by qualified and paid government schoolteachers. Occasionally some of the pupils at the state school of Ambohivohitra were successfully trained for the old French BEPC[4] which enabled them, in theory at least and now and then in fact, to go to the good schools available at Ambositra.

Since 1975 however the general decay of the state and its agencies has also affected Ambohivohitra. This is most obvious in the fact that the road has become impassable—or at least no transport available to the villagers can travel on it. As a result Ambositra, which used to be only three hours or so away until about 1970, is now practically two days' walk away. This has meant that the administration has become intermittent at best, since by now there is only a single administrator. This man is expected to pay frequent court to his superior in Ambositra, and has therefore to stay in that town most of the time.

The school in Ambohivohitra has suffered too. First of all educational aids such as books, paper and biros have become very scarce. More significantly, the increasing remoteness of the place has made school-teachers, who normally come from small towns in the area around Ambositra, unwilling to take up posts in the village or, if they do, stay there. Equally disruptive has been the fact that the Malagasy government insists on paying school teachers every month in person in Ambositra. This means that for at least one week of every month there is no school in the village, while the teachers collect their wages. Also the school week has recently been reduced to four days as no school is now held on market days.

Equally damaging has been the increase in the number of school-children, with no compensating increase in the number of teachers at least since 1970. The population of Mamolena is representative of the general increase in population. It has increased by 45 per cent between 1971 and 1989, but of course this means a much greater proportional increase in the numbers of children, and the population of school age has in fact more or less doubled over the period.

This has not only affected the quality of schooling in Ambohivohitra; it has also meant that the slim chance once available to Mamolena pupils of attending school in this village has vanished, since there is now literally no room for them there.

The disappearance of state administration and schooling in the last two decades has been compensated in part by the growing presence in the area of the Catholic Church, with largely foreign funding. For Ambohivohitra, and especially for Mamolena, it is the Catholic Church which has become much the more important source of contact with the outside world.

The Catholics established themselves quite securely in the Zafimaniry area during the 1930s, and in 1967 the local missionary began to build a massive, very ugly and totally inappropriate stone church in Mamolena. The money for this church and many others like it came largely from the selling of Zafimaniry carved artifacts to dealers and tourists in Antananarivo and beyond. This selling of artifacts generated large revenues for the priest, who employed the money in a programme of church building worthy of an averagely wealthy medieval cardinal.

The building programme stopped abruptly when the present incumbent replaced this priest in 1972. The new man set out to rescue the church from its building obsession and used the money for small scale development projects which, unlike most development projects undertaken in Madagascar, have actually proved on balance beneficial to the recipients.

The significance of the unfinished church in Mamolena for our concerns is that it has housed a church-run school on and off for about the last twenty years. This church school was started as a stop-gap measure by the Catholic Church until such a time as the government should decide to provide the village with its own school. This it has regularly promised to do since the 1930s but the promise has yet to materialise. In 1985, the administration told villagers that if they put up a building for a government school a fully trained school teacher would then be appointed. The school was erected at considerable expense by the villagers but it is now derelict and no teacher has ever come.

The church school has been run by a number of teachers who have always lived in Ambohivohitra and who have passed the BEPC. In most cases the teacher had benefited from at least one year's school experience in Ambositra. The school has never succeeded in training anybody to the level of the BEPC but it has, in at least three cases, trained pupils sufficiently well that they could be accepted and cope with teaching for the BEPC in Ambositra.

The school was open fairly regularly in the 1970s but during the 1980s it has had a much more troubled history and was in fact closed several times, including one long period of five years when no schooling was available.

One result of this is the variable amount of schooling received by the people of Mamolena depending on their ages. Those under twenty-five are, as a direct result of the recent troubled history of the school, relatively poorly schooled, with low levels of literacy. Those between twenty-five and forty are relatively well schooled and were probably in most cases fairly literate when they left school. Among these were at least two ex-pupils, probably more, who are fairly advanced because they benefited from further schooling in Ambohivohitra and Ambositra. However, for reasons discussed below, these stars have, without exception, left the village of Mamolena and are now living somewhere else. Finally, among the over forties the situation is very uneven. Some—those who went to school in Ambohivohitra—received fairly good education and in many cases can still read and write, though with difficulty. The majority are, however, totally unschooled since they were children at a time when there was no school in Mamolena.

What happens in school is ultimately modelled on European, mainly French, models of secular and church education. However, because the facilities available in the school are so different from what most of the readers of this chapter are used to, a short description, drawn in a modified and shortened form from my field notes for part of a fairly typical day in 1989, will evoke the reality of what is actually being discussed when we are talking of schooling.[5]

A Day at School

It is ten past eight. The children are all gathered in small groups in the village under the eaves of a couple of houses waiting for the door of the church to open as a sign that the teacher has come. He appears and prepares to put a conch to his lips but before he can do this the children rush out of the village towards the school in high good humour in spite of the pouring rain.

The barefoot teacher is eighteen. This schoolteacher came close to getting his baccalaureat after two years at school in Ambositra. His salary is unclear; his predecessor got 10,000 FMG a month (approximately three pounds sterling[6]). He certainly does not get more than 20,000.

The church is much like an unfinished garage except for the fly-blown religious pictures, which are old posters of Europeans being crucified, nursing babies or growing amazing white beards. The benches on which the children sit are very rough-hewn pews, six inches off the ground. Two short rows at the front are better and attempt to be rickety desks. The only school equipment is a tiny, worn-out blackboard.

All the children are dressed in incredibly ragged, and by now mud-coloured clothes. They are clearly very cold. However, all seem to be enjoying themselves. The children in this first session are divided into two groups. On one side of the aisle there is a large group of children of approximately 7–10 year olds (about forty of them), in the other aisle a group of 10–12 year olds (about thirty).

The first part of the proceedings (15 minutes) is catechism done with great care by the school teacher who explains about the ascension of Christ. Then the secular teaching begins. The younger children basically have three items on the curriculum which take more or less equal time: reading, singing and drawing.

They are asked to draw on their slates a picture of a house, something which they are asked to do at least once a week and they do this relatively well, with great enthusiasm. The houses are entirely stereotyped but the degree of elaboration varies.

The singing consists of a total repertory of five songs, which they sing again and again throughout their school career, hardly ever learning new ones. They did the singing with great gusto and with obvious enjoyment. Among the songs, three in all this morning, are the National Anthem and a Malagasy version of *Alouette* . . . It is striking how crude and simple this singing is in comparison with the subtle polyphony of the funeral wake songs which the same children will sing whenever anybody dies in the village.

Reading is the most important part of the teaching. It consists of reading a couple of simple sentences which use similar words and which are written on the blackboard. The reading is first recited in unison by the whole class with little difficulty. Then each row of children by themselves are asked to read in unison. This is more difficult. The reading in unison takes on the character of chanting. However, since the same sentences are put up on the board day after day (for several months) it is not clear how far the whole thing is an exercise in reading or memorising.

The older group of 10–12 year olds have a similar programme except that the reading exercise is slightly harder. They are also asked to write in books or on slates. Today this is exclusively copying the copperplate model of individual letters written on the board by the teacher, but on other days they copy the complete sentences which they read.

At half past nine there is a break and the children pour outside. There the children themselves organise a tug-of-war with a liana between the boys and girls, with the two sides winning about an equal number of times. At quarter to eleven the young ones leave.

My feeling about the proccedings is that in spite of the very poor content of the teaching, the atmosphere is excellent, relaxed and under control. This was in part due to the pleasant and unchallenging attitude of the children and the skill and good humour of the teacher.

The behaviour of the boys and girls is strikingly different. With the notable exception of two girls who behave exactly like the boys, the girls when interrogated are *menatra* (shy), looking away, sideways or to the ground and ultimately dissolving into embarrassed giggling, to such an extent that some have to sit down before finishing what they have to say. The boys are confident, witty, their eyes shining. They all seem to be treated in the same way by the teacher however.

After eleven the older ones (approximately 12–14) come in. They will stay until one. They are a much smaller group, thirteen in all, nine boys and four girls. It is significant that there are so few and so few girls. Marriage and economic activity soon removes the children from school. The girls however, because they marry much younger, are removed by marriage sooner than the boys.

All the children who are there can read and write to some extent. They read more complicated sentences from the board, first in unison and then individually. Then they copy them in their books. They learn a little pointless French vocabulary which is pronounced by both teachers and pupils in an unrecognisable way.

Besides this, the children do lengthy sums, such as writing every interval of 50 between 2,500 and 10,000, as well as simple problems. The answers to these sums are written in exercise books and corrected individually. On the whole, the mathematics demanded of the pupils, which they do with difficulty, is infinitely easier than mathematical sums which are being done daily by the same children in dealing with money, thereby confirming the findings reported by Lave (1988).[7]

There are also some bizarre grammatical exercises concerning stress in Malagasy. What was taught made no sense to the teacher, the pupils or me.

Sometimes, once a fortnight or so, but not on the day these notes were taken, there is a little geography—learning the names of the provinces of Madagascar and sentences concerning France, the USA, the USSR,

Jerusalem, Bethlehem and Rome—and a little science in the form of reading and copying sentences like 'Water boils at 100 degrees'. (I later asked the pupils what degrees were, and found that they had no idea.)

Although the content of the teaching is not very different for the older and younger classes, what was striking was the difference in atmosphere. In the case of the older children I got the impression that the schoolteacher, although still amiable, felt that he was wasting his time and this feeling was shared by the pupils. The atmosphere of this second half was gloomy, unpleasant . . . defeated. The explanation for this is all too simple: teaching at this level is meant to be directed towards passing the exam which replaces the old BEPC, but all the pupils and teachers know that there is no possibility that anybody will get through. At this stage the school represents something which is normally insignificant in the village as opposed to more 'developed' places in Madagascar: the intrusion into the village of an image of a society of which the villagers have to see themselves as the lowest echelon.

*   *   *

Although the older pupils may regard it as impossible for them, as villagers, to achieve academic success, they nevertheless share one thing with everybody else in Mamolena, and with everybody I know in Madagascar, educated or not; that is, they are absolutely convinced of the *value* of schooling and literacy. I find this conviction surprising and it is worth considering what might account for it, at least as far as the inhabitants of Mamolena are concerned.

The first and most obvious explanation would be that education is seen by the Zafimaniry as a potential avenue to social success and wealth. There is no doubt that much government and Church propaganda encouraged this idea and the people of Mamolena know of a few success stories from other villages to which they sometimes referred. However as far as their village is concerned clear cases of people for whom education led to good jobs are non-existent.

Education makes it possible to be elected to, largely unpaid, local administrative posts since these require at least some ability to read and write. However, whether these positions are really desired by the Zafimaniry is far from clear and it is a question to which I shall return below.

There is also an awareness that those who were successful at school have tended to leave the village and to settle in big towns such as Ambositra and the capital of Madagascar, Antananarivo. There, some of these people have been successful and others not, but this success has been unrelated to their education.

Perhaps more relevant to the valuation of school and literacy is the villagers' knowledge that the children of these more mobile village parents have been able to attend better schools in the larger centres. It is also known that in some cases at least, these children have obtained government employment—hence academic success might be said to have borne fruit at one generation's remove.

However, seen from the village, this kind of success is double-edged. Firstly, although people realise that once upon a time government urban jobs were lucrative and led to prestige and high standards of living, they also know that this is no longer the case. Villagers are continually commenting on the lack of jobs in town, the terrible living conditions of the urban poor and the fact that government employees are badly and irregularly paid at a time when the price of the foodstuffs which they must buy is rising. People know what is happening. During my recent visit, the only discussion of possible future social success through education which I heard in the village concerned a girl who was being considered for acceptance as a novice in a nunnery.

Emigration to urban centres which is made possible by education has, however, an even more protound drawback as villagers see it. People in Mamolena and other places like it have their own powerful understanding of the nature of success, and this involves having as many children, grandchildren and other descendants as possible, either in the village itself, or at least in the locality. The very children who may do well at school, leave the village and eventually produce children who can perhaps achieve some success in the outside world, become at the same time lost to their parents and grandparents, and so actually diminish their older relatives' success and prestige within the village.

*   *   *

The reason for the high valuation of schooling and literacy must therefore, at least today, lie somewhere else than in the practical advantages it can confer. I would argue that this continuing valuation can only be understood when we move beyond the social-economic context discussed above, to locate what is taught in school in a different context as well, that of the organisation and valuation of knowledge in the village—that is, the way villagers think about knowledge when (as happens most of the time) they are not in, or specifically referring to, the school environment. When we put school knowledge within that context it becomes possible to understand somewhat better both why the villagers should value school-knowledge, and how they use it. The strength of the explanation depends on the fact that, as we shall see, the schooling villagers receive does not seem to affect their organisation and philosophy of knowledge; instead, school knowledge is itself interpreted within the terms of the village home culture. This finding is in accord with a number of recent studies of schooling (Willis 1977; Scribner and Cole 1981) which document the strength of home culture and the weakness of school culture.

The strength of home culture, in Mamolena at least, is not surprising to an anthropologist who has carried out field work in the traditional manner, noting daily life as it occurs, not focusing on a pre-defined 'problem', while it might escape the research approach of those who have focused on education even when thinking of themselves principally as anthropologists. This is because the home theory of knowledge and the evaluation of different types of knowledge are completely linked with the way such things as the body, gender, maturation, the nature of the living world and the understanding of productive and reproductive processes are all envisaged. In other words, it is by understanding things which at first appear totally remote from education and literacy that their meaning for the Zafimaniry can finally be grasped.

In sketching the ethnography of knowledge among the Zafimaniry I am aware that much of what I have to say also applies in lesser or greater degree to many other Malagasy. I am also aware that the discussion provided here can only be cursory and indicative. Since I am arguing that a much broader than usual cultural view is necessary in order to understand the uses of literacy and schooling, I can unfortunately present only a partial account of those factors in the limited available space.

Like most Malagasy, the Zafimaniry stress how the passage through life is one of fundamental transformation, so that little of the person is considered as fixed simply because of ancestry. For them, living human beings are best thought of in terms of what they are transforming from and into rather than as fixed entities. This transformation affects their bodies, their genders, their minds, their use of language and their appropriate spheres of action (Bloch 1986 and 1989). It is on the last three of these aspects that I shall concentrate here. The process of transformation is gradual, with no sharply marked discontinuities, but for the sake of presentation it can be divided into three principal stages.[8]

Zafimaniry concepts regarding the bodily aspect of the transformations associated with maturation are reminiscent of those of other Malagasy people (Bloch 1986; Huntingdon 1988). There is a general idea that children start life all soft and bendy but that as they mature, which occurs principally as a result of receiving the blessing of their ancestors, they straighten up both physically and morally. This transformation is not only evident in the material parts of the body but also in such less tangible aspects of the person as their style of speaking. The young speak in an unformalised tumble of words and unfinished sentences. The old often use near-formulaic expressions phrased in an archaic and fixed style. All this, as in other parts of Madagascar, is seen as part of a general process of hardening, drying, becoming more fixed, more ancestral and more moral.

In many symbolic ways, as people go through life the Zafimaniry house gradually becomes a substitute for the body. We can distinguish three stages in life; the first is when the person is not yet linked to a house and their body is likewise soft and undetermined, the second is the period when, as part of a married couple, they are developing themselves through their descendants and their house, and the third is when they start to separate themselves from normal human activity and are becoming ancestors, but for the Zafimaniry this means merging with the ancestral houses, the structure of which becomes the object of ancestor worship.

This general process of maturation has for the Zafimaniry yet a further side. It is associated with the idea that the different stages in life are also linked with appropriate spheres of activity and therefore with appropriate types of knowledge. The young, that is those who are not yet married and so are not yet associated with a house, are typically thought of as hunters and gatherers, carrying out these activities in the forest. Because young men marry later this period is longer for males. This association of the young with the forest and hunting and gathering is not merely to be understood in terms of a type of productive activity. The young are in many ways also seen as sharing the characteristics of their quarry. They are said to be like animals or even wild plants: unreliable, forming and breaking personal links promiscuously, amoral, mobile, interested in this and that.

For the Zafimaniry the typical way of doing things at this stage in life is playing, and hunting and gathering is seen by them as a type of play. Zafimaniry children play in ways which are familiar, for example imitating adult activities by making mock houses where they cook, playing at the rituals of adults, or sometimes they play more organised games such as knuckle bones or hopscotch which they score in extremely complex ways. But above all they play with wild plants and animals.

What is particularly interesting in this type of play is that it involves a combination of encyclopedic knowledge and scientific experimentation. For example, the boys in Mamolena make, apart from the ubiquitous whipping tops out of wood and liana, pop guns with bamboos and other forest plant materials. Similarly they make windmills, often with tails which direct them constantly into the wind. What is more, the brighter among the children are very happy to discuss the principles which make these toys work. Accompanying this practical and theoretical physics is a great fascination with practical and theoretical biology which involves playing with and examining animals, often in an extremely cruel way.

I was particularly struck by the scientific nature of this type of play when, as a result of a cyclone, an unknown bird, actually a sea bird never seen in those parts, was blown down near the village. It was brought triumphantly into the village by a group of children who began to examine it. They were particularly amused and interested by its beak which had two strange openings which they decided must be its nose. Then they discussed the peculiar hooked character of this beak which they felt meant that it must be a bird of prey, but they worried about what animals it could catch given its small size. Then they noted its wing span and they decided that it must 'fly high'. Finally they noted its webbed feet and decided that it must be a water bird and probably came from the sea and had been blown to the village by the high wind.

It is difficult to imagine a better organised biology lesson, but the manner of the transmission of this knowledge and the language in which it is put is totally informal, hardly ever consisting of complete sentences. In the discussion over the sea bird the children interrupted each other and pushed each other. When adults joined in, which they did with clear interest, they seemed ashamed to be participating in such frivolous activity and would move away as soon as anybody else appeared. It was obvious from their attitude that for them, as for everybody else, this was not really serious subject matter. This attitude towards knowledge about wild things is shared by everybody and is linked, not simply to the fact that this is stereotypical children's knowledge, but also to the fact that the wild things themselves are seen as of no significance to the wise since they are fluid and impermanent. This is so in spite of the fact that objectively, in terms of nutrition and other important activities, forest products are very economically significant, a fact I never found anybody willing to admit.

Activities and knowledge about wild things are thus linked to the non-house status of the young. Marriage and the beginning of the association with a house make such play inappropriate. This change occurs sooner for girls than for boys, who in the later stages of their bachelorhood develop a special version of the wild theoretical child knowledge stage associated with hunting which is linked with adventure away from the village.[9]

The married period is associated with the development, fixation and 'becoming permanent' of the house. This process in turn is associated with agriculture, which is seen as the means of sustenance of the family in the house. Because the house and marriage are viewed as a joint male-female activity this is also true of agriculture and the Zafimaniry continually comment approvingly on the mutual cooperation between husband and wife which is necessary and right for agricultural tasks.

Not surprisingly the knowledge appropriate for this period of life is, and is seen to be, governed by the principle of utility. The type of discourse in which it occurs is largely about practical matters, is perfectly shared by men and women and most typically occurs between husband and wife. As is the case for farmers everywhere, their detailed knowledge about soils, weather, plant-species and prices is awe-inspiring. However, as with the play-knowledge of the young, most of this knowledge is implicit and is therefore difficult to describe.

It would be wrong, however, to believe that this type of knowledge is never verbalised. It is manifested either in practical problem-solving or else sometimes in discussions after work. The language in which these matters is discussed also reflects the notion of utility. It is serious, calmer and more organised than the language of the young concerning wild animals and plants; conversations on these topics are often half whispered and include long pauses expressing reflection, calculation and doubt. People do not interrupt each other, they sit in proper positions. These types of dialogues usually take place at appropriate times for talk of this sort: after breakfast, after the last meal of the day or at certain stages during visits from relatives.

The practical agricultural knowledge of middle life is part and parcel of often repeated activity but it would nonetheless be misleading to think that it cannot occsionally be used for context free or innovative speculation, as has sometimes been suggested by psychologists (Perkins 1988).

For instance, because the Zafimaniry are faced by three incompatible calendars they continually discuss ways of aligning them and for this use mathematical principles infinitely more complex than anything taught in school. Similarly, discussion of supply and demand and how to take advantage of price fluctuations according to the timing of harvests revealed rich operative ability. Again they employed good scientific hypotheses, the result of innovative thinking in a new situation, to explain the spread of a pig epidemic by the fact that people did not wash their feet properly before entering a village, by the wind, or by people buying infected pig meat in other villages, then throwing away the bones which were then gnawed by the pigs ... [10]

After middle age comes a stage of life which can be labelled 'elderhood'.[11] Gradually the period of life when the married pair are primarily concerned with producing the nurturing descendants gives way to the period when the couple become elders. As we have noted above, this means on the one hand that they are becoming almost like ancestors and on the other that at the same time they are becoming merged with the fixed, hardening and beautifying house. Men slip in to the role of being an elder more easily and more clearly than women although women may also attain the status of elder, only more rarely and more uncertainly.

Being an elder is a status but it is also a style of behaviour which the person adopts when he is being an elder. This is marked by posture and linguistic code. He tends to speak very quietly, using formalised and fixed language which is highly decorated and full of quotations and proverbs. When an elder speaks he addresses nobody, apparently not caring if he is heard or not, ignoring the fact that others may be speaking at the same time since a specific linguistic exchange would negate the almost other-worldly character of what he is saying.[12]

The wisdom of the Zafimaniry elder is much less politically relevant than that of the Merina.[13] It is treated, rather as the person themself is treated while they are speaking, with respect, but with a sense of being kept at arm's length from practical life, almost of being ignored.

The discourse of elders, however, is not merely marked by form, it is also marked by content. In other words elderhood also implies a particular form of knowledge. Elders are associated with the image of straightness, hardness and permanence, of morality, of fixity in time and space (marked by the holy house) but also with clarity[14] and truth. This is because the wisdom that emerges with elderhood contrasts both with the chaotic fluctuation of life characterised by wild things which typically concerns the young and with the process of getting a living which is the primary concern of the middle aged, and which is also linked with dialectical change, although of a more orderly kind. The wisdom of elders is authoritative, it is beyond question and in a sense even beyond human life, since the elder is often represented as merely speaking the words of the ancestors who are merged with the house.

The Zafimaniry elder has become fixed and therefore like an inanimate object. What he is allowing to be expressed through himself is therefore of no practical value since it concerns things on a time scale different from human life; it is not referential but constitutive; it is worthy of being expressed and displayed for itself; it is wisdom. What is mainly spoken in such talk are blessings and special forms of thanks which are also a kind of blessing. Otherwise it tends to be *tantara*, a word which is often translated as 'history', since the contents tend to be genealogies of people and places as well as information on the geography of previous significant places and descriptions of how things should be done at rituals. *Tantara* and eldership are inseparable.[15]

Overall therefore the Zafimaniry view knowledge as one of these three kinds, each associated with different ages of life. Youth is speculatively playing with wild plants and animals. Middle age is concerned with practical knowledge and the maximisation of utility. Elderhood is concerned with history. As we pass from the knowledge of youth to the knowledge of elderhood we move along an axis of increasing fixity and of categoricality, but also of decreasing relevance for dealing with the environment.

*   *   *

The Zafimaniry therefore have a meta theory about different kinds of knowledge which is associated with different styles of communication and which is itself part and parcel of much more general concerns such as the maturation of the body and the person, the nature of human society and its relation to the non-human world of plants, animals and places. It is within this relatively organised system of beliefs about different types of knowledge that the Zafimaniry try to place the knowledge which is transmitted at school.

In terms of content school knowledge is seen as being of the same kind as the 'wisdom' of elders. It also comes from an absolutely authoritative beyond, which one respects but does not want to come too close to. It is therefore presumed to be categorically true but, at the same time, to be irrelevant knowledge as far as practical activities are concerned. It is not considered to be a source of information about the empirical world.

Such an association of school knowledge with wisdom explains the uncritical acceptance of everything taught at school. The Zafimaniry attitude to such knowledge is that, of course it is true and one should know it, of course it cannot be questioned since it is true, and of course it is neither fun nor relevant. The apparent anomaly which struck me so strongly in the field—that the intellectual and practical value of what was taught in the school was so poor compared with what was daily available out of school—did not matter at all to my fellow villagers. What one was taught in school emanated from such prestigious sources that it could not and should not be concerned with the practical or with the empirical world. Above all it should be, like the elders and their knowledge, beyond dialectic.

This having been said, however, school knowledge cannot in every way be that simply assimilated into the pre-existing system. This is because Zafimaniry theories of knowledge assume a homogeneity between the type of knowledge and the kind of person who professes it. If school knowledge is a form of 'wisdom' it is being transmitted by the wrong kind of people to the wrong kind of people since it is taught by the young to the very young. Furthermore, the problem is made worse by the fact that the type of communicative code that is appropriate for the transmission of 'wisdom' is inappropriate for either pupils or schoolteachers.

The problems which these anomalies pose are partly resolved and partly avoided in a number of ways. One of the ways of avoiding the problem is not giving the young a chance to display the fact that they have this 'wisdom'. So in assemblies and so on they are not given a chance to speak and pontificate and, in the village context, school knowledge is kept back by the young, until, as elders, they may finally occasionally use it as a decorative extra to *tantara*.

The problem caused by the fact that schools give 'wisdom' to the wrong persons is, however, acute when school knowledge occasionally gives authority. This occurs when it leads to the possessor of such knowledge obtaining an administrative position of some kind. This is not really a problem in Mamolena since nobody holds such a position, but in Ambohivohitra for example and in another nearby village the problem clearly exists.

In this other village there is a young man in his thirties who holds an official administrative post. He was chosen for this post mainly because of his success at school, as the job requires being able to read and write. His position is an embarrassment to every one including himself, as a short anecdote will show. Shortly before leaving the field I had said to people in Mamolena that I was interested in seeing the ancient tomb of the founder of that other village. At the market that Wednesday, after having bought three litres of rum, the elders of Mamolena suggested that we should go to that other village to ask for permission to go to the tomb, perhaps because this would offer an occasion to drink some of the rum. We first went to the elders of that village and the request proceeded with usual Zafimaniry decorum, then as we were leaving we met the young official on the path and my co-villagers decided that we should ask him also for permission. From the first this caused problems because both the way you sit and the order in which you drink implies relative seniority and nobody could decide on precedence. This was settled in the end and things went well for a while and we addressed the young man by his administrative title of *President*. Then, thanks to the effects of the rum, a new note of irony began to creep into the way the elders addressed the official. They began to call him *Raiamandreny* (elder) and to behave towards him with increasing mock humility. The president did not know where to put himself and finally slunk away.

Schooling is therefore by and large not used out of school in Mamolena, and when it is used it quickly becomes problematic. There is one area of schooling however which does intrude and which needs to be considered separately and that is the use of literacy. Literacy is above all a communicative technique, but since communicative style, person and knowledge are totally welded together for the Zafimaniry, the use of literacy in the village presents the same problems as the use of the 'wisdom' from school.

As discussed above, the Zafimaniry associate different stages of life and different types of knowledge with different forms of communication. For them these different types of communication vary along a continuum from a point where the subject matter and the content are seen as ephemeral to one where it is seen as concerning permanent things conveyed in a language which reflects that fixity. Working with this type of notion and with a view of writing as a technology which immobilises speech, it is not surprising that they, like the Merina a century before,[16] see writing as appropriate for 'wisdom' and conversely as a sign of 'wisdom'. This categorisation therefore has a great influence on the way writing is received and used.

First of all we need to consider the reception of writing, mainly in printed form, which originates outside the village. This comes in three forms:

1. There are the communications from the administration which are mainly read by the administrator in Ambohivohitra in the presence of the villagers from Mamolena who are summoned to listen.
2. In many houses in the village there are old pages from French magazines which are sold in markets and are used for house decoration. For example in the house where I lived during field work there was a double page from a fifteen-year-old *Express* which showed adver-

tisements for, on one page, a bra and, on the other, a credit card bearing the amazingly inappropriate message: *Maintenant avec ma carte Bleu je ne suis plus jamais pris a court.* The picture showed an elegant couple with the man being presented at the end of the meal with a bill he clearly could not pay. As far as I could judge nobody ever made the slightest attempt to read this.

3. Those who attend the make-do service run in the church on Sunday are read to by the catechist from the Bible. There are two striking aspect of these readings. First of all, as the relatively young man painfully and sullenly reads the same texts, week after week, the elders stand all together in a row at the back of the church, doing something like presiding, and in this way removing whatever authority the catechist might gain from his profession of 'wisdom'. Secondly, it is clear that what is read on such occasions is almost totally meaningless to the hearers and they never show the least interest in its content. This is perhaps because the language is very difficult to understand as a result of the total disregard for punctuation which characterises the catechist's way of reading. It is also because of the strangeness of the content. For example, a text which came up again and again was the Bible story of the miraculous fishing expedition which involves the casting of nets on either side of the boat, but the Zafimaniry have no experience of fishing from boats with nets. To make matters worse, the translation renders such words as boat by the totally inappropriate Malagasy *sambo kely* which means 'little ocean liner' or 'tanker'.

In fact none of this matters much and the content of these different written messages is all treated in much the same way, a way which is totally consistent with its being assimilated to the 'wisdom' of the elders. All these messages, whether government communications, bra ads, or scripture, are all presumed to come from an immensely powerful beyond and because of this they are taken to be true without question, but also because of this, these messages are not, nor expected to be, informative in a practical way or expected to be immediately relevant to anything in one's life or one's environment. Any attempt to try to analyse what the stuff might mean by ordinary people would be both subversive and imprudent.

Written material produced outside the village does not, therefore, pose a problem for the village theory of the distribution of knowledge. Written material produced inside the village, however, does potentially pose such a problem in much the same way as the use of school knowledge by the young administrator does. This is because those who can write tend to be the fairly young and therefore not appropriate exponents of 'wisdom'. By and large, however, the problem is solved by making the actual writers appear to be scribes for the wisdom of the elders.

There are two kinds of writing which normally emanate from the village. Firstly, there are the messages, four or five lines long, that are sent to neighbouring villages inviting the villagers to rituals or announcing death. Although these are often written by the young, because their form is completely fixed they are seen as emanating from a kind of village 'collective will' of which the elders are the epitome.[17]

Secondly, apart from these totally standard letters there are other, rare, but very important letters which are occasionally sent to, or received, from distant kin and which give important news. One very interesting aspect of these letters is their form which itself suggests the oratory of elders since it is totally modelled on the oratorical exchanges which characterise the special forms of greetings which a returning relative should address to the elders of his family.

On such occasions the returnee, after a lengthy and totally fixed section of the 'how are you' kind of exchange, gives a standardised account of what she has done during her absence. The response is as follows: first a standardised greeting section again, then thanks for the information which should repeat as exactly as possible what has been said by the returned person, then a brief standardised account about what is new in the village. This speech is answered by the returnee in a similar manner. She will thank the elder for the news and then will repeat it.

The general effect of this procedure is that it transforms the fluid events recounted into fixed *Tantara* spoken and endorsed by the elder. In this way knowledge which bore some of the characteristics of that appropriate to middle age is converted into the wisdom of the old in that the speech of the young has somehow been 'taken over'.

Letters follow this pattern too in that they consist of the same kind of greetings, then replicate the previous letter, if there has been one, then they give new news (three or four lines at most), then they sign off with other conventional phrases.

Writing a letter again puts the facts beyond doubt and makes it part of the domain of the absolute truth, like the received writing from the church, the government or the old magazines. Here however there is a difficulty. Such information should emanate and be received by the elders but on the whole the elders are rarely competent readers and writers. The problem is however not great. The action is represented as the junior person writing under the dictation of the elder and reading the letter to the elder who thus becomes the true recipient. This is somewhat of an ideal scenario since what tends in fact to happen is that everyone gets into a huddle trying to make as much sense as they can of the paper . . . but this is what the Zafimanry say should happen.

This way of representing writing so that it appears to emanate from those in authority negates any of the cognitive and revolutionary potential writing has sometimes been said to have (Goody 1968, 1977). This is because the basic rules concerning knowledge out of school have somehow reorganised the school knowledge to their logic. This might however be considered to be due to the institutionalised nature of letter writing. However, even in cases of innovative uses of writing in the village the control of literacy by the young does not seem to have any significant effect. This is what appears in the following example which is particularly interesting in that it involves precisely the situation which Goody suggested would have fundamental sociological implications since it concerns the writing-based criticism by the literate young of the oral record professed by those in authority.

When I had returned to Mamolena in 1989 after an absence of seventeen years this caused such surprise and interest that I found people falling over themselves trying to be helpful. By then they had decided that what I had been trying to do during my earlier period in the village was to learn *Tantara* since this was the only possible explanation for what I had been doing from within their theory of knowledge. As a result, when the villagers realised that I had come to do the same thing again we began to talk about the history of the village. Then, very soon into this discussion, a middle-aged man whom I had known as a child produced a school note book of sixteen pages filled with neatly written material which turned out to be a history of the village consisting largely of genealogies and I was told that all I needed was in there. I thought the Goody 'great divide' had occurred while I had been away.

In fact I soon realised that my past presence in the village was not unrelated to the existence of this document. What had happened was that I had spent a lot of time talking with a highly respected blind elder, sometimes recording what he said, but most of the time taking notes which I would write up in the evening. This clearly was *Tantara* and the villagers had decided that they too wanted a permanent record of this *tantara* for themselves since they rightly knew that the elder would not live long. They therefore approached a young man and asked him to do what I was presumed to have done, that is to write at the elder's dictation the history of the village.

This was the document which was produced. In a sense exactly the scenario predicted by Goody occurred. As the book was brought in, two elders in a spirit of subdued competition were telling me their version of the *tantara* of the village. Although they were disagreeing on some points, this disagreement was quickly hidden through use of the normal Zafimaniry displays of politeness appropriate among elders. This was not so easy for the written record. The man who had brought in the book began to check the oral against the written and from time to time he pointed out that what was being said did not match up with what was written there. This caused temporary discomfort but in fact it was quickly dealt with. These impertinent interruptions were sometimes listened to in puzzlement but soon they were simply ignored. The fact that it was a young man who was using writing in this way meant that he could not really intervene in the exposition of 'wisdom' by elders. This however did not mean that the book itself was treated with disrespect. The very opposite was the case. The book was clearly a most treasured possession and when it was put away it was given a small offering of rum.

Again the social and cultural framework had subdued the implication of schooling and literacy to its rationale and had meant that, whatever intrusive potential such elements might have, they were rapidly tamed. Thus neither writing nor schooling have made any significant difference to the basic organising principles governing the evaluation of knowledge, rather literacy and schooling have been put to use to reinforce previously existing patterns. Although this is so in Mamolena, it would be dangerous to assume that this is so in other parts of Madagascar and that it would be so in different circumstances. For example, even in Zafimaniry village peopled by descendants of slaves the situation is not quite the same and schooling does have more significant social implications. Several factors seem to have come together in Mamolena to create this state of affairs. These include the poor economic situation of the country, which has led to the weakness of the educational institutions and the lack of jobs for those with education, and the peculiar suspicion of state authority characteristic of the Zafimaniry and which is probably due to their specific history. Nevertheless, a crucial factor is, I believe, the significance of the way the Zafimaniry view different types of knowledge, which, as we saw, is inseparable from their beliefs about bodily maturation, the person, the nature of society and the plants and animals which inhabit the natural world.

It is consideration of this latter type of context which seems to me to be lacking from most discussions of schooling and literacy. The traditional problematic of the social and psychological sciences has tended to define in advance what is relevant to such research. What the Zafimaniry case shows, is that the empirical enquirer cannot afford to do less than try to observe life in almost any and every aspect.

Notes

The research on which this work is based was financed by the Spencer Foundation of Chicago. I would like to thank Fenella Cannell for assistance in preparing this chapter.

1. Like the recent article by Street (1987) which takes a similar line, the title of this paper is intended as an indirect tribute to Hoggart's famous book *The uses of literacy* (1957).

2. For further ethnography on the Zafimaniry, see Vérin 1964, Coulaud 1973. Bloch 1975b.

3. The names of villages in this paper have all been changed to maintain confidentiality.

4. This exam, which in French schools was a low level qualification, was very significant in Madagascar until the level of higher qualification, the Baccalaureat, was lowered.

5. From my earlier field work there and from the recollections of older villagers, I believe that such a day is basically similar to any schoolday in the past in Mamolena and not all that different to what went on in similar schools in the area for the last fifty years, apart from the fact that no serious attempt is now made to teach any French.

6. 1989 exchange rate.

7. This is in part due to a special difficulty most Malagasy have with Arabic numerals. In most dialects of Malagasy, including Zafimaniry, numbers are spoken the opposite way to the way they are written. This obviously causes problems in the learning and teaching of arithmetic. Official Malagasy, a language which the government has attempted to introduce to overcome dialectical variation, puts the digits in the European order and in school there are occasional attempts to teach this way. Clearly, however, neither the teacher nor the pupils can actually use this way of talking about numbers in their sums or in ordinary speech and the attempts to introduce 'official Malagasy' seem only to create further confusion.

8. In fact the intermediary stages between these main stages are also very interesting but cannot be discussed here.

9. This includes looking for valuable trees deep in the forest as well as going on wage work.

10. Here are a few further examples: (i) It was explained to me that Taro does not grow so well now that the forest has retreated. This was attributed by a Zafimaniry to the fact that by now the *decayed vegetable matter* of the forest does not wash down into the swiddens so well any more. (ii) Winnowing from a basket on the head as opposed to winnowing with a tray, requires a really scientific approach since the height of the basket is calculated in terms of the strength of the wind so that the rice lands fairly separate from the chaff. The weaker the wind the higher the basket. The process produces three piles in a continuum: one rice, one chaff, one mixed, and so on. The interaction of height and wind speed was perfectly explained to me by a woman who noticed me watching her winnowing. (iii) When filling up his granary with the rice from his harvest, a young married man is measuring it out in numbers of baskets by putting one grain of maize for each *daba* in a small box as a mnemonic. He further informs me that he will not touch the rice before September, when the price rises. Until then he will buy some if he has to. For this he will go to a market in the wet rice-growing area where it will be cheap and where later he hopes to sell dear.

11. The Malagasy term is *Raiamandreny*. It does not denote an absolutely fixed status and can indeed, in some contexts, simply mean parents. It can be applied to both women and men but is more often applied to men.

12. Actually one can distinguish two forms of elder speech. One is of the extreme formalised kind and is used for blessings and thanks: the other, a little more assertive, is used for *Tantara*. This will be expanded elsewhere.

13. For the characteristics of the oratory of Merina elders see Bloch 1975a, pp. 5–12.

14. See Bloch (1995a, b).

15. The Zafimaniry make a very sharp distinction between *tantara* and *Anganon*, normally translated as 'tales', and they explain the difference by saying that one is

true while the other is not. (Not that *Anganon* are necessarily untrue but that they lack the categorical truthfulness of *tantara*.) What 'true' in this case means, is to be believed 'beyond question'. It can also be qualified as clear, *mazava*, which again implies that it cannot be doubted (see Bloch, forthcoming, b).

16. See Bloch 1989.

17. In fact, often the letters do not exist as such but people will say that a 'letter' *Taratsy* (lit. 'paper') has been sent or received to say that an invitation or notification has been formally done.

References

Bloch, M. 1975a. *Oratory and political language in traditional society*. London: Academic Press.

_____. 1975b. 'Property and the end of affinity', in M. Bloch (ed.), *Marxist analyses and social anthropology*. London: Malaby Press.

_____. 1986. *From blessing to violence: history and ideology in the circumcision ritual of the Merina of Madagascar*. Cambridge: Cambridge University Press.

_____. 1989. 'Literacy and enlightenment', in K. Schousboe and M. Trolle Larsen (eds.), *Literacy and society*. Copenhagen: Akademisk Forlag.

_____. 1995a. 'People into places: Zafimaniry concepts of clarity', in E. Hirsch and M. O'Hanlon (eds.), *The anthropology of landscape*. Oxford: Oxford University Press.

_____. 1995b. 'The resurrection of the house', in J. Carsten and S. Hugh-Jones (eds.), *About the house: buildings, groups and categories in holistic perspective*. Cambridge: Cambridge University Press.

Coulaud, D. 1973. *Les Zafimaniry: un groupe ethnique de Madagascar à la poursuite de la fôret*. Antanarivo: F. B. M.

Goody, J. (ed.), 1968. *Literacy in traditional societies*. Cambridge: Cambridge University Press.

_____. 1977. *The domestication of the savage mind*. Cambridge: Cambridge University Press.

Hoggart, R. 1957. *The uses of literacy*. Harmondsworth: Penguin.

Huntingdon, R. 1988. *Gender and social structure in Madagascar*. Bloomington, IN: Indiana University Press.

Lave, J. 1988. *Cognition in practice*. Cambridge: Cambridge University Press.

Perkins, D. N. 1988. 'Creativity and the quest for mechanism', in R. J. Sternberg and E. E. Smith (eds.), *The psychology of thought*. Cambridge: Cambridge University Press.

Scribner, S. and Cole, M. 1981. *The psychology of literacy*. Cambridge, MA: Harvard University Press.

Street, B. V. 1987. 'The uses of literacy and anthropology in Iran', in A. Al-Shahi (ed.), *The diversity of the Muslim community*. London: Ithaca Press.

Verin, P. 1964. 'Les Zafimaniry et leur art. Un groupe continuateur d'une tradition esthétique Malgache méconnu', *Revue de Madagascar*, 27: 1–76.

Willis, P. 1977. *Learning to labour*. Farnborough: Saxon House.

Chapter Twelve

Why do Malagasy Cows Speak French?

In this short chapter I look at how French is used by Malagasy peasants when addressing their cattle or when drunk. Their use of French, which the peasants consider totally foreign, is linked to the fact that it implies a type of hierarchical relation, which they associate with the colonial period and which they find difficult to express in their own language.

*　　*　　*

When I started field work among Malagasy peasants in 1964 the inability of nearly all of them to speak French made preliminary contact naturally difficult. However, looking back on these early days with a lot of long-term personal knowledge of the people concerned, I realise that the problem was made worse by the fact that the little French that they *did* know they were very unwilling to use and that they positively avoided revealing the extent of their knowledge. It was therefore extremely surprising to find that these same peasants always addressed their cattle in French. When driving herds to pasture, using cattle for ploughing, stampeding rice fields or pulling the carts which are essential both in agriculture and in the trade of rice, planks and reeds in which so many are involved, the cattle are shouted such orders as: "a droit, a gauche, allez . . . etc." Why suddenly the switch to a little known and hostile language when talking to animals? (For it must also be mentioned that French was also commonly used for ordering dogs and other animals about.)

Perhaps the answer will become clear when we look at the few other contexts when French is used in villages. I said the peasants avoided French but there was one exception. When drunk, usually on market days or on family ceremonies, people I had never thought could say a single word in French would suddenly launch into long tirades addressed to me or to other villagers. These drunken speeches, however, were marked by other characteristics than a choice of language. Malagasy speech usually is, as a recent worker on the island confirmed (Elinor Keenan of the University of Pennsylvania), so tuned as to draw attention away from the speaker in order to avoid any aspects which might suggest boasting.

Aggression is studiously avoided in relation to the way other peoples are addressed; unqualified active imperatives are almost unknown, direct contradiction of any statement would be a serious assault and hardly ever occurs since elaborate circumlocutory devices are used for denial. In almost two years in a Malagasy village I only heard two verbal disputes with people shouting at each other and in a village context such disputes could not have been kept private. Even for those disputes the people concerned punctuated their abuse by the phrase "God bless you" in order to diminish the apparent violence of their contradictory positions. This normally extremely polite speech behaviour contrasts sharply with the way the drunken peasants spoke in French. Their lack of grammatical control of the colonial language means that not much significance can be attributed to either their choice of vocabulary or of construction. But their intention was perfectly obvious from other non-linguistic signs. Their manner was boastful, aggressive, even hectoring. They talked of the excellence of their performance, of the superiority of their culture, of their skills both amorous and technological, even of their wealth and their strength. Most significant perhaps was that they ordered people about, often aimlessly but often repeating to them as orders the injunctions of the Government to work hard to pay taxes, etc. Even more characteristic, and I have seen this many times, they acted like gendarmes, stopping people on their way to the market and demanding in a peremptory manner their identity cards and the receipts for the poll tax which all Malagasy must carry at the risk of being put in gaol and also searching to see whether they were carrying bootleg rum and tobacco.

Another situation where French is used in a peasant context is linked with the shows of semi-professional minstrels who are invited as entertainers on all great occasions of either public or private rejoicing: on Independence Day, for marriages or for secondary burials. The shows put on by these minstrels are composed of very varied elements—poetry reciting, often specially composed for the occasion, the singing of long moral tales, dancing, extravagant speech-making and acrobatics. It is in connection with the dancing and acrobatics that French is used. For these activities there is always a character who acts as a slightly ridiculous leader, blowing a whistle from time to time and shouting orders in as violent a voice as possible. His behaviour is reminiscent of a gym master and a sergeant major. The orders are nearly always in French.

Finally, there is an entirely different context in which French is used and this is obviously the most significant. French is used extensively for Government administration. Madagascar became a French protectorate in 1895 and in 1896 the French made it a colony and tried to administer the island through a French-type civil service, the higher echelons of which were

Frenchmen and were backed up by the French Army. From that time until independence all administration and contact between colonised and colonisers took place in French. The matters which most concerned the peasants were the payment of taxation and, perhaps even more important, the carrying out of various forms of forced labour. These involved the uncontrolled exercise of power through the medium of French. All relations with all members of the administration, whether Malagasy or French, had to be carried out in French. All absolute orders came in French. To a certain extent since the coming to independence of Madagascar in 1960 things have changed. Malagasy has become an official language and all official documents are bi-lingual, French-Malagasy. Politicians and administrators make their speeches in Malagasy and much of the day-to-day administration is carried out in that language. However, much French remains. The highest administrators are often Frenchmen speaking no Malagasy and so the original decisions are made in French and are often untranslatable because the French legal jargon cannot be adapted by administrators at the lower levels who are anxious not to misinterpret them. The names of officers involved are French names and so are other aspects which refer to the French administration system. In the end the peasant receives Government orders in Malagasy with the crucial part still in French. Nothing has really changed for the orders from the all-powerful administrators remain basically in a foreign language. The speeches of Ministers, Prefects, and Headmen are, and must be, stuffed with French terms and phrases.

The reason why Malagasy cows speak French is by now apparent. Just as French is used for communication by the totally powerful colonials or administrators to the totally powerless peasants, the totally powerful cattle owner addresses his totally powerless cattle in French using the analogous model of the colonial relationship which contrasts so sharply with the entirely different social relationship between peasants which are transacted in Malagasy. The fantasies of the peasant that for a short illusory time he has placed himself in relation to others in the way the cattle owner is to his cow, or the administrator is to his subject, are acted out in drunkenness or in plays. One language is for one type of social relation, another for another radically different type.

As man is to beast, Government bureaucrat is to village cultivator. The model and symbol of one relation has been transposed into another.

P.S. James Woodburn significantly tells me that the Hadza talk to their dogs in Swahili.

Index

Abelson, R. P., 19(n9), 53(n5)
Abu-Lughod, L., 102
African sacrifice, 63
Agriculture, Zafimaniry, 28, 30, 92, 182–183
Ambohivohitra, 173–174, 185–186
Ambositra, 173
Anakara, 135
Ancient and Medieval Memories, Studies in the Reconstruction of the Past (Coleman), 70
Anderson, J.R., 8
Andrianampoinimerina, 138–139
Anganon, 108, 191(n15)
Antaimoro, 132–141, 145
Antambahaoka, 132–138
Anthropology
  approach to memory and history, 68–69, 82–83, 114–115
  cognition and theory in, 3–5, 39–43, 46–47
  combining psychology and, 52(n3)
  and debate over knowledge and literacy, 154, 162
  explicit knowledge and methods in, 15–18, 22–27, 36
Apprenticeship learning, 7
Arabic culture, in Madagascar, 131–135, 136–137, 145
Aristotle, 70–71
Artefacts, 57–63
Astrologers/diviners, 135–150
Astuti, R., 78
Atran, S., 5, 54–58, 59, 62, 63(n1)

Autobiographical memory, 115–117, 119–124
Ayache, Simon, 158

Baddeley, A. J., 68, 69, 115
Balance, Zafimaniry concept of, 31–32, 35
Barthema, Ludovico, 132
Bartlett, Frederick, 68, 81, 122, 123
Bauer, P., 56
Bechtel, W., 19(n12)
Behaviour, social, 50–51, 193–194. *See also* Social relations
Behaviourism, 50
Berlin, Brent, 41, 55, 56
Berthier, H., 139
Besy, Arthur, 155–156, 157, 159, 160–161, 169(n1)
Betsileo, 138
Betsimisaraka, 169(n1)
Bible, 159–160, 187
Bicolanos, 74–77, 81–82
Bilek, 87
Bloch, M., 19(n14)
Bohannan, Laura, 153
Bourdieu, P., 23, 37(n7)
Bowerman, M., 6
Breedlove, D., 55, 56
Brown, R., 6
Buffon, G. L., 162

Callet, R. P., 158
Calligraphy, 166–167
Cannell, Fenella, 74–76
Carey, S., 56
Carpentry, Zafimaniry, 28–29

Carruthers, Mary, 73, 115
Carving, Zafimaniry, 28–29, 33, 34, 93
Catholic Church, 86–87, 174
Chamberlain, Basil Hall, 169(n4)
Childbirth, 91–92
China, 153–154
Chomsky, N., 72
Christianity
  and Madagascar, 135, 158–160
  and theories on narratives, 101
  See also Catholic Church
Churchland, P.M., 11
Churchland, P.S., 11
Classificatory concepts
  formation of, 5–7, 14
  and living kinds *versus* artifacts, 55, 56–57
  and Madagascar directional system, 143, 144
Clifford, James, 40
Cognition
  connectionism in, 11–14
  living kinds *versus* artifacts in, 54–63
  relation of language to, 19(n10)
  relation to culture, vii
  as represented in narrative, 101–102, 110–112
Cognition in practice (Lave), 172
Cognitive apparatuses, 9–11
Cognitive organizing, 10–11
Cognitive relativism, 101
Cognitive science/psychology
  and anthropology/ethnography, viii, 3–5, 17–18, 23–27, 36, 40–41, 43–44, 47, 49, 51–52, 52(n3)
  and conceptualizations of time, 110
  connectionism, 45–47
  experiments in language/knowledge relationship, 44–45
  in explaining religious symbolism, 54
  and memory studies, 117, 119, 126
Cohen, G., 68, 69, 115
Coleman, Janet, 70
Communication. *See* Speech/conversation
Comoro Islands, 131–132

Compatibility, mutual, 30–31, 88–89, 97(n9)
Computers, 11, 12, 13
Concepts
  of individuals in history, 69–83
  of living kinds *versus* artifacts, 55–63
  relation of language to, 44–45, 49
  socialisation and formation of, 50–51
  of time through narratives, 101–102
Connectionism, 3, 11, 12–14, 24–27, 45–47
Connerton, Paul, 115
Context
  and memory, 118, 119, 120
  and schooling/literacy, 171–172, 190
  and Zafimaniry narrative, 110
Contrapuntal conversation, 29
Cross-cousin marriage, 32
Cultural model, 37(n2)
Cultural relativism, 101
Cultural variability, xvii–xviii, 37(n4)
Culture
  as common knowledge, 45
  as creating the individual, 69
  effect of literacy on, 131
  home *versus* school, 179–190
  relation to cognition, vii
  role of language in, 14–15
  traditional view of, 4, 15

da Cunha, Tristan, 132
D'Alembert, 162
D'Andrade, R., 18(n3), 41
Danielli, Mary, 147
Death, 78–79, 80
de Certeau, M., 105, 111, 112
Délivré, 112
Democracy, 153
Deschamps, H., 140
Diderot, D., 162
Dispute settlement, 29, 35
Domain specificity, 54–63
Domestication of the Savage Mind, The (Goody), 152
Dreyfus, H., 15, 17, 18(n7)
Dreyfus, S., 15, 17, 18(n7)

Dualism, 79
Dubois, H., 138, 149
Dubois, R., 63(n5)
Duby, George, 125
Durkheim, E., 39, 117, 143, 149, 163–164

Economy, Madagascar, 172–173, 190
Eickelman, D. F., 72–73
Ellis, W., 138
Emotional states, 119
Encyclopedie, 162–163
Endogamy, 74
Enlightenment, 162–164
Ethnography
    combining psychology and, 52(n3)
    and connectionist theory, 46–47
    Sperber and interpretive, 43
    See also Anthropology
Ethnoscience, 5
Europeans
    intrusion into Madagascar, 132, 134
    view of knowledge, 168
Evans-Pritchard, 41

Fanambarana, 31
Fananbarana, 90, 92
Ferrand, G., 137, 138
Fertility, 89
Fieldwork, Zafimaniry, 37(n1), 102–110, 111–112. *See also* Anthropology
Fiji, 102, 111
Finnish anthropology, 67–68
Firth, 162
Flacourt, E. de, 135–136
Fodor, J. A., 19(n10), 54
Folk psychology
    ethnographers' use of, 16, 23, 44, 47
    of knowledge and history, 69–70
    and mind models, 11
Fomba, 146–150
Foraging, 28, 181
Fort Dauphin, 135
Fortes, M., 76
France, Merina in, 80. *See also* French
Frazer, Sir James, 3

French
    in Madagascar, 135, 148, 159
    and Madagascar war of 1947, 86, 96, 118
    Malagasy use of, 193–195
Functionalism, 39, 153, 154, 163–164
Fundamentalism, 40–42

Gadamer, 101
Geertz, Clifford, 40, 41, 47, 52, 102
Gender differences, 29–30, 177, 182, 183
Goody, E., 7
Goody, J., 69, 131, 148, 152–154, 162, 163, 164, 165, 167–168, 189
Gough, Kathleen, 154
Government
    Madagascar and centralized, 141
    in Mamolena, 172–173
    use of French by, 194–195
Griffiths, David, 140
Growth. *See* Maturation

Halbwachs, Maurice, 117, 126
Harris, Marvin, 52(n2)
Hastie, James, 139
Haudricourt, A.-G., 7
Hawaii, 102, 111
Hearth, 34–35, 59, 91
Hébert, J. C., 150(n5)
Hermeneutic process, 52
Hertz, Robert, 39
Historians, memory studies by, 114–115, 116–117, 125
History
    Bicolano view of, 75–76, 77
    as constructed in narratives, 100–102, 105, 106–112, 117–126
    as creating the individual, 69
    Madagascar written, 158–159
    versus memory, 116–117
    Merina view of, 78–80
    Plato and Aristotle on, 70–71
    psychology/anthropology approach to, 68–70, 81–83
    Sadah view of, 71–74

Hoggart, R., 190(n1)
Holland, Dorothy, 18(n5), 115
House-based societies, 58, 87–88, 93
House posts, 34–35, 59, 90, 91, 97(n12), 98(n15)
Houses
  and Madagascar directional system, 141, 143–144, 144(fig.)
  Zafimaniry holy, 95–96, 98(nn 18, 19)
  and Zafimaniry maturation concept, 33–35, 58–59, 61, 62, 87, 90–97, 180–181, 182
  as Zafimaniry nonverbal narrative, 109–110
Hupsey, John, 122
Hutchins, E., 18(n3)

Idea of a Social Science, The (Winch), 101
Identity
  and autobiographical memory, 81–82, 116
  Bicolano view of self, 74–77
  and cultural views on knowledge, 168–169
  Merina view of self, 78–80
  Sadah view of self, 72–74
Ideograms, 153–154, 164–167
Ideology, transmitting, 161. *See also* Transmission, knowledge
Ie, 87
Ileto, R., 102
Imerina, 138–140
Immigration
  Merina in France, 80
  and the Sadah, 74
  See also Migration
Inference, 123, 125
Innovation, 14–15
Interdisciplinary study, 114–115. *See also* Anthropology; Cognitive science/psychology
Introspection, 16
Islam, in Madagascar, 131–135, 150(n1)

"Islamic education and its social reproduction" (Eickelman), 72–73
Islands of History (Sahlins), 102

Japan, 87–88, 153, 164–167, 168–169
Johnson-Laird, P. N., 8, 13, 37(n2), 122
Jones, David, 140

Kabary, 156–157, 159
Keenan, Elinor, 157, 193–194
Kilwa, 132
Kinship organization
  relation with concepts of history, 72, 76–77, 78
  stem family systems, 87–88
  Zafimaniry, 26, 47–51, 87
Knowledge
  Bicolano view of, 75–76, 77
  and domain-specificity, 57
  Enlightenment on, 162–164
  ethnography and explaining cultural, viii, 7–15, 24–27, 43–44
  explicit *versus* inexplicit, vii, viii, 15–16
  Islam view of, 72–74
  Japanese view of, 165–167
  literacy and the nature of, 152–154, 167–169
  and literacy in Madagascar, 154–161
  Madagascar and supernatural, 140, 144–150
  Merina dualism in concept on, 79–80
  organization of, 46–47
  Plato and Aristotle on, 70–71
  relation to language, 44–45, 110–111
  schooling and cultural, 172, 179–190
  See also Literacy; Transmission, knowledge

Labour, wage, 28, 173
Language
  and cognition, 19(n10)
  and cultural knowledge, 4, 5, 6–7, 11, 13–14, 44–51

and innovation, 14–15
limitations/role in ethnography,
  15–16, 23–24, 25
in Madagascar, 131–132, 136, 155,
  193–195
Qur'an and Arabic, 137
See also Narrative;
  Speech/conversation
Lave, Jean, 7, 14, 172, 177
Learning
  Bicolano view of, 75–76, 77
  and classificatory concepts, 5–7
  concept formation, 37, 50–51
  everyday tasks and non-linguistic,
    7–11
  in Japan, 165–166
  as linking domains, 57
  Sadah/Islam on, 72–73
  and structuralism, 18(n4)
  See also Literacy; Schools
Leroi-Gourhan, A., 7
Lévi-Strauss, C., 39–40, 44
  and historical narratives, 101, 105,
    109
  and house-based societies, 58, 87, 93
  on knowledge and literacy, 154
L'Insurrection Malgache de 1947
  (Tronchon), 85
Literacy
  and cultural context in Madagascar,
    171–172
  and debate on the nature of
    knowledge, 152–154, 162–164,
    167–169
  effect on culture of, ix, 131
  in Japan, 164–167
  in Madagascar, 132, 135–141,
    146–150, 154–161, 175,
    176–177, 192(n17)
  and memory, 69, 125
  and Muslim view of learning, 73
  as representing world views,
    111–112, 148–150
  Zafimaniry attitudes toward,
    178–190
Literacy and Traditional Society
  (Goody), 152, 154

Living kinds, 54–63, 63(n1)
Locality, 29
London Missionary Society, 140, 158
London School of Economics, 67–68,
  71
Luria, A. R., 68

Madagascar
  Arabic culture in, 131–135, 150(n1)
  colonial war in, 85–86
  language use in, ix, 193–195
  literacy and astrology in, 135–150
  literacy and knowledge in, 154–161,
    168, 171–190
  map of, 133(fig.)
  narrative/memory in, 102–110,
    111–112, 117–118, 119–121
  views of identity and history, 78–80
  See also Zafimaniry
Madelung, W., 73
Malinowski, B., 8, 16, 39, 41, 52
Mamolena, 172–173, 174–185
Manakara, 132
Mananjary, 132
Mandler, M., 56
Marcus, George, 40
Mariano, Father Luis, 132
Markham, E. M., 6
Marriage
  Zafimaniry concepts on, 28, 30–32,
    58–59, 61, 87–95, 182
  Zafimaniry rituals of, 89–90,
    97(n10)
  Zafimaniry system of, 47–51
Marx, K., 163–164
Matitanana, 132
Maturation
  and oratory in Madagascar, 156, 159
  Zafimaniry concepts on, 27–29, 33,
    60–61, 62, 180–185
  See also Identity
Mauss, M., 7, 143, 149
Memory
  academic disciplines on, 68–70,
    81–83, 114–115, 126
  autobiographical *versus* semantic,
    115–117

as constructed in narratives,
    100–102, 108–112, 118–124
explicit *versus* inexplicit, ix
and literacy, 69, 125
Plato and Aristotle on, 70–71
Sadah view of, 71–74
and structuralism, 18(n4)
and Zafimaniry colonial war, viii–ix,
    85–86, 96–97, 106–108, 117–118
See also History
Memory in the Real World (Cohen), 68
Mental models, 11–12, 24–27, 37(n2)
and memory, 122, 123, 125
obvious nature of, 26, 36, 37(n3)
and Zafimaniry conceptualizations,
    26–37
Merina, 77, 78–80, 82, 87, 97(n5),
    111, 112
astrology and, 138–150
oratory and knowledge for,
    156–161
Metaphors, 61
Migration, 74, 80, 138, 178–179
Minstrels, 194
Mnemonic devices, 119, 120, 150(n5).
    See also Memory
Mohammed, Prophet, 71
Moiety system, Zafimaniry, 32, 35, 48,
    50–51, 95, 98(nn 14, 17)
Morality
and compass directions, 141–142
and concepts of history, 69–70, 71
Zafimaniry concepts of, 27–28, 108
Multiple parallel processing, 25
Munthe, Ludvig, 158
Muslims, 72–73, 74

Narrative
and historical memory, 110–111,
    118–124
nonverbal, 109–110
as representing world views,
    100–102, 131, 148–150
Zafimaniry types of, 103–110
Neisser, Ulrich, 68, 115, 122, 124
Nigro, G., 115, 124
Nonverbal narratives, 109–110

Objectivism, 41–42
Obscurantism, 162–163
Occupation, Zafimaniry maturation
    and, 28–29, 181
Olson, D. R., 69
Oratory, 155, 156–161, 168, 169(n2).
    See also Speech/conversation

Parry, 152
Participant observation
combining psychology and, 52(n3)
as ethnographic method, 4, 16–17,
    25–26, 39
Pasyon and Revolution (Ileto), 102
Philippines, 74–77, 102
Piaget, J., 18(n4)
Placing the Dead (Bloch), 79
Plato, 70–71
Play, 181–182
Politico-economic system, literacy and,
    153–154. *See also* Government
Population, 174
Portuguese, 132
Post-modernism, 42
Potential
and concepts of history, 69–70
Sadah view of individual, 72, 73
Power, political
and oratory in Madagascar,
    159–161
and use of French, 194–195
See also Social status
Prototypes, 49, 50, 55
Proust, M., 116
Psychology
approach to memory and history,
    68–70, 81–83, 114–115, 116
and contexts in education, 172
folk, 11, 16, 23, 44, 47, 69–70
value of anthropology for, viii
See also Cognitive science/psychology
Psychology of Memory, The (Baddeley),
    68

Quinn, Naomi, 18(nn 3, 5), 37(n5),
    115
Qur'an, 137, 140

Radama (Lehidama), 138, 139
Raison-Jourde, Francoise, 158
Rationality, 101
Raven, P., 55, 56
Recall, *versus* remembering, 118–119.
   See also Retention
Recognition, 89
Reisman, Karl, 29
Religion
   Bicolano spirit world, 75
   Islam in Madagascar, 131–135
   and literacy, 163
   and Zafimaniry, 86–87, 97(n3)
Religious symbolism, 54, 57–58, 63
Remembering, *versus* recall, 118–119.
   See also Retention
Remembering (Bartlett), 122
Reproduction, 30
Retention, 9–11, 12, 118–119,
   121–122. *See also* Memory
Rey, P., 56
Ricoeur, P., 101, 106, 110, 111
Rituals
   blessing and oratory in Madagascar,
      156–157
   connectionist theory and explaining,
      46
   as representing world views, vii
   symbolism in, 54, 57–58
   Zafimaniry, of return, 105, 108, 188
   Zafimaniry birth, 92
   Zafimaniry house, 34, 58, 91, 95,
      98(n16)
   Zafimaniry marriage, 31, 89–90,
      97(n10)
Rosch, Eleanor, 55
Rousseau, J., 162, 163
Rubin, David, 122
Ruud, J., 142

Sadah, the, 71–74, 76–77, 80, 81
Sahlins, M., 102, 107, 110, 111
Schank, R. C., 19(n9), 53(n5)
Schemata, 45–47, 53(n5), 122
Schmitt, J-C., 120
Schools, Madagascar, 139, 158,
   171–190, 191(nn 4, 5, 7)

Science
   and debate on literacy and
      knowledge, 153, 162–163
   and ethnography, 40, 52
   Zafimaniry knowledge and,
      181–182, 183, 191(n10)
   See also Objectivism
Secularization, of writing, 140–141
Seibert, J., 6
Semantic memory, 115–117,
   119–121
Sentential linear model, 11–12, 14,
   23
Sexual relations, Zafimaniry, 88,
   89–90
Siblings, 32
Sikidy, 139
Socialisation, 50–51
Social relations, 50–51
   elders and knowledge in, 185–186
   knowledge as linked to, 153,
      157–158, 161, 163–164
   and Malagasy language, 193–194
Social status
   astrologer-diviner, 145–148
   and education in Madagascar, 179,
      191(n11)
   and house associations, 87
Social structure
   scribe aristocracy in Madagascar,
      138
   Zafimaniry, 27, 47–51, 87, 97(n4)
Sociology, 114–115
Sorabe, 137, 138, 142, 148, 150(n2)
Southeast Asia, 77, 87–88
Speech/conversation
   and memory, 117, 121–124, 126
   Merina astrologer/diviner, 146
   Merina dualism in, 79
   and Zafimaniry maturation stages,
      29, 180, 182–184, 191(n12)
   See also Oratory
Sperber, Dan, 8, 18(n4), 43, 54–55, 68,
   83, 115, 122, 123
Strauss, C., 18(n3)
Street, B. V., 190(n1)
Structuralism, 5, 6, 18(n4), 44, 49, 154

Symbolism
    cognitive theory in explaining
        religious, 54, 57–58, 63
    and linking living kinds and artifacts,
        57–63
    and Madagascar directional system,
        141–142, 143(fig.), 144(fig.)
    Zafimaniry house, 34–35, 87,
        90–96

Taboo (Ruud), 142
Tamatave (Taomasina), 138, 154–155
Tanala, 132
Tananarive, 139, 149, 155
Tantara, 108, 109, 111, 112, 184, 188,
    189, 191(nn 12, 15)
Tantaran ny Andriana (Callet), 158
Tapa maso, 31, 89–90
Tapa sofina, 89
Taro, 91, 191(n10)
Taussig, Michael, 40
Technology, 160
Terminology
    Malagasy for "written thing," 131
    Zafimaniry for inherited goods, 95
    Zafimaniry for "land," 63(n4)
    Zafimaniry for "people," 63(n5)
    Zafimaniry for rebels, 86, 97(n1)
    Zafimaniry for tree/wood, 59, 60
    Zafimaniry kinship, 47–51, 93
Teza, 33, 34–35, 60–61, 93
Thailand, 88
Time
    narratives as revealing concepts of,
        101–102, 110
    in Zafimaniry narrative, 105, 106
"Time, Person and Conduct in Bali"
    (Geertz), 102
Toren, C., 52(n3)
Trano masina, 35
Transformation
    and Bicolano self-identity, 75–76,
        77
    and Merino view of history, 78
    and Zafimaniry view of life, 180
    See also Maturation
Transmission, knowledge, 18(n1)

    and historical memory, 120–126. *See
        also* Narrative
    inexplicit, ix, 14
    Madagascar and literacy in, 161
    role of literacy in, 164, 165
Trees, 32–33, 59–63
Tronchon, Jacques, 85
Tulving, E., 116
Turner, T., 18(n4)

Uses of literacy, The (Hoggart),
    190(n1)

Veiled Sentiments (Abu-Lughod), 102
Vezo, 78
Vigotsky, 68
Vintana, 144–145
Visual imagery, 122–124
Vohipeno, 132
Voltaire, F., 162
vom Bruck, Gabrielle, 71, 74

War, Madagascar colonial, 85–86, 96,
    106, 118
Watt, I., 148, 152, 163
Weber, M., 52, 163–164
Westermarck, Edward, 67–68, 70
Whitehouse, H., 115
Wilson, D., 123
Wilson, W., 8
Winch, P., 101
Wood, 32–33, 59–63, 93
Woodburn, James, 195
World view
    as identifiable through narrative,
        100–102, 110–112, 131, 148–150
    Zafimaniry, 27, 35–37
Writing. *See* Literacy
Writing systems, 153–154

Yemen, 71–74

Zafimaniry, 37(n1)
    field work and narrative among,
        102–110, 111–112
    houses and symbolism, 58–63,
        87–96

memory of colonial war/village
    return, viii–ix, 85–86, 96–97,
    106–108, 117–118
mental models, 26–37
religion, 86–87, 97(n3)

schooling and literacy, ix,
    172–190
social structure, 27, 47–51, 87,
    97(n4)
variation, 37(n4)

Printed in the United States
71980LV00005B/301-336